BACKPACKING

Fifth Edition

R. C. Rethmel

 Burgess Publishing Company
Minneapolis, Minnesota

Preface

Backpacking has been an intriguing subject, and a favorite outdoor activity, to the writer for many years. Most of us have a certain "explorer instinct." We would like to know and see what is beyond the next bend in the river, or over the next mountain, or in the canyon far below. A backpacker can find out for himself and enjoy the healthful exercise, the fun of camping out, and many other benefits in doing so.

An experienced backpacker can go into a remote area for a week with a 35- to 40-pound pack on his back and live very adequately, shut off from all outside communication. In fact, in many cases he will live more comfortably and eat equally as well as others who take to the highway with a full trailer-load of equipment, in spite of the fact that the highway travelers will probably make daily stops to replenish certain foods and supplies. Specific information on just how the backpacker keeps down the weight of his pack, however, is not very plentiful. Therefore, the primary purpose of this book is to set forth this information in terms that the average hiker can understand. A particular effort has been made to be very specific rather than to discuss the various applicable subjects in general terms.

My background includes a long term as a Boy Scout and Scout leader. For many years I have made frequent backpack trips into the Gila Wilderness in southwestern New Mexico and into some of the other wilderness areas. On many of these trips I have been organizer and leader of small groups of adult sportsmen. Checklists and pretrip plans, as well as notes made during and after pack trips, led to the original publication of this book. I never make a backpack trip that I don't learn something. Hence there has been a frequent updating of the material in this book.

I recently spent an entire summer backpacking in the Canadian Rockies. Much of the time I made a particular effort to travel those trails where I knew there would be a fair population of other backpackers. I did this so that I could meet and talk with some of the most experienced backpackers and also see their equipment "in action" on backwoods trails and in backwoods camp areas. I wanted to get the other fellow's viewpoint and compare it with my own experience and background. I also spent considerable time in visiting and talking with Canadian wardens who were backpackers and other government personnel who were knowledgeable on the subject of backpacking.

Please keep in mind as you read through this book that the material herein applies specifically to backpacking. Otherwise you may squirm a bit in your chair when you read such recommendations as to take no duplicate clothing on a week-long backpack trip except for socks, to use a sheet of plastic for rain protection (under some conditions), or to use certain freeze-dried foods which may cost fifty cents or more for one ounce.

For those readers who are old hands at backpacking, it is hoped that you will be broadminded about the amount of detail included in this book. After reading the book you may feel that you would like to express your opinion on some recommended procedure, technique, or item of equipment, based on your backpacking experience. If you have comments of any kind, either general or specific, I would appreciate receiving them in a letter or note addressed to me at P.O. Box 1526, Alamogordo, New Mexico 88310.

Well, we were going to talk about backpacking—so pull up a log, get a little closer to the campfire, and we will get started.

Alamogordo,   R. C. (Bob) Rethmel
New Mexico

Acknowledgments

A number of people contributed to this revision of *Backpacking*. Some of them must remain anonymous. They were the backpackers I met on the trails in the United States and Canada; we held brief conversations, often without removing our packs, and passed on. In some backwoods camps I observed the practices, some good and some bad, of other backpackers in the area. Sometimes we conversed and at other times I just observed from a respectful distance. I learned something from most of these contacts, even from those who seemed to be doing "everything wrong."

Lou Clemmons of Gig Harbor, Washington, made important photographic contributions to this revision. Lou also furnished some very worthwhile suggestions on certain portions of the text. Fred Curtis of Calgary, Alberta, Canada, also had helpful comments on some of the text. For the cover photo I am indebted to William A. Lee, Edmonton, Alberta, Canada, with whom I did some backpacking in the Canadian Rockies.

The part on "Backpacking with Children" is based largely on my experience of backpacking with my own children. However, the Fred Mulholland family of Tampa, Florida and the Owen Thero family of King of Prussia, Pennsylvania furnished photographs and some helpful comments for this part. Both Owen and Fred are accomplished backpackers. They can be very proud of having carefully and thoroughly indoctrinated their children to wilderness backpacking.

Several manufacturers of backpacking equipment supplied photographs and these are acknowledged where they appear in the text.

June 1974   R. C. R.

Contents

1

Introduction

WHY GO BACKPACKING?

People go backpacking for a variety of reasons. Backpacking can take you into beautiful scenery that may lie just a few miles beyond the roadhead. It can provide an inexpensive vacation. It is certainly healthful exercise, if you are in reasonably good physical condition to start with. Entire families, frequently with children as young as five or six years of age, have backpacked into some of our forest and wilderness areas. In addition to the objectives of photography, rock collecting, fishing, relaxation, or whatever else you may be after, there is a tremendous satisfaction in being able to carry your "house" on your back for a week and to live comfortably in the woods, shut off from all outside communication. It takes skillful planning, and this too is part of the fun in backpacking. If you want some unusual fishing, wildlife study, or just plain solitude, you leave a lot of the competition behind when you pack into areas where only your two feet can carry you.

Persons interested in technical mountain climbing find that backpacking is useful and necessary in carrying their climbing gear and supplies to a base camp, from which they will do their climbing. Sportsmen use backpacking equipment and techniques in getting to good hunting and fishing grounds, which are frequently more than a day's travel from the roadhead. Thus, to some persons backpacking is simply a necessary means of moving equipment

and supplies into an area in order to accomplish another, more primary objective. Many others find backpacking in itself an enjoyable and exhilarating sport, especially when done in an area that is isolated and attractive from a scenic standpoint. For those in Boy Scouting and Girl Scouting, backpacking brings together the basic skills which they have learned and puts them to good test.

In this "modern day civilization" it is possible for a person to go from the cradle to the grave and hardly draw a deep breath. He may never have a problem in seeking shelter from the elements or a need to build a fire from natural materials and cook his own food. You can go through life and never experience the fatigue and pleasure of real physical exhaustion. A drink from a cool mountain stream on a hot day, the smell of a pine forest, and the taste of a fresh-caught mountain trout are pleasures that are available to practically everyone in reasonably good health, if they will but make the effort and take the necessary initiative. Psychologically it is good for us to have new problems and new experiences that are different from the pattern of our everyday living. We all need some adventure in our lives, if only for a few days each each year. Backpacking is a wholesome, invigorating activity that will provide a physical and mental atmosphere which is a pleasant change from our daily routine.

Trail trips, using riding horses and pack horses or mules, are common, especially in the West.

1

These certainly have a very important place as a means of seeing and enjoying our wilderness and forest areas. Without them many persons would never know the pleasure and general well-being that come from packing into a remote area. They do have certain limitations, however. On the average pack trip by horse, reasonably good trails must be followed. If you want to explore a deep and rugged canyon, or some other difficult terrain, the horses must frequently be left behind. There is also the matter of water and forage for riding and pack animals. Along some of our well-used wilderness trails, forage, in particular, can be a problem. Even though you may be a good rider, unless you have had considerable experience with horses and pack animals on trail rides (wrangling), their care is best left to experts. When the night is dark, the grass is thin, and a horse starts getting visions of the home pasture, he can travel surprisingly far, even if he is hobbled. Throughout a horseback trip, constant consideration must be given to the care and well-being of the horses, and this detracts considerably from the time that is left for other pursuits. Therefore, such pack trips are frequently made up of formally or semiformally organized groups of ten to twenty persons or more, plus hired guides and wranglers. The privacy and individual decision that is inherent to a small party of backpackers is impossible on such trips. The techniques and experience required, however, dictate that most persons must join such a group if they are to participate. By no means a small consideration is the cost, usually ranging from $30 to $40 per person per day. However, these remarks are not intended to discourage you from taking such a trip. If a trail trip by horse is your chosen way of seeing a remote area, then by all means take it. A well-conducted trail trip will be an experience which you will long remember.

PHYSICAL CONDITION

In a discussion of backpacking, the matter of physical condition usually comes up. It is true that good physical condition is important. However, many persons well past middle age go backpacking regularly. Grandmothers and grandfathers have hiked the Appalachian Trail. If you are in reasonably good physical condition you can probably backpack. Obviously you should select a pace, suitable terrain, and a reasonable pack load which is commensurate with your age, hiking ability, and backpacking experience.

To a considerable degree your technique and "know-how" are deciding factors in how long you can stay out (on the trail) and how comfortable you will be (whether you will enjoy the trip or will decide to give up backpacking).

BE PREPARED

On a backpack trip into a remote area, you must not only be a hiker but you (or other members of the group) must be a camper, cook, doctor, pathfinder, and many other things. On an automobile camping trip, or on any other trip that keeps in touch with civilization, forgotten items of equipment can be bought at the nearest store. If your equipment needs repair, you require medical attention, you need a change from your own cooking, or you require some other service, you can usually buy that service. Your money won't help you on a backpacking trip in a wilderness area. You are on your own.

YOUR EQUIPMENT

You will find some references in this book to specific brand names of equipment and food. These are brands which the writer has personally used on backpack trips and found to be satisfactory for the job. This is *not* meant to imply that there is not another product which may be equally as good. You may wish to try other brands or your own substitute equipment, and that is certainly your choice to do so. However, before taking off on an extended backpack trip it is recommended that you thoroughly try out all such equipment and food at home, or on a very short backpack trip, just in case they do not work out as planned. This cannot be emphasized too strongly.

SHOPPING FOR EQUIPMENT

You can easily spend several hundred dollars on special equipment for use in backpacking. On many items, however, you can improvise or "make do" with equipment that is already around your home or with substitute items that are locally available. A list of some of the firms that sell special equipment for use in backpacking is given in Appendix A. It is recommended that you order the catalogues of some of these suppliers and browse through them. This "window shopping" won't cost anything, and it will add to your knowledge just to read through these catalogues. This book will outline what is desirable in the way of effective and lightweight backpack equipment, but it will also give particular emphasis to pointing out acceptable substitutes for special (and frequently expensive) equipment. If you keep on with backpacking, you will probably want to replace some of these substitute items with better equipment. It is recommended that you do this *gradually*, however, and gain some experience and knowledge as you go along, so that you can spend your dollars more wisely.

Before spending large sums of money on new backpacking equipment you should become acquainted with other backpackers, if possible, and seek their advice. Also, you can go backpacking in mild weather with less expensive gear than is required for cold or foul weather backpacking. You can learn a lot on "trial" backpack trips, with persons who are knowledgeable backpackers, by observing their equipment and asking questions. Perhaps you can join a club that backpacks regularly.

Some of the newsletters and periodicals, such as *The Signpost*, *Summit*, and *The Trail Walker* (see OTHER LITERATURE in the Appendices) have a classified ad section in which you may find satisfactory used equipment advertised at considerable cost reduction from new equipment. You can also run your own classified ad in such periodicals or even in your local newspaper. Backpackers go "in and out of business" in much the same way as people involved in any other sport or hobby do. Some people invest in good, expensive equipment (perhaps hastily) and then give up the sport. Others discard certain equipment in favor of more sophisticated gear as they advance and become more knowledgeable. If you are outfitting an entire family for backpacking, including young children, it can be quite expensive. You should not overlook the fact that there are other families that have done the same thing before you. Young children of other parents may have outgrown clothing, sleeping bags, and other gear. In some cases you may even be able to borrow such equipment, and if you are careful with it there will be no harm done.

PACK WEIGHT

As for every other kind of outdoor activity, there are equipment, clothing, and techniques which are especially pertinent to backpacking. This book sets forth information on these and other applicable subjects that will enable you to properly prepare for a backpack trip and to hit the trail with confidence. It would not require nearly so much skill and planning for a backpack trip if the matter of weight did not need to be continually considered. The pack weight, in turn, is interrelated with equipment, clothing, food, and technique. Your equipment and clothing can be perfect for backpacking but, if you plan for and take the wrong foods, your pack weight will grow out-of-bounds. Those persons who like to "throw a few things together and take off" when they go camping had better prepare themselves for a drastically different approach if they plan to do some serious backpacking. Assuming that you or the group leader possess the necessary "know-how" to plan and conduct an interesting and safe backpack trip, and that you have proper equipment, then the single most important factor affecting your enjoyment of the trip is the weight of your pack. Consider it carefully.

You should not plan to carry a loaded pack totalling more than 40 pounds. This applies to the average adult male backpacker, with average experience, for a trip lasting up to a week or ten days. A 50-pound pack may feel quite comfortable when you are walking around in the living room or in the backyard at home for a few minutes, but five or six hours on a mountain trail can be quite different. If you have a special purpose for going into the wilderness, say for commercial type photography, and you choose to carry 10 or 12 pounds of photographic equipment, then it is going to be difficult to keep the total pack weight under 40 pounds. However, the average backpacker should not be carrying this much special purpose gear. If you are of small body build, or not accustomed to backpacking, you should eliminate all nonessential equipment and clothing to keep the total pack weight betwwen 25 and 30 pounds. The irony of it is that the experienced backpackers will have least difficulty in keeping their packs light, while the beginners (who are most apt to really suffer from a heavy pack) will find it more of a problem. However, it can be done if you are willing to spend sufficient time in planning and preparation. The chapters that follow tell how.

2

The Pack

BACKGROUND

Your pack is your home on your back. In your pack you will need to carry shelter, food, extra clothing, cooking and eating utensils, and all the other gear required to travel and live comfortably in the back country. If your trip is to be pleasurable your pack load must be comfortable. Your pack is your most important item of equipment (except for boots, which are really an item of clothing).

Over the years many styles of packs have been devised for carrying loads on the trail. A man's back, in relation to the rest of his skeletal structure, was not properly designed for carrying heavy loads. Yet, by trial and error, the back has been proven to be the optimum place to position large loads which are being carried for relatively long distances.

When I was of high school age I made a four-day backpack trip from the south rim of the Grand Canyon to the north rim and back again. My "pack" for that trip consisted of an Army blanket with essentially all equipment rolled inside. The blanket was then tied into a horseshoe shape and was worn over one shoulder. A canteen was carried on a strap over the opposite shoulder and a cooking pan dangled from the blanket roll. By frequent changing of the pack from one shoulder to the other I endured the trip. However, I would have welcomed almost any of the packframes that are commercially available today in place of that blanket roll.

The Army packboard used a piece of curved plywood for mounting a canvas panel that rested against the back. The load was lashed to the packboard. I have used such a pack and these packboards are still available in some Army surplus stores today. The Trapper Nelson packboard has been carried by many thousands of backpackers over the years and I have also owned and used one of these. This packboard also has a straight wooden frame, with a single large backpanel. It has a large canvas packbag, much too deep to keep the load close to the wearer's back, no side pockets, and no waist belt. The Trapper Nelson is still available in some stores today, but its design is obsolete.

AUTHOR backpacking in Grand Canyon at 16 years of age. Note horseshoe-shaped blanket roll, which served as a "pack."

5

THE MODERN PACK

Thus the backpack has undergone many changes in design and materials, in both the packframe and the packbag. Many of these changes have taken place in fairly recent years. Most backpacking for pleasure involves carrying 25- to 45-pound loads for substantial distances, over reasonably good trails. For this purpose the most widely accepted backpack today is the contoured aluminum frame, with a fitted packbag to match. Many styles and innovations of the contoured aluminum packframe and fitted packbag have been developed and changes are still being made. Yet the fundamental requirements of a good packframe and packbag seem to be pretty well agreed upon by both the majority of backpackers and the designers, in spite of the many variations. What the next few years will bring I doubt that anyone knows, but most assuredly there will continue to be some changes.

PACKFRAME CONSTRUCTION. Aluminum tubing is most commonly used for packframe construction, although magnesium tubular frames are also available and are somewhat lighter. The frame should be constructed so as to hold the load close to the wearer's back and to provide for placing the load as nearly as possible over the center of gravity of the body. To accomplish this, a good packframe will have the general shape of an elongated "S" when viewed from the side.

The two outside vertical rails of the frame (about 1″ in diameter) are usually joined by three or more horizontal crossbars of lesser diameter, curved outward to provide for holding the load away from the wearer's back. (The open ends of the vertical rails should be plugged with plastic caps to prevent entry of dirt and water.) Two or more small-diameter vertical tubes join the horizontal members to provide greater strength and rigidity. The tubular aluminum (or magnesium) frames in many of the best packframes have welded joints which join the cross members to the vertical rails. These are often heli-arc welded, which refers to the fact that helium gas was used in the welding process. Good workmanship in the welding process is of the utmost importance. The welded joints should have an irregular, handmade appearance. Inspect each individual joint carefully and reject any frame which has even a slight crack in the welded joints. Brazed, soldered, and bolted joints are also used. Such packframes may be satisfactory, depending upon the quality of workmanship. The reputation of the manufacturer is an important consideration.

In buying a packframe, you can make a simple test of rigidity and strength by setting the

A useful modification to the packframe is the addition of four of these "D" rings to the two top and two bottom clevis pins. Rope, drinking cup, etc., can be suspended from the rings. Photo by Lou Clemmons.

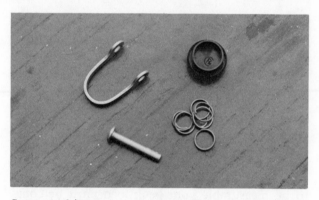

Some useful spare pack parts. Clockwise, starting at upper legs: Aluminum U-rings for attaching lower end of shoulder strap to frame, frame end plugs, clevis pin, split rings. Photo by Lou Clemmons.

frame upright on the floor, bracing the bottom ends of the rails with your feet, and then attempting to twist the tops of the rails, using a *reasonable* amount of force. In frames having welded or brazed construction there should be very little "give" and the joints should remain intact. In bolted construction there may be some "give" but the frame should regain its original configuration, with no detrimental defects, when the force is released.

As you view the packframe from the top, you will see that the curved horizontal members provide a concave configuration to allow for holding the packbag away from the wearer's back.

BACKPANELS. On most packframes there are two wide canvas backpanels wrapped around the vertical frame members so that the pack load bears on the hiker's back through these panels. The panels should be adjustable up or down on the frame to fit the individual, with the lower panel resting on the slope of the buttocks.

Typical tubular aluminum packframes, of good design, with matching packbags.
(Stuff bag mounted to packframe is also shown.)

The packframe-packbag combinations shown above are typical of many that are available from mountaineering and backpacking equipment shops, sporting goods firms, and large mail order firms. This general type of packframe-packbag is the most widely used by backpackers today.

The Trapper Nelson   Army packboard

For serious backpacking these packs have been largely replaced by the contoured, tubular aluminum packframes, which have better weight distribution, waist belts, and other desirable features. The Army packboard will carry large and odd shaped loads and is sometimes useful in hunting, in packing out a quarter of game. For normal backpacking it leaves much to be desired.

Most of these backbands have a turnbuckle arrangement so that the backband can be drawn very tight ("drum tight") as it should be. A few packframes have a large, single backband of nylon mesh, rather than separate backpanels.

SHOULDER STRAPS. Shoulder straps should be attached high on the frame. They should be wide where they bear on the shoulders and narrow where they pass under the arms. Usually there are optional holes in the crossbar to which the strap is fastened to provide for varied placement of straps. The straps should ride close to the neck, never far out on the shoulders. They should always be firmly attached to the frame, rather than having a "floating" arrangement which will allow the pack to move either up or down or from side to side. Padded shoulder straps will be found on most of the good packframes. If the shoulder straps on the packframe are not padded, or the padding does not seem to be adequate, shoulder pads can be purchased separately and installed on the straps. Buckles at the bottom ends of the strap provide for length adjustment to suit the individual wearer. When you are wearing a loaded pack the top point of attachment of the shoulder straps to the crossbar should be above the level of your shoulders, never at the same level, and *never* below. (This would indicate the full load being borne by the shoulders.)

WAIST BELT. A good waist belt is one of the most important features of a good packframe. It will help to hold the frame and load close in to the body and will take a good part of the load off the shoulders (up to 75 percent or more). On quite a few packframes the waist belt is not a full belt. Rather it is two half-belts, each attaching to the bottom end of one of the vertical rails, and each half meeting in front of the wearer in a buckle arrangement. The two half-

Hip belt on pack frame. This type of hip belt is available as a separate accessory and will attach to many packframes.

belt approach is considered by some backpackers to be less desirable than a full belt. However, there are many satisfied owners of packframes which have the two-piece belts. Other packframes have a wide (4 inches or more), well-padded belt which completely encircles the waist. Two-piece belts tend to "clamp" the frame tight to the back, whereas a full belt allows some "floating" of the packframe as you hike. All waist belts should have a quick release buckle for quickly jettisoning the pack in an emergency situation.

If your packframe does not have a full waist belt, hip belts are available as a separate accessory (cost about $6). They are usually 4 inches or more in width, with generous padding. They can be attached to most packframes.

When in proper position a hip belt should fit *very tightly* across the hips. It is important to keep the belt that holds up your trousers free of canteens, sheath knives, and similar equipment which will interfere with the waist belt.

LOADING. The pack load should ride close to the back and high on the back but not be top-heavy. Where the terrain is very rugged or steep climbing is to be done, the center of gravity of the load needs to be kept low, so as not to throw the wearer off balance. In most backpacking over reasonably good trails, the heaviest items in the load need to be near shoulder level. This is accomplished by mounting the packsack high on the packframe and by packing light objects in the bottom of the packsack, heavier objects near the top. The sleeping bag is usually lashed to the lower part of the packframe.

When a good packframe is properly loaded, the center of gravity of the load will be very nearly over the hiker's hips. The hiker will feel comfortable when walking in essentially an upright position, bending forward only very slightly to balance the load. In order to keep the center of gravity of a substantial load close to the back, the frame and the load on it need to be high, wide, and not very deep toward the rear.

ACCESSORIES. An accessory sometimes used with packframes is a tumpline. This is a strap that generally fastens near the bottom of the frame and has a padded area that bears on the top of the head. However, unless your head and neck are thoroughly accustomed to use of a tumpline you probably will not find it very comfortable if used for more than a few minutes at a time. It is not recommended for the average backpacker. Somewhat more useful accessories, for some situations, are clamps which mount along the vertical frame members (tubular

Extension frame. A useful addition to the packframe is this extension frame that fits to the top vertical rails. A typical use is to lash foam pad and tent to the extension frame. (Cost about $4.00.) Photo by Lou Clemmons.

Added "D" ring in use, supporting a coil of rope. Photo by Lou Clemmons.

Pocket for pack strap, handmade from denim material. Can be used to carry such items as sunglasses, compass, notepad, pencil, etc. Photo by Lou Clemmons.

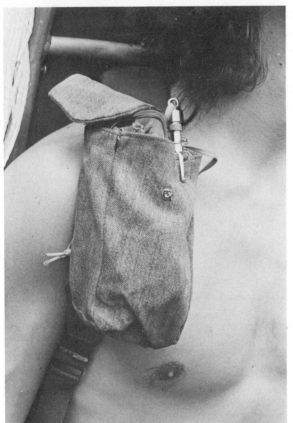

frames) for lashing various items of equipment. A removable shelf, which mounts to the lower part of the packframe, is also available. Extension bars are available, as an accessory, which will mount to the top of some packframes and increase their usefulness for some types of loads (such as an additional sleeping bag in a family group, a tent, or a similar light, bulky load).

THE PACKBAG

A good packbag is an important complement to a good packframe. It should be large, commensurate with the size of the packframe. This is not so you can carry an extra heavy load, but rather because it is easier to pack equipment in a roomy bag in a systematic manner, and so that it can be found more quickly when you want it. In general, packbags come in full length (covering essentially the full length of the packframe) and in three-quarters length. The three-quarters length bag is the least expensive and remains the most popular but its popularity is probably due as much to versatility as price.

ATTACHMENT. If possible, purchase a bag that is intended for the frame you buy. This will provide a better fit and ensure that the points of attachment and method of attachment of bag to frame are commensurate with one another. Method of attachment of bag to frame is usually by clevis pins, using either a long locking wire going through all pins along one rail of the packframe or individual split rings in the clevis pins. The grommets through which the clevis pins fit to attach the bag to the frame are worthy of careful inspection to see that they are properly inserted and not likely to tear loose. Other points of stress on the bag should also be inspected for sewing quality. Reinforced stitching (bar tacks) should be used at the end of all seams or points of strain. Synthetic thread should be used in all sewing throughout the bag, since it is stronger and does not rot as cotton thread does.

MATERIAL. The best bags are made of waterproof coated nylon duck. Some bags are only water-repellent but waterproof is preferable. If it is raining, you will want to keep every drop of water out of the bag that you possibly can. The question of "breatheability" of the fabric is not applicable here, as it is in tents or clothing. If you have a damp article of clothing in your packbag it should be inside a plastic bag or other waterproof cover where it cannot dampen the other contents of the pack. If the sun is shining, damp articles are best hung on the outside of the pack where they can dry as you hike along the trail.

The side of the waterproof nylon which has the waterproof (urethane) treatment should be on the inside of the packbag. The outside surfaces of your packbag are subject to scuffing and abrasion which have a tendency to rub away the waterproof coating. Although the inside surfaces of the bag are subject to a certain amount of rubbing and abrasion, it is not nearly so severe as that on the outside surfaces, if the bag is properly packed.

The basic packbag may be one large compartment, or it may be divided. A common arrangement is one large upper compartment and a comparatively roomy lower compartment, extending the full width of the bag, with a generously long zipper for separate access to contents. This makes for easy access to certain items, especially items that may be used frequently during the day, without opening the large, main compartment. Some bags incorporate a light metal frame in the upper (large) compartment for the intended purpose of holding the compartment open for easier loading or unloading.

POCKETS. The better packbags have outside pockets, frequently two on each side and a large, relatively flat pocket at the rear. These pockets should have zippered closures and are worthy of some careful consideration and inspection since

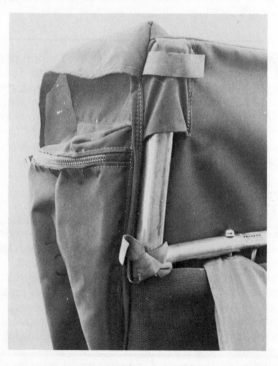

One method of attaching packbag to frame. (Clevis pins are a somewhat better method.)

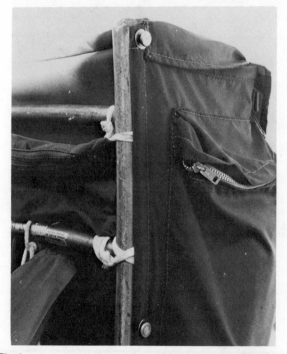

Clevis pin attachment of packbag to packframe. Tie tapes hold a small "homemade" zippered bag containing trail snacks, etc., in place.

you will probably be using them rather frequently during the day. Nylon zippers are the best type of closure for the zippered pockets. Metal zippers are least desirable since they are prone to rust and sticking. However, I have a packbag with metal zippers that has seen many years of use, in all weather, and the zippers have never been a problem. A very important feature of all zippered closures is a generous sized flap which completely covers the zipper, with the pack loaded (zipper under tension). These flaps should keep out water and dirt. When you buy a new packbag, check over the inside of the packbag pockets for possible loose ravelings of thread along the seams. When these get stuck in the zipper, in camp or along the trail, it can be very annoying. In general, the manufacturing processes used in the better packbags eliminate this problem.

The top flap on the packbag should be of generous size, so as to cover the main (top) opening completely and also to provide protection to a jacket or other article of clothing, etc., which may be rolled and placed under the flap in the final step of packing the bag. A map pocket located in the flap is an important feature and it should be of generous size. A Velcro tape closure for this pocket may be helpful. The flap is usually fastened in closed position by nylon cords tied to the flap at the corners through grommet holes and fastened to "D" rings located about two-thirds of the way down the back side of the bag. A strap and buckle closure may also be used.

STUFF BAG

As stated earlier, the packbag is normally placed high on the packframe, with the heaviest items of the load near shoulder level. Since the sleeping bag is relatively light, it is usually strapped to the packframe below the packbag, and is contained in a strong, waterproof stuff bag. It cannot be stressed too strongly that the stuff bag should be of strong, abrasive-resistant, *waterproof* nylon. It should have a drawstring opening and a generous-sized flap to protect the opening. Your sleeping bag is not a rugged piece of equipment. If it gets torn or wet it is not going to do the job you want it to. As a further aid to assuring that your sleeping bag will stay dry, it is recommended that it be contained in a large polyethylene bag, in addition to its regular stuff bag. The polyethylene bag can be somewhat larger than the regular stuff bag but never smaller. The best approach to getting the sleeping bag inside both bags is to first partially stuff the sleeping bag into the polyethylene bag. Next insert the polyethylene bag into the regular stuff

Stuff bag, containing sleeping bag, strapped to lower part of pack frame.

bag and continue stuffing the sleeping bag simultaneously inside both bags.

As you travel along the trail there will be rest stops and other stops during the day when you will be removing your pack load. In setting your pack load on the ground, use reasonable care to select a spot that is free from stones, sticks, or any sharp objects that might penetrate the stuff bag and perhaps damage the sleeping bag inside.

SHOPPING FOR A PACK

You will probably have your packframe and packbag for a long time. Some careful shopping is called for if you are to have a combination that you will be satisfied with. A poor pack load can mean many hours of misery on the trail, whereas a substantial load contained in a good packbag which is mounted on a good frame can be carried in relative comfort.

Talk to other backpackers about their packs. Visit mountaineering stores and other shops and try on some of their packframe-packbag combinations. If possible, rent or borrow a pack for a short trail trip. If your budget is limited it is recommended that you concentrate on first obtaining a good, well-fitting *packframe*. The best packbag will never make a comfortable load if mounted on a poor packframe. On the other hand, an inexpensive packbag can be purchased, or even made at home, and will do the job. Or, you can place your equipment in a tarp and lash it to the packframe. It may not be as convenient as a good packbag (with pockets, etc.), but if the load is properly fastened to a good packframe, it will be comfortable.

Quite a few cheap imitations of good packframes, many foreign made, have appeared on the market in recent years. It is particularly recommended that your packframe-packbag combination be purchased from a reputable backpacking equipment supplier or one of the large mail order firms. Be sure to check it over thoroughly and determine that it meets the basic requirements as outlined herein. You cannot get much "feel" for the comfort of a packframe-packbag combination by simply putting it on with no load in the packbag. Some stores will have a simulated load you can use. Or, you may have to carry your own, say a package of books wrapped in a blanket and tied into a bundle.

You may expect to pay at least $12 for a satisfactory packframe and up to $25 or more for some. A packbag to fit the frame will range in price from about $15 to $30. The packframe-packbag combination will generally weigh from 3½ to 4¼ pounds with 4 pounds being a good average weight for an empty pack in an adult size.

RUCKSACKS

A rucksack is a small pack that is usually supported entirely by the shoulders. It rides quite low on the back, compared to a packframe They are used primarily for day hikes and overnight trips, where light loads are to be carried. They are of particular use to climbers and skiers because the center of gravity of the load is much lower than with a packframe. They do not have the tendency to throw the wearer off balance, as does a packframe load with a high center of gravity. However, with most rucksacks a load of more than 20 to 25 pounds is uncom-

A small rucksack for day hikes. Photo by Lou Clemmons.

fortable. Even then you need to lean "into" the load to keep your balance. There are frameless rucksacks and also rucksacks with a light metal frame to give "shape" to the load. Many backpackers never use a rucksack. For the average hiker their primary use is for day hikes.

FRAMELESS RUCKSACKS. For carrying a jacket, rain gear, lunch, first aid equipment, etc., on a day hike a frameless rucksack is often used. For loads of 10 to 20 pounds a frameless rucksack is usually preferable to carrying a large packframe and packbag. In the frameless type the load will bear directly against the back. If it is a large load it can generate quite a bit of heat and sweat and be uncomfortable on a hot day. It is best to buy a fairly large rucksack and plan to fill it only loosely. If a loaded rucksack is packed tightly it will tend to bounce against the back with each step and make for a very uncomfortable load. It is also important in packing the rucksack to have clothing or other soft material in the area that will be riding next to the back.

Rucksacks are often made roughly triangular in shape, with the peak of the triangle riding near the nape of the neck. They are frequently made of canvas, which is relatively rugged and tends to retain the original shape of the sack. Nylon is also used. Nylon rucksacks have the capability of being folded and compacted into a small bundle for stowing. Some backpackers carry such a rucksack inside their packbag for day trips that they plan to make from a base camp. The average frameless rucksacks range in weight from about 1 to 2 pounds. Cost ranges from about $5 to $20.

FRAMED RUCKSACKS. For greater loads, of roughly 15 to 30 pounds, framed rucksacks are available. The frame tends to give shape to the load and to keep various objects in the rucksack from poking into the hiker's back. With a few exceptions (a few sophisticated designs have weight-bearing belts) the load is still borne entirely on the shoulders. When it reaches the 25- to 35-pound category it is often best to go to a packframe-packbag combination.

Framed rucksacks are usually somewhat larger and a pound or more heavier than the frameless type. Costs range from about $12 to $40.

BELT POUCH. Rather than stuffing your pockets with a few items of equipment needed for a very short hike, it is a good idea to use a belt bag or pouch. These usually take the form of a small zippered compartment that simply slips on your belt. The cost usually ranges from about $3 to $8. However, it is not difficult to make a simple belt pouch if you choose to do so.

FANNY PACK OR WAIST PACK. The fanny pack or waist pack is usually a fairly large zippered compartment measuring roughly 12″ x 4″ x 4″. It is contoured to fit around the waist and has its own waist strap with buckle. Its use is generally limited to short day hikes in good weather. Cost is usually $6 to $9.

Waist pack

Waist pack being worn by author

The "waist pack" is useful for day hikes. When you know absolutely that a few small items of equipment and your lunch and canteen will suffice for the hike you are taking, this is a good way to carry your few items of gear.

3

Sleeping Gear

SLEEPING BAGS

Backpacking requires the expenditure of a lot of physical energy. If you are to recover this energy and be prepared to start each day with renewed strength and enthusiasm, then you must sleep soundly and comfortably at night. Few things are more important on a backpack trip than your bed. It is one of those factors. like a good pack and good boots, that can mean the difference between an enjoyable trip and one where you wish you had stayed home. Don't try to drive any "hard bargains" in purchasing a sleeping bag for backpacking. A good sleeping bag, purchased from a reputable manufacturer or supplier, is a wise investment, a pleasure to pack, and a joy to use. With reasonable care it will probably last for many years.

The first backpackers carried blankets, and later old style rectangular bags that left much to be desired from the standpoint of weight, warmth, bulk, and other important factors. It was not unusual in the old days for a backpacker to carry 10 to 12 pounds of blankets, or a rectangular-shaped bag weighing 8 or 10 pounds. This is no longer necessary. Modern methods of construction and modern filler materials have made available good sleeping bags weighing from 3 to 5 pounds that will provide the necessary warmth and comfort required by the most discerning backpacker.

For backpacking use the rectangular shape sleeping bags have given way to the "mummy" shape. A mummy bag, in contrast to the rectan-gular-shaped bag, essentially conforms to the shape of your body, being wide at the shoulders and tapering toward the feet. The rectangular bag has much more room in it than is necessary to confine your body, and thus it weighs more than a mummy-shaped bag which will provide equivalent warmth. The air inside the sleeping bag must be heated by your body before you will become warm. It takes considerably longer to heat the excess volume of air in a rectangular bag than in a mummy shape.

FILLER MATERIAL. The warmth of a sleeping bag is a primary consideration. Warmth in turn is determined by the *loft* or *thickness* of the insulating material. The greater the thickness the greater the dead air space which is created around your body and thus the warmer the bag will be.

Many types of filler material have been used in the making of sleeping bags. Two important considerations are compressibility and weight. For backpacking it is desirable to compress the bag into a reasonably small space for ease in carrying. Weight is also a primary consideration in any item that must be backpacked.

The down of the northern Canadian domesticated goose has long been considered the best filler for high quality sleeping bags for backpacking. It can be compressed repeatedly and will still regain its original volume when the pressure is released. One ounce of good down will fill a space of over 500 cubic inches.

Top quality goose down has become quite

scarce and expensive in recent years. As a result, some manufacturers are substituting duck down, or a blend of goose down and duck down, in their sleeping bags.

Good duck down comes quite close to being the equal of goose down insofar as the factors of compressibility and loft are concerned, and is used in many good quality bags. Incidentally, in goose down the color of the down makes no difference in the quality. Gray goose down is as satisfactory as white down. Also, a few small feathers are present even in the best quality down.

As a rough check on the quality of down, you can feel through the covering of the bag for lumps that indicate the presence of pin feathers. You can also check the bag label, which is required by law to state the nature of the filling, but there can be a great deal of variation in fillings covered by the various descriptive tags on sleeping bags, even though the tags would all appear to indicate high quality filler. Avoid any sleeping bag if the label indicates that it contains reprocessed down. Bags can be compared somewhat by laying them out on a flat area, fluffing them up, and noting the loft. The bag with the most loft will be the thickest and warmest. Since you cannot see the filler material, this is another important reason for buying your sleeping bag from a reputable manufacturer. Down bags range in price from about $50 to over $100.

Cheap sleeping bags are available which contain inexpensive filler materials such as kapok, orlon, celacloud, and a long list of others, which can be quite confusing to the inexperienced. Many of these fillers have a tendency to mat and pack into lumps, thus losing their insulating value, which was probably very poor to start with. Some of the fillers are attractive to vermin. An exception is Du Pont Dacron Fiberfill, which is now available in two different varieties. Du

Pont Dacron "88" (polyester fiberfill) has been used for some years in making sleeping bags. For many years it was the best of the synthetic materials available. It is resilient and not very fluffy. It will not pack into lumps. Many rectangular-shaped sleeping bags, over the years, have been made from Du Pont Dacron "88." A very few suppliers carry mummy-shaped bags made of this filler material. A well-constructed mummy-shaped bag, containing 3 to 4 pounds of Dacron "88," is satisfactory for temperatures down to about freezing. The big advantage of such sleeping bags is their relatively low cost, about $25 to $40. A disadvantage is their high bulk and lack of compressibility.

A rather recent development in synthetic fiber materials is Du Pont Dacron Fiberfill II. This material compresses much more readily than Dacron "88." It also recovers quickly from compression and can be refluffed. In fact, its compressibility is roughly 90 percent of the compressibility of goose down. It takes about 1.4 pounds of Fiberfill II to equal the insulating value of one pound of goose down. An important characteristic to the backpacker is that Fiberfill II is virtually *waterproof*. It can be water-saturated and still retain essentially its original loft. Also, a wet Fiberfill II sleeping bag is much easier and quicker to dry than a wet down bag. In the field, water can be wrung from a wet Fiberfill II bag, the bag dried for a short period, and it is ready for use. In fact, after being wrung out by hand, the still damp bag can be used immediately with relative comfort. Still another important consideration is that Fiberfill II is much less costly than down and hence the finished sleeping bags are less expensive. They are not yet as inexpensive as you might expect, however, considering the difference in cost of the filler materials. As manufacturing experience is gained the price will probably improve. Mum-

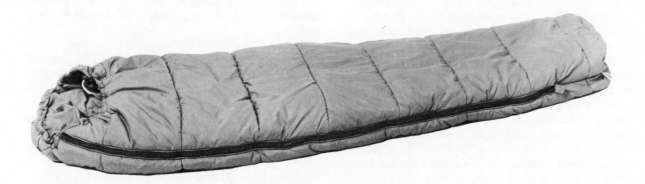

This sleeping bag uses Du Pont Fiberfill II as an insulating material. Photo courtesy of Mountain Products Corp., Wenatchee, Washington.

my-shaped sleeping bags suitable for backpacking, using Fiberfill II as an insulator, are now available from a number of suppliers of backpacking and mountaineering equipment. Jackets and parkas are also available which use this material as insulator. Cost of sleeping bags is about $45 to $70.

Some sleeping bags used for backpacking utilize open cell polyurethane foam as an insulator. Sleeping bags using this material have been on the market for a few years. Open cell urethane foam is another of the few materials that will still insulate when damp. A thoroughly soaked sleeping bag which uses this material as an insulator can be wrung out in the field and can be used immediately with relative comfort. A disadvantage when it comes to packing these sleeping bags is their relative bulk and stiffness. They compress very little and about twice the storage volume is required as for an equivalent down bag. However, an advantage in this regard is that a sleeping pad or mattress is frequently not required when using such a bag. The urethane foam used as an insulator is often a sufficient pad in itself between the sleeper and the ground. These bags do not "conform" or drape about the body as do most sleeping bags which are made from more conventional materials. However, some backpackers have found these bags to be quite acceptable. From a weight standpoint such sleeping bags are competitive with conventional bags, especially if the backpacker eliminates a separate pad or mattress. These sleeping bags range in price from about $40 to $60. Trail Tech Company of Corona, New York, is a manufacturer of urethane foam sleeping bags.

CONSTRUCTION. Most mummy bags are designed so that the sleeper's head is completely enclosed by the bag proper, leaving only the face exposed. A single drawstring provides for drawing the bag tightly around the head. On a cold night this is important because it prevents the escape of warm air from the sleeping bag. Some sleeping bags come from the manufacturer with a tie tape threaded around the circumference of the head opening. When you are snug in the sleeping bag you reach up from the inside with your hands and tie a nice bow knot in the the tie tape. However, this frequently presents a problem later on. When you wake up, either during the night or early morning, and sleepily reach up to quickly undo the bow knot in the tie tape, you may find that it has relapsed during the night into a good solid knot. Not being able to see the knot you are trying to untie makes the job no simple matter, and being somewhat captive inside the sleeping bag may give you claustrophobia quickly. The solution is to use one of the small spring-loaded drawstring clamps in the tie tape, as stocked by most supplies of backpack equipment. They weigh only about 1 ounce. They are simple to use and effective.

Some mummy sleeping bags have a hood for covering the head which can be left open and lying flat in warm weather. The hood will have a drawstring for drawing it tight around the head when the weather is cold. Most bags designed with separate hoods also have a drawstring around the shoulder area to shut out the cold air at that point when the hood is left open.

The outer and inner fabric used in the shell construction of down sleeping bags must be downproof, so that the down pods will not work their way through the bag covering and be lost. Many manufacturers of quality down sleeping bags use 1.5 to 1.9-ounce ripstop nylon. This material is essentially downproof, breatheable,

Sleeping bag which uses open cell urethane foam as an insulator. Photo courtesy of Trail Tech.

Spring-loaded drawstring clamp, installed on sleeping bag drawstring.

and strong (good tear resistance). It is also wind-resistant and fairly water-repellent. Taffeta is a nylon material with characteristics similar to those of ripstop nylon. It is also used for shell construction in some of the quality sleeping bags.

A basic aspect of sleeping bag design is the cut of the inner and outer shells. In a differential cut the inner shell (next to the sleeper's body) is cut smaller than the outer shell. This type of cut supposedly has the advantage of allowing the filler to loft more freely about the sleeper's body. However, many quality bags are made with the inner shell having the *same circumference* as the outer shell. Manufacturers who use this design claim that the inner shell drapes more closely around the sleeper's body, thus leaving fewer air pockets to be heated. Quite a few manufacturers who previously used the differential cut have abandoned it in favor of inner and outer shells of the same diameter.

A well-made sleeping bag will have additional room at the foot end in the form of a special elliptical or box-shaped construction rather than a flat envelope. This prevents the feet from thrusting into the filler material and thus creating a thin spot or cold area.

To provide uniform warmth in a sleeping bag, it is important that the filler material be kept evenly distributed around the sleeper's body. In down bags the filler material is contained in tubes or panels. In a very few inexpensive sleeping bags these tubes run longitudinally, from the head to the foot. However, the filler tends to shift within the tubes, and in the longitudinal tubes shifts toward the foot of the bag. The better sleeping bags have circumferential filler compartments, or a variation of this, which is the *chevron* pattern. Panels are usually constructed of nylon netting, which is light and compressible, and does a satisfactory job of preventing down shift between compartments.

One of the indications of quality in a sleeping bag is the *stitching*. It should be uniform. Nylon thread is generally used. Check the stitching in difficult-to-sew places, such as the hood of the bag. There should be a double row of stitching at points of stress. Eight to ten stitches per inch is about right. Cheaply made bags may have much longer stitches. Backstitching or tacking should be used at the end of a row of stitching for reinforcement.

In shopping for a sleeping bag be sure to get one that is long enough. If you are six feet or taller in height, this requires special consideration. If you should purchase a sleeping bag that is a bit too short, you will regret every night that you spend in it. You should get inside the bag. With the hood closed there should be ample room at the shoulders and at the foot end. With your body stretched out your feet should not press against the ends of the bag. Make sure you can draw the hood tightly and securely about your head.

Internal Construction of Down Bags. The internal construction of the sleeping bag is of primary importance. A well-constructed sleeping bag having 2 pounds of high grade goose down filler material may easily keep the sleeper warm at temperatures down to 5° or 10° F. A poorly constructed sleeping bag using exactly the same filler material may be cold at temperatures well above freezing. Good construction means extra workmanship and good workmanship and a higher cost, but it is a very important factor. There are essentially five basic types of internal construction used in down sleeping bags.

A *quilted* or *sewn through* construction is used in some of the inexpensive sleeping bags. It is the least satisfactory of the various types of construction because it permits cold spots at the stitch-through points. The best quality sleeping bags have panels or baffles sewn to the inner and outer shells. In a *box* type of construction baffles are used which form individual compartments at right angles to the inner and out fabric. In this type of construction there is some tendency for the down to fall away from the baffles. This may result in cold spots.

The *slant tube* or *slant wall* type of construction is used by many manufacturers of high quality sleeping bags. The slant tube minimizes

Down-filled baffle on sleeping bag, along full length of zipper, prevents cold air from entering bag.

Sleeping bag with side-mounted zipper (down-filled). Photo by Lou Clemmons.

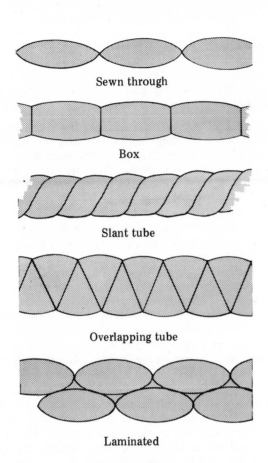

Sewn through

Box

Slant tube

Overlapping tube

Laminated

Sleeping Bag Construction

the shift of the down. At the same time when pressure is released from the bag the down regains its maximum loft.

The *overlapping tube* type of construction is efficient in restricting down shift. However, it somewhat restricts the down from reaching its maximum loft when the pressure is released. There is also some penalty in added weight and cost, because of the additional paneling required.

The *laminated* type of construction is essentially two quilted type sleeping bags sewn together so as to eliminate the cold spots. Such construction makes the bags heavy because of the extra layers of fabric. Very few sleeping bags use this design.

ZIPPERS. Some sleeping bags are made without zippers. You simply put them on like a sock. If the weather is warm, you push the bag down from the head and shoulders, for more ventilation. Most of the better quality sleeping bags have zippers. A zipper adds a bit to the weight and is a possible source of heat loss. However, the possibility of heat loss at the zipper can be

countered by a well-designed, down-filled flap. The down-filled flap or tube should be constructed so that it cannot be easily moved out of position when the sleeper rolls over.

The best zippers are nylon, rather than metal. The nylon zippers do not freeze and are lighter in weight. A nylon zipper is not cold to the touch, as is a metal zipper. Double sliding zippers which can be zipped from top or bottom are recommended. In shopping for a sleeping bag check all modes of zipper operation. Check to see that the down tube or flap, which prevents cold air from entering at the zipper closure, gives complete coverage and that it is not easily caught in the zipper. Also the draft tube should not easily be moved out of place when the sleeper turns during the night.

Whether to buy a bag with a full-length or half-length zipper primarily depends upon intended use. If you are going to be using your sleeping bag mostly for warm weather backpacking, you may want a full-length zipper, for a wider range of temperature control. If most of your backpacking is in cool weather, a half-length zipper may suffice.

Whether the zipper is located on the top of the sleeping bag or on the side is usually not of great importance. In the case of a husband-wife team who buy two sleeping bags with the thought of zippering the two together, a full-length, side-mounted zipper will be necessary. In such cases it is important to check the operation of the zippers to see that they are compatible. Most full-length zippers on quality sleeping bags are side mounted and are 70 inches or more in length.

LINERS AND COVERS. A liner can be used in your sleeping bag to aid in keeping it clean. Depending upon material and construction, a liner will also add some warmth. Commercially made liners are available from some manufacturers of sleeping bags. It is not difficult to make a sleeping bag liner yourself from muslin or other suitable material. If you plan to use a liner it will be necessary to purchase a sleeping bag which has an internal system of snaps and tie tapes, in order to keep the liner in place during use. Otherwise it will get hopelessly and uncomfortably twisted around your body during the night. I have used a liner in my sleeping bag in the past, but found it to be generally unsatisfactory. When it wasn't caught in the zipper it was frequently twisted uncomfortably about my body (sometimes both at the same time).

There is no doubt that it is desirable to keep your sleeping bag clean. However, this can be accomplished by other and simpler means than using a sleeping bag liner. First, you can bathe fully before going to bed. This is not always practical. However, it is no great chore to wash at least your head and face and hopefully your feet. In addition you can sleep in a pair of pajamas. These can be very lightweight, as an aid only to keeping your bag clean, or they can be of such material (flannel, dacron suit, etc.) as to provide additional warmth. If you feel you may overlook washing your feet before crawling into your sleeping bag at night sew a "foot" or "bootie" to each leg of the pajamas. The pajamas will then keep the foot area of your bag clean, as well as the main portion. The area of your sleeping bag that will often become soiled rather soon is the *head end.* This is usually the result of oil and dirt in the hair. A small homemade "night cap" or hood to cover your hair will prevent this soiling. In cold weather a wool stocking cap is often worn by backpackers at night for warmth. If kept clean, this will suffice to protect the bag from hair oil and dirt. You will find that wearing the items described will keep your sleeping bag just as clean as using a liner and it will be much more comfortable to sleep in.

A cover for your sleeping bag, to keep it clean, is generally not recommended. You will find that it has about the same nuisance aspects as a liner. If you use an adequate ground cloth, with a pad or mattress of at least knee length, you will find that the outer shell of your sleeping bag will stay reasonably clean for a long time. The sleeping pad or mattress will give protection from abrasion on the ground side.

CLEANING DOWN SLEEPING BAGS. A down sleeping bag when thoroughly dirty is difficult to clean. It is also very easy to permanently damage a down bag in the cleaning process. Most backpackers take more than casual care of a down bag to see that it does not become dirty in the first place. Probably the average owner also tolerates a soiled bag somewhat longer than he normally would because of the known hazards in cleaning.

Spot cleaning of the nylon shell is relatively easy and harmless. Spots are simply sponged with lukewarm water and mild soap, and then rinsed with plain lukewarm water. The bag is then hung up to dry. A complete and thorough washing of a down bag is something else. A wet down bag should never be lifted by its shell. The weight of the wet down will tear out the internal baffling of the bag. The best place for washing is the bathtub in your home. Again, use lukewarm water and mild soap. Place the dry bag in the tub of water and work it with your hands, being very careful not to scrub, twist, or yank the bag. You can gently press, squeeze, and massage the bag while it is lying in the bottom of the tub. Again it must *not* be lifted, even partially, by its *shell.* When you are satisfied that the soap and water have done the job, drain the tub, leaving the bag lying in the bottom. Then slowly refill the tub again with clear lukewarm water. Continue to massage and manipulate the bag until all evidence of soap has been removed. This will require the tub to be drained and refilled a number of times. In the last rinsing gently *squeeze* (not wring) as much water from the bag as possible. You can then remove the bag from the tub very carefully by placing both arms under the folded bag so that the entire bag is supported. It can then be put in a front loading clothes drier which is set on low heat. Placing a pair of clean tennis shoes in the drier will help in breaking up clumps of wet down and also assist the buildup of static electricity which is necessary for the bag to regain full loft. Repeated cycling on low heat will be necessary. When the sleeping bag is dried to the point where it is only slightly damp it may be removed and hung outdoors for final drying.

An alternative to hand washing your sleeping bag is to find a reputable dry cleaner who is experienced in the dry cleaning of down sleeping bags. In choosing a dry cleaner it is best to select one who has a known reputation for the satisfactory cleaning of down sleeping bags, and this narrows the choice considerably. Your sleeping bag may need to be mailed to an out-of-town cleaning establishment. The sleeping bag should be carefully air-dried after the dry cleaning, for two reasons. First, any cleaning solvent remaining in the bag may deteriorate the goose down. Second, dry cleaning fluids are toxic and have been known to kill sleepers who used them before they were thoroughly aired. Eight to ten days of air drying are not too much. If you are in doubt as to where to send your sleeping bag for dry cleaning, consult with a backpacking and mountaineering equipment supply firm for their recommendation.

OTHER SLEEPING GEAR

ROUGHING IT. A bed made on the bare ground will not provide the comfort that most people need for a good night's sleep. Most of us require something a bit softer. There was a time when a person could take an axe or hatchet and cut limbs from live trees in order to make a bough bed. That time is past. Don't do it! Leaves, grass, and other similar materials can also be used to provide a foundation for your sleeping bag. However, the time required to gather such materials and the likelihood that you won't find them when and where you want them add up to the fact that you should plan to carry a pad or mattress of some sort on which to lay your sleeping bag. It should also be pointed out that most bough beds, as well as beds made from other natural materials, would look pretty sad in comparison with a good air mattress or foam pad. Especially after such beds have been slept in for four or five hours, they leave much to be desired. Try to imagine, too, some nice, large, sticky, stained areas on your good sleeping bag, caused from the pitch in the pine or balsam boughs.

Most important is the fact that the gathering of any natural materials for making a bed (including grass, leaves, etc.) *can no longer be condoned* from an ecology standpoint.

AIR MATTRESS. The average person will sleep comfortably if his head, shoulders, and hips are properly supported. Your legs can extend past the edge of the mattress onto the ground and it will make little difference. A hip-length air mattress weighing under 2 pounds is suitable for backpacking. For very short backpack trips the added weight of a full-length mattress may not be important, but on longer trips it will be. An air mattress made of plastic (vinyl) material will be lightest in weight for a given size. Such a mattress will also be the most

subject to tears and pinholes from twigs, pine needles, sharp stones, and other material lying on the ground where you choose to make your bed. You should go over the ground very carefully (on your hands and knees) before you put down an air mattress, and remove all such objects. If you use a plastic air mattress, be sure it is in new condition. After they have been lying around for a few months (even though they are not used much), plastic air mattresses will start to develop pinholes that will about drive a person crazy trying to keep them patched. Your ground cloth (discussed later) will give some protection from puncture, but plan on spending some valuable camp time (and sleeping time) in locating and patching air leaks if you use a plastic air mattress. A few years ago a discarded plastic air mattress was one of the more common items of trash that one sometimes found at abandoned campsites in the backwoods. Today very few backpackers use them.

The best air mattresses for backpacking are made of coated nylon fabric. A typical air mattress of this type, in hip-length size, is about 22″ wide by 48″ long and weighs about 28 ounces (no pillow). Cost is about $11. Such mattresses will take a lot of fairly rough treatment. Air mattresses made from other materials are available but most of them are too heavy for backpacking use. A patch kit should always be carried with an air mattress, so that any necessary repairs can be made on the spot.

Blowing up an air mattress, if you should decide to use one, might be considered one of the "occupational hazards" of backpacking. It takes a lot of huffing and puffing. After a hard day on the trail you may get light-headed and pass out. In a group, a lightweight air mattress pump might be a justifiable item of equipment. However, it would be unusual to find many persons in a group using air mattresses.

BACKPACK AIR MATTRESS. A typical air mattress for backpacking, made of coated nylon fabric.

A distinct disadvantage of an air mattress is that it provides only very poor insulation between your sleeping bag and the ground. This is an area where you particularly need good insulation. This is because the filler material on the ground side of your sleeping bag (especially down bags) is compressed when you are lying on it.

When you inflate an air mattress for the night, don't blow it up too hard. It should be fairly limp. When you lie on it and can just barely feel your hip touch the ground at one point, it is about right. Lay it out so that the valve end is near your head. Then you can easily reach over and let a bit of air out if it is too hard. Or, if it is too soft, roll off to one side and blow it up a little. When you first wake up in the morning, reach over and open the air valve while you are still lying on your mattress. This will save a little time later on in getting the air out. Lying on the hard ground will also provide additional incentive for getting up. In packing your air mattress, try not to fold it in the same pattern each time since this will cause the mattress to weaken along the seams where it is repeatedly folded.

URETHANE FOAM PADS (OPEN CELL). The urethane foam pads, ranging in thickness from 1″ to 2″ or more, are quite popular among backpackers. Most persons find that the cushioning effect and the relatively firm support provided by a foam pad is far superior to an air mattress. Theoretically an air mattress would seem to be ideal for providing maximum comfort to a tired body. However, it does not. Based on personal experience and that of other backpackers, I find that most persons achieve a much better night's sleep when using a foam pad in contrast to an air mattress. The foam pads also provide good *insulation* between the sleeper and the cold ground, whereas an air mattress provides essentially no insulation.

A short urethane foam pad, 24″ by 48″ and 1½″ thick, weighs about 1¼ pounds, which is about one-half pound lighter than a good air mattress of equivalent size. A disadvantage of the urethane foam pads is their bulk, and this is a major factor. A pad of the above dimensions rolls into a bulky package having a diameter of about 9″. When rolled tightly for carrying on your packframe the roll must be secured by wide straps. If rope is used the pressure exerted by the tightly rolled cylinder will cut into the foam.

Another disadvantage of the urethane foam pads is that they are open cell construction. They will readily absorb water. They should therefore be enclosed in a cloth cover to keep out moisture. A cover which uses waterproof nylon on the bottom side of the foam pad and cotton on the top side is good. Your sleeping bag would have a tendency to slide around if the top side (next to the bag) were nylon.

CLOSED CELL FOAM PADS. The ensolite pads are closed cell foam. No cover is needed for these pads. They will not absorb water and they provide excellent insulation. An ensolite pad will provide about three times as much insulation as an open cell urethane foam pad of equivalent thickness.

A popular size of ensolite pad is 21″ x 56″, of ⅜″ thickness and weighing about 1¼ pounds. Although a ⅜″ thick ensolite pad is not as comfortable as the thicker urethane foam pads, many backpackers find ensolite pads to be a very acceptable compromise, considering weight, bulk, insulation, and general comfort. I have used a ⅜″ thick ensolite pad on many backpack trips and find them to be very acceptable. When rolled for attaching to the packframe a 56″ pad is about 5″ in diameter.

Another popular type of closed cell foam pads are the Blu-Foam (Volarafoam™ is similar). These foam pads weigh less than half an equivalent size ensolite pad and they also cost less. I have used these pads and find them to be very satisfactory. The following are some comparison figures between ensolite and Blu-Foam:

TYPE	SIZE	WEIGHT	APPROX. COST
Ensolite	⅜″ x 21″ x 56″	1¼ lbs.	$5.00
Blu-Foam	⅜″ x 24″ x 48″	6 oz.	$3.00

I have observed that on the trail more and more backpackers are seen carrying closed cell foam pads. This applies to summer as well as cold weather backpacking, so evidently many hikers consider the lighter weight and less bulk of the closed cell pads to be an acceptable compromise of comfort.

Closed cell foam pads (ensolite on left, Blu-Foam on right). Photo by Lou Clemmons.

GROUND CLOTH. It is extremely important that your sleeping bag be kept dry. It should also be kept clean, insofar as possible. If you are sleeping inside a floored tent a ground cloth should not be necessary. If you are sleeping in the open a ground sheet is recommended.

If you lay your sleeping bag directly on the ground it will probably get dirty, and possibly wet. Even though you may be sleeping on a full-length mattress or foam pad, you cannot count on these to keep your sleeping bag off the ground. You will be rolling around a bit during the night and some parts of your bag will contact the ground. For one person a ground cloth about 3 feet wide by 7 feet long is recommended.

The least expensive ground sheet will be a piece of plastic (polyethylene), of 3- or 4-mil thickness. A ground cloth made of coated nylon will be much more durable. Some of the backpacking equipment supply firms sell such cloth by the yard. It is certainly not difficult to make your own ground sheet out of coated nylon and it is recommended that you try it.

Stones, sticks, pine cones, etc., should be removed from your bed site before spreading out your ground sheet. It is suggested that you mark the top side of the ground sheet with the word "UP," using a felt tip marker, and that you always place the opposite side next to the ground. In this way you will avoid getting your sleeping bag and mattress dirty by putting them down on the side of the ground sheet that was next to the ground the last time it was used.

PILLOW. Most backpackers improvise a pillow in preference to carrying one as an additional item of equipment. A jacket or other clothing, placed inside the stuff bag used for your sleeping bag, makes a satisfactory pillow. For maximum comfort it should be stuffed only loosely, not full.

Some backpackers may purchase an air mattress with an attached pillow. If you do this make certain that the pillow and the main mattress each have separate valves for filling. If there is only one valve, air will enter the pillow part when you lie on the mattress, making the pillow much too hard for comfort.

If you want to carry a separate pillow, there are air pillows available which weigh 4 to 6 ounces. As with an air mattress, the pillow should never be blown up hard. It should be quite limp for maximum sleeping comfort.

4

Shelter

It is recommended that some type of shelter be taken on every backpack trip. If it is the time of year when rain is very unlikely, then the shelter can be regarded as an emergency measure and the simplest type of protection may suffice. If you are going into an area where rain may be expected, you will want to provide yourself with more substantial protection. Travel in the high mountains, at a time of year when rain or snow, and possibly high winds, may be expected requires substantial protection, usually in the form of a well-made, commercially designed and fabricated tent.

The background and experience of the hikers is also important. When you are taking young children on a backpack trip, under any conditions, some type of tent is desirable. It gives them an added sense of security, which is important when they are being indoctrinated to backwoods travel. The same can be said of many women and girls. The psychological aspect should not be important to experienced male backpackers, and they may be willing and ready to take some gamble with respect to the weather. However, even the latter types will generally take some emergency shelter. Getting thoroughly soaked and possibly chilled and having a camp full of wet gear is no fun, regardless of your experience and background.

In some areas a tent or enclosed shelter of some kind may be required simply for reasons of privacy. In a crowded backwoods campground a sheet of transparent plastic doesn't offer much privacy. Getting dressed and undressed inside a sleeping bag, or trying to, is usually not very practical. However, it should not be overlooked that plastic sheeting is available in black and other colors (nontransparent) if privacy is the main concern. A coated nylon tarp is also nontransparent, and with some improvising will offer privacy that would be acceptable to most male backpackers, if not to women and girls.

In some seasons, and depending on the particular locale, protection from *insects* is just as important as protection from adverse weather. Insects may be in the form of hordes of mosquitoes or black flies, or crawling ants, bugs, and no-see-ums on the ground. These can make for a poor night's sleep.

On a cool and windy night, the wind sweeping unchecked over your sleeping bag can greatly reduce its ability to keep you warm. In a stiff wind a tent can increase the effectiveness of a sleeping bag by as much as 10 to 20 degrees.

PONCHOS

An adult size poncho will be roughly 54″ x 90″ in size. Ponchos made of polyethylene material are available but a coated nylon poncho has much greater tear strength, is generally more comfortable to wear, and is recommended. Many such ponchos have grommets in the corners (you can easily add more) and are suitable for use as an emergency tarp for rain protection at night. Ponchos are available which cover not only the hiker but also his pack. Such ponchos will be about 54″ x 105″ in size.

A poncho such as described above should not be laid directly over your sleeping bag, when used for rain protection at night. It should always be pitched over a ridge line (see page 36) and maximum ventilation provided, even though the size of the poncho may limit the peak height when pitched to 1½′ to 2′. There must be free circulation of air under any such waterproof covering, or excessive condensation will result.

TARPS

Polyethylene tarps are available in many thicknesses. Some are sold at hardware stores as painters' drop cloths. The very thin variety may weigh as little as 6 ounces for a 9′ x 12′ size. However, these are very fragile and must be very carefully handled and kept away from bushes or tree limbs while being erected. Otherwise they will billow with the slightest breeze and be torn before they are erected the first time. They are usually pitched over a ridge line, in "pup tent" fashion, and weighted along the ground edge with smooth round rocks. Unless you have had experience with such tarps, and are willing to take the time and patience to erect them properly (and keep them patched), don't bother with them, even for emergency protection against unlikely rain.

Heavier polyethylene tarps are available in 2 mil to 4 mil thicknesses (.002″ to .004″). A 9′ x 12′ size will weigh about 2 to 4 pounds. Some will have grommets for tying in place, or you can install some grommets yourself, if you have the equipment. In installing grommets, glue an extra square of polyethylene or cloth over the area where each grommet is to be inserted and they will not be so likely to tear out in a stiff breeze. Tarps without grommets can be guyed in position by placing small, smooth stones on the inside surface and tying the guy rope around the stone where its outline protrudes through the other side of the plastic. An even better method of fastening such sheets where no grommets are present is to use Visklamps. This is a small rubber ball and clamp arrangement which works like a garter. They are inexpensive and are available from mountaineering supply shops.

Polyethylene tarps which are reinforced with nylon thread are available from mountaineering shops. These are much more durable than the same weight of nonthreaded poly tarp.

If you are "tarp-minded" the best tarp will be a sheet of coated nylon varying in weight from about 2 to 4 ounces per square yard. Ripstop nylon, about 2.2 ounces per square yard, is good. It is strong, tear resistant, and waterproof. Those purchased from mountaineering shops will have grommets installed and the area around each grommet will be reinforced with an added square patch of cloth. It is not difficult to make a nylon tarp. It will be less expensive than the same size which is made commercially. The coated nylon cloth can be purchased by the yard from a number of mountaineering and backpack equipment supply shops. Seams should be planned so that they will run perpendicular to the ground, rather than horizontal, when pitched in the position that you would normally use the tarp. All seams should be coated with urethane seam sealant. For sewing nylon cloth, cotton-covered polyester thread is recommended.

Tarps can be pitched in many configurations. The configuration used will often depend upon the particular terrain where you find yourself when it comes time to make camp. Sometimes a large log, 3 or 4 feet in diameter or more, can be used as the "front" of your tarp shelter and the tarp can be erected in a position slanting from the top of the log to the ground. Probably the most used configuration is to pitch the tarp over a ridge line in an A-frame or pup tent fashion. In this configuration, with a steep sidewall, it will usually shed water readily. In other configurations it is quite likely that there will be some places in the roof which will sag and collect water. If it rains this will mean that you will have to "dump water" from these sagging places at regular intervals, by pushing up from the inside with your hand. If you are asleep at night while the water is collecting in puddles on certain portions of your roof, it may start to leak long before you are aware that there is a puddle there.

TUBE TENTS

The tube tents are used by some backpackers as emergency shelter. They are waterproof (when new) but there are drawbacks. Even though the ends of the tent are open, there will be some condensation inside. Rain falling on the outer edge of the ground side will usually run toward the center, wetting your sleeping bag and other articles which are on the ground surface of the tent. If you attempt to partially close the ends of the tent you must be very careful. It is extremely important that the tent *not* be closed tightly. If this is done the sleeper will use up the available oxygen in the tent and may suffocate. If you decide to try such a tent, you should mark a particular section (with a felt tip marker) that is to go next to the ground. Thereafter, always pitch the tent with that section on the ground side (rather than as a wall). The ground side will develop pinholes and leaks, and if the tent is pitched so that that side is on a wall, your tube tent will leak.

Another drawback of these tents is that you should carry poles, for the front and aft ends. Trying to find a level spot, with good drainage, between two trees that are positioned so as to accommodate a ridge line, is quite a task.

The polyethylene tube tents leave much to be desired. This is evident from the number of such tents that one sees discarded at campsites in the backwoods. (The owner "forgot" to carry it out with his other litter, when he found it didn't do the job intended.) Some mountaineering shops have discontinued selling tube tents because they have become such a common item of backwoods litter.

If you are on a limited budget and are seriously considering a tube tent, I would recommend that you consider making a tent yourself from reinforced plastic sheeting. This refers to the polyethylene sheets that have been reinforced with nylon thread, making them much stronger and tear resistant. (Eastern Mountain Sports is one source of such sheeting.) Buy a sheet about 8 or 9 feet long and of sufficient width to accommodate the desired number of persons when pitched over a ridge line, or between poles. The "floor" will be a separate ground cloth, spread over pine needles, or whatever the terrain offers. Reinforce the edges of the front and aft ends of the tent with cloth adhesive tape. To these reinforced edges, sew a triangular piece of mosquito netting, fore and aft, of sufficient size to accommodate the end opening when pitched. The mosquito netting at the front end should have a zipper sewn down the vertical center, from the peak, to allow entry. Additional cloth adhesive tape can be used at intervals along the longitudinal ground edge to provide for insertion of a grommet at that point. You now have a tent which will not sweat and is essentially mosquito proof, and rain blowing in a bit from the open ends will not run the length of the floor (as in a tube tent) and wet the contents.

ONE-MAN BACKPACK TENT

Sleeping in the open, with only the sky for a roof, can be a delightful experience. You can watch the tall pines sway in the breeze and view the starlit sky, unhampered by a "roof" over your head. Depending on the season, however, mosquitoes and other "peskies" may make your night in the open pretty uncomfortable. With a little ingenuity it is not difficult to make a one-man tent, suitable for most backpacking, which will provide protection from insects, rain,

reptiles, and rodents. I frequently use such a one-man tent that I planned and fabricated, and which meets these requirements. This tent is essentially a cover for your sleeping bag, with some additional room at the head end for a few items of clothing or equipment. The tent is about 8 feet long, 28 inches high at the head end, and 17 inches high at the foot end. The main tent is made of nylon mosquito netting. A plastic fly sheet can be used for rain protection, although I generally use a coated nylon fly. Including the coated fly sheet and stakes, the tent weighs about 44 ounces. With such a tent you dress or undress outside. There is not room inside unless you are a real contortionist. You slip into your sleeping bag at the same time you slide into the tent. However, it answers the requirement for a lightweight, inexpensive shelter. Instructions for making this tent are given in Appendix C.

It is a pleasant experience to lie in this tent at night, with the head end of the fly sheet drawn back, and watch the starlit sky overhead. If you want protection from rain or wind, you simply fasten the head end of the nylon fly sheet back in place and you are in business. A tree or bush at the head end, for fastening the ridge line, is all that is required for supporting the tent. A stick 18 or 20 inches long, under the ridge line at the foot end, keeps that end off your sleeping bag.

Backpacking literature frequently shows a ridge line strung between two trees, supporting a tube or other type tent. However, even in a forest of trees it is seldom that you will find two trees, the right distance apart, with level ground between them suitable for pitching your tent. It is possible, but not very likely, that you will find such a spot when you need it. Finding one tree or large bush, with fairly level ground nearby, as

ONE-MAN BACKPACK TENT. Note "bathtub" floor constuction. A waterproof fly is used over tent to give protection from the elements. Instructions for making this tent are given in Appendix C.

required for the one-man backpack tent just described, is not so much of a job.

FOREST TENTS

There is a wide range of tents available for general backpacking use which are generally referred to as forest tents. Such tents are intended for use *below* timberline, where the primary requirements are protection from rain (possibly snow), insects, and, to some extent, storage of gear out of reach of birds and rodents. The effectiveness of a sleeping bag (low temperature range) is also increased when used with a tent. Very high winds, deep snow, and severe cold are not normally encountered in the use of such tents, as contrasted with tents designed for high altitude mountaineering use.

The conditions which are expected to be encountered in your backpacking are important factors to consider in the selection of such a tent. The number of persons who will be using the tent (possibly a family with children) is also a factor. The most popular size tent in this category usually accommodates two or three adults.

A *waterproof* floor is important. If much camping in wet weather is expected it is best to choose a floor construction in which the floor material extends up the sides of the tent, also the front and aft ends, about 6 to 8 inches. This is generally referred to as "bathtub" or simply "tub" construction. Even though the site selected for the tent has imperfect drainage, a tub floor will usually keep water out of the tent.

A prime consideration is *breatheability* of the tent material. If the tent does not breathe so as to allow body moisture given off by the occupants to escape, it will be damp inside, regardless of the weather outside. This requires that the main tent be made of *water-repellent* material, rather than *waterproof*. Maximum ventilation should be provided in the tent design, even though the material is breatheable, to keep condensation to a minimum.

A common style of forest tent is the *A-frame*. It will normally have a screened front and a screened rear "window" of generous size. A modified A-frame may have low side walls, and possibly additional netting along the top edge of the sidewall, for maximum ventilation. Such a tent will usually serve the purpose in mild rain showers, shedding the rain satisfactorily and still not drenching the occupants in their own sweat. Selecting a tent site in a protected area or in the woods, as contrasted to open terrain, will increase its effectiveness.

In hard rain, or in a prolonged rain, a water-repellent tent will sooner or later start to leak.

Therefore, with many such tents a waterproof fly is used. This is pitched over the main tent and the combination will usually provide protection in the most severe and prolonged rain.

You may have possibly located a water-repellent A-frame type tent which is generally satisfactory for your intended use but which does not have a separate rain fly. In that case, especially if you are on a limited budget, you should seriously consider buying the waterproof material and making a rain fly yourself. For an A-frame tent a fly sheet is not difficult to make. It should extend well out over the fore and aft ends of the tent. If you anticipate the need for a sheltered area in cooking with a backpack stove, it is particularly important that a generous overhang be provided at the front end, since that is probably where you will be using your stove, in foul weather.

A-frame tents may have a true A-frame pole arrangement at the front and aft ends. Some have A-frame poles at the front, for easy access to the tent, with a single pole at the aft end. Others have single poles at both ends. An A-frame pole arrangement withstands high winds better than the single poles, but this would not normally be a problem in camping below timberline. Some A-frame tent designs have a lesser height at the rear, often referred to as "low enders." This design saves a bit on weight with no significant decrease in utility.

There are many other shapes of tents in the general category of forest tents. Some are of pyramid shape, with stand up room. Others are igloo-shaped, without ground stakes. In general a tent with waterproof floor and separate rain fly should weigh about 3 pounds per person, including poles and stakes. That is, a two-man tent should weigh about 6 pounds. Cost of forest

A typical A-Frame tent, good for all-round use at normal altitudes. Photo by Lou Clemmons.

type tents varies from about $30 for a simple A-frame, two-man tent, without a separate rain fly, to about $90 for the more sophisticated tents.

ALPINE OR MOUNTAINEERING TENTS

For use in the high mountains and above timberline an alpine or mountaineering tent, made by a reputable manufacturer of mountaineering equipment, is recommended. Such tents must not only withstand snow and rain, but winds of 75 to 100 miles per hour. Two-man tents of this type are often of the A-frame design but they must have much better materials and workmanship, and other features, than an ordinary A-frame tent intended for low altitude use. Good design and adequate performance of such a tent is not merely a matter of convenience. It can mean the difference between life and death, in adverse weather.

Cooking inside the tent is sometimes necessary in prolonged severe weather. Therefore a *vestibule* at the tent entrance or a *cook hole* in the floor (frequently both) is desirable. The cook hole is a section of floor, roughly 30 inches in diameter, which is zippered in place so as to be removable for cooking. This permits stove and utensils to be set on the bare ground and some spillage can occur without soiling the tent or other equipment. A vestibule at the front of the tent is very worthwhile. Ofttimes, cooking can be done in the vestibule (much safer than in the tent) in weather that would prohibit cooking outside the tent.

A good mountaineering tent will have the customary separate fly for rigging over the main tent. It may also have double entrances, with one entrance being of tunnel design. With a tunnel entrance two tents can be joined together. Also, zippered entrances may freeze up under certain weather conditions and a tunnel entrance is preferable from this standpoint. Where zippers are used nylon zippers are much preferable to metal zippers.

The best tents are constructed with a *catenary* cut. A line stretched between two points will never be straight. It will always sag, even from its own weight. This curve is called a catenary. All tent ridges which are sewn straight across between suspension points will sag and this causes wrinkles in the fabric. Pulling on the ridge of the tent to correct this will not do the job and will put a lot of strain on the tent. Therefore the best tents are designed with a catenary curve in the ridge. Some also have "pullouts" which are flaps of cloth on each side of the tent to which a rope line is fastened. When pulled taut this eliminates flapping of the side of the tent and sagging. It also provides more interior room.

A good alpine or mountaineering tent will cost about $110 to $150 and up. A tent of this type will not be required by the average backpacker when backpacking in normal weather and camping at timberline or below.

USE OF TENT

The floor of even the best tents is not very rugged. Choose your tent site carefully. Go over the ground on your hands and knees and remove pine cones, rocks, twigs, etc., that may cause abrasion and possibly a hole in the tent floor. Some backpackers carry a polyethylene sheet of 2 to 4 mil thickness, to be placed under the tent floor. This keeps the ground side of the tent floor clean and also increases the life of the floor. In trimming such a sub-floor sheet to size be sure to cut it *smaller* than the tent floor. If the edges

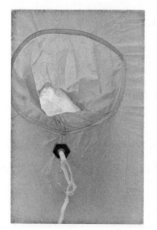

Typical mountaineering tent for high altitude use. This tent has a semicircular zippered cook hole in the floor, and loops at front and rear peaks (inside) for clothesline. Rainfly (not shown) extends below the sidewalls to keep tent dry in all weather. Design provides good stability in high winds. Photo courtesy of Holubar, Boulder, Colorado.

Ventilation tunnel, viewed from inside and outside tent. Photos by Lou Clemmons.

TABLE 4.1 RECOMMENDED SHELTER

Item	Approximate Weight (Ounces)
Tent (one-man tent, as described in Appendix C, or similar design)	36
Tent stakes	8

OR

Two-man tent; one man sharing half the weight, assumed at 6 pounds for tent, fly, poles, stakes, or 48 ounces per man. (Weight includes small whisk broom and sponge, for keeping tent clean.)	48

TABLE 4.2 OPTIONAL SHELTER

Item	Approximate Weight (Ounces)
Nylon tarp; 8' x 11' ripstop nylon, for one man	26
Stakes for tarp	7
Rope for tarp; $\frac{1}{8}$" nylon parachute cord, 30'	2

OR

Nylon tarp; 11' x 12' ripstop nylon, for two men, each man sharing half the weight, by carrying compensating load of other common equipment	40
Stakes for tarp	9
Rope for tarp; $\frac{1}{8}$" nylon parachute cord, 45'	3

of the ground sheet extend beyond the tent floor, rain will fall on the exposed plastic sheet and water will probably run under the tent, just where you don't want it.

To keep the floor of the tent clean on the inside it is a good idea to carry a small whisk broom for sweeping out loose debris. When entering the tent it is best to remove hiking boots, or crawl around on hands and knees. A small sponge is helpful in removing dirt and stains from both inside and outside surfaces of the tent. A tent should not be washed. If on occasion the tent must be rolled up and packed when damp it should be aired and dried at the first opportunity.

With proper selection of a tent site it should not be necessary to ditch a tent. Ditching leads to erosion and mars the ground surface. Contouring the ground to form "hip holes," in preparing a bed site, is in the same category.

Normally it is best to carry tent poles for erecting a tent. Finding suitable trees, with a level space in between for erecting a tent without poles, cannot be depended upon, even in a forest. Tent stakes should also be carried. Aluminum and high-impact plastic stakes are available which are strong and light in weight. They are available in many sizes and shapes, for effectiveness in a variety of soils.

5

Clothing

For mild weather backpacking you will need very little special clothing. Usually some of the clothing that you already have will do the job, except for possibly hiking shoes or boots. This does not mean that "any old thing" will do for clothes on a backpack trip. It will not. With some searching and a little ingenuity, however, you can usually find clothes among those you already have that will suffice. *Never* take any worn-out article of clothing (or equipment) on a backpack trip with the idea that it will probably last and after the trip you can throw it away. Every item should be in good condition, and there should be no doubt about it. Various articles of clothing are discussed in the following paragraphs, pointing out the important requirements of each item. Your clothing should give you maximum protection from the sun. You will take less risk with heat exhaustion, save on drinking water, and avoid sunburn if you keep this in mind. Sunburn on a backpack trip is *serious*, and every precaution should be taken to avoid it. Sunburned shoulders, especially, can be a catastrophe. Therefore, long-sleeved shirts, long trousers, and a broad-brimmed hat are advisable. At the same time you will get more protection from nicks and scratches caused by rocks and bushes and from poison ivy, etc. Long-sleeved shirts and long trousers also offer significant additional protection against snakebite, compared to bare skin, where rattlesnakes (or other poisonous snakes) may be encountered. All clothing should be a little loose fitting rather than a little too tight.

Clothing must *breathe*. This is demonstrated when you wear a pair of rubber hip boots or a rubber slicker on a warm day. Your perspiration cannot escape to the outside and evaporate. Depending upon the amount of exertion, humidity, and other factors, your clothes soon become damp and uncomfortable. Keep shirts and other clothing clean, insofar as practicable, and keep them dry. When clothing becomes sweat or rain soaked it loses a lot of its insulating value. You can easily become chilled when you allow your clothing to get damp.

In general, girls and women wear the same type of outer clothing on backpack trips as men. Long-sleeved shirts, long trousers, and a brimmed hat are recommended.

If you are backpacking into high mountain country or if the trip is to be made in winter, special clothing and rain gear will probably be necessary, as well as special techniques. Weather in high mountain country is frequently unpredictable, at any season. Before going into such country you should have had ample experience at lower elevations. Also, you should not attempt high mountain backpacking unless there are capable persons in the party who are thoroughly experienced in the special equipment and techniques required.

HAT

A few persons backpack without a hat; however, a hat is definitely recommended. The head and neck are very sensitive to changes in temperature. If your head is uncovered a lot of heat loss will occur from the head in cold weather. In the summer sun a hat can mean the difference between being comfortable and being too hot, or possibly becoming sick and dizzy from the sun. It can also prevent sunburn, which is important.

For mild weather backpacking any comfortable hat, reasonably soft and flexible, with a broad brim, should be satisfactory. An old felt hat is good. A few holes cut in the crown will make it cooler. The *Crusher* hat, sold in many backpack equipment shops, is a good hat for backpacking. It weighs about 3 ounces. The white *tennis* or *glacier* hats, with wide brim, are also good. In the hot sun your hat should be worn with the brim turned down, so as to shade the eyes and provide protection for the upper face and ears. Hats made from preshrunk, water-repellent poplin material are also good. Summer hats should be light in color to reflect the sun rays. In hot weather it is best to wear your hat with the crown pushed up, rather than creased, so as to provide maximum *air space* around the head.

To avoid losing your hat in a brisk wind, a *chin strap* is important. You can easily attach a chin strap. Punch a hole in the brim just above each ear and thread a leather thong around the back half of the brim circumference on the top side and down through the holes. Tie the thongs under the chin or use a slide fastener. You will usually need to roll the brim of the hat up in back (or turn it down) to keep the top of your pack from bumping against your hat as you hike along the trail. (This can be very annoying.)

Heat is lost from the body primarily through the extremities (legs, arms, and head), particularly the head. Therefore, in cold weather it is important to wear a hat that will prevent such heat loss. Many hikers wear wool stocking caps for this purpose. A stocking cap can also be worn in your sleeping bag if you are sleeping a bit cool. For very cold weather a balaclava is often used. This covers not only the head but also the neck and lower face as well.

RAIN HAT. A separate rain hat will not normally be necessary. For rain protection a poncho or rain jacket will usually be carried and these will have a hood that protects the head

GLACIER HAT. Provides good protection from sun.

CRUSHER HAT. Note that the top of the pack is well above the hat. The Crusher hat, worn here, is soft and flexible. The annoying "bumping" of the rear part against the pack, that occurs with many broad-brimmed hats, is avoided.

STOCKING CAP. Good headgear for cold weather daytime use and for wearing in sleeping bag on cold nights. Photo by Lou Clemmons.

and neck area. If for some reason you are hiking in predominantly rainy weather you may prefer a separate rain hat. The sou'wester type rain hat, with a wide brim that pulls down to protect the face and neck, is a popular type.

SHIRT

For summer a light cotton shirt, worn next to the undershirt, is recommended. Synthetic shirts do not absorb sweat satisfactorily. A wool shirt worn over this will provide significant additional protection. Many persons find that wool, when worn next to the body, causes their skin to itch and become uncomfortable. The cotton shirt underneath the wool shirt will usually take care of this problem.

The heavy cotton flannel shirts (also called chamois shirts) are quite popular among some backpackers. They are very soft on the skin and absorb sweat readily. Persons highly allergic to wool usually like these shirts.

In cool, wet weather wool has an advantage in that it will keep you warm even though it is wet. Two popular brands of wool shirts are Pendleton and Woolrich. A light or medium weight wool shirt is recommended over the heavy jacket type.

If the shirttail is worn outside the trousers in hot weather you will be cooler because of the added ventilation provided. For wearing outside the trousers, a square cut shirttail is a little more convenient than the long tapered shirttails. However, a long shirttail provides needed additional warmth in cool weather. Shirts should normally have long sleeves. These will give protection against sunburn, and cuts and scratches from brush, and provide added warmth in cool temperatures. A plaid design will not show dirt as readily as a solid color. Light colors will be cooler in hot weather. Two generous-sized pockets, with button top or flap, will prove useful. Before starting out check all buttons and resew those that are loose.

TROUSERS

Long trousers, without cuffs, are recommended. In cool weather they are needed for warmth. They also protect the legs from scratches and insects. In the hot sun they perform the important function of preventing sunburn. Trousers should not be formfitting, but comfortably loose. Large, roomy pockets are desirable.

Some hikers prefer blue jeans for backpacking in mild weather. Some blue jeans may be satisfactory, but many are formfitting and too narrow and tight. They do not allow sufficient freedom of leg movement.

In cool, wet weather *wool* trousers should be worn. An old pair of dress trousers may be satisfactory. In mild weather a cotton trouser will usually do the job. Work trousers are usually generously cut and satisfactory for backpacking.

An elastic waist band to hold your trousers in place, rather than a belt, will be most comfortable. When the waist strap on your pack is drawn tight, a conventional belt and buckle is going to interfere a bit. One solution to the problem is to wear heavy duty suspenders to hold up your trousers. Even if you don't normally wear suspenders you will probably find them useful and comfortable in backpacking.

Some hikers prefer shorts, rather than long trousers, for added freedom of movement and ventilation. If you do wear shorts it is also recommended that you carry long trousers in your pack for cool weather and for part-time protection from the sun, insects, etc.

Trousers should be a little short rather than too long and should fall 2 or 3 inches above the heel of your boot. Don't load the pockets down with equipment. If you have a packsack with outside pockets you can put in those pockets most of the items that you would normally want to carry in your trouser pockets, and they will be almost as accessible. Otherwise put such items in a small bag near the top of your pack.

SWEATERS AND JACKETS

The mornings and evenings in the mountains can be very cool, even in summer. At these times a fairly heavy jacket or sweater will feel very comfortable. Once the sun comes up, however, and you are hiking, you will warm up fast. A heavy jacket may weigh 2½ to 4 pounds, and many times it will only be used for an hour or two in the evening and again in the morning.

It is very important to keep in mind that the *layer system* should be used in selecting clothing for protection against cold, rather than wearing a single heavy garment. Then, as the temperature and your level of exertion change, you can shed or add clothing as necessary to stay comfortable.

For early morning and evening wear, in fairly cold temperatures, a sweater, vest, or jacket can be worn. Down will be the lightest in weight for the protection afforded. For very cold weather the down jacket should have an attached hood. It then becomes a parka. In addition it is usually a good idea to carry a nylon shell jacket for protection against wind. Depending upon wind and humidity, the combination of net underclothes, light cotton shirt, medium weight wool shirt, wool trousers, down jacket and wind shell jacket is usually good for temperatures as low as 20° F. Protection for head and hands is also important in cold temperatures to prevent heat loss in those areas.

An anorak is a pullover parka made of a single layer of water- and wind-repellent cotton. It usually has a large zippered pocket across the front. If you should buy such a garment be sure to get one of generous size. When they are tight fitting, they are very difficult to get into and out of, over other layers of clothing.

It cannot be stressed too strongly that you should avoid sweating if at all possible, especially on a cool or cold day. You may start hiking on a cool morning, wearing a sweater, jacket, or other protective clothing. Exertion will produce body heat and you will soon become warm, and may perhaps start to perspire. Stop immediately! Remove your outer jacket. Take off your hat for awhile. When the head is uncovered much heat is lost from the body through the head area. Open up the neck of your shirt. When you stop, or slow down in your exertion, you may need to put some of your outer clothing back on. In other words, be continually aware of your level of exertion, the relative outside temperature and wind, whether you are becoming warm to the point of perspiring, etc. *Don't allow your clothing to become sweat soaked.* It will lose its insulating value if this happens, and you may become chilled and sick—possibly very sick.

GLOVES AND MITTENS

For normal summer backpacking few hikers bother with gloves. However, at certain seasons a pair of lightweight gloves may be desirable to protect the hands and wrists from insects. In a work party, where clearing of brush, digging, and similar jobs are to be done, gloves will offer some protection against blisters.

Heat is lost from the body mainly through the extremities and this includes the hands. When your hands get cold you can put them in your pockets. However, if much cool weather is expected a pair of gloves may be desirable for warmth. Gloves offer greater versatility than mittens when you are working. You can do many jobs while wearing gloves, but mittens must usually be removed even for very simple

NET UNDERSHIRT. The fishnet construction holds your outer shirt away from the skin. In cold weather your outer shirt and jacket should be closed at the neck and wrists (elastic or knitted cuffs on jacket and preferably a hood) to prevent the escape of warm air at these points. The air pockets provided by the net construction will then be heated by your body and will aid in keeping you warm.

In hot weather your shirt neck should be open and your sleeve cuffs loose, to allow maximum air circulation. The net construction, holding your outer shirt away from the skin, allows perspiration to evaporate without soaking the shirt. This is important in keeping your body cool. Wearing the shirttail of your outer shirt outside the trousers will provide still more circulation.

DOWN VEST. The down vest, made by the author, provided an interesting weekend project. It weighs ten ounces. In combination with a flannel shirt and light windbreaker jacket it keeps the wearer comfortable at temperatures to 20° F (in low humidity). It was made from a kit (precut materials) which is now available from a number of sources (See Appendix A).

tasks. However, mittens offer much more warmth in cold weather. (Your fingers need the "companionship" of one another, in cold weather, if your hands are to stay warm.) Some backpackers wear mittens over a very thin pair of wool or silk gloves, in really cold weather. Simple tasks can usually be performed by removing only the mittens and the thin gloves offer some protection during such periods.

SOCKS

The socks that you wear with your hiking boots are very important. They should either be new or in new condition, without darns or patches. On a hiking trip don't try to get by with old well-worn socks or the thin socks that you usually wear with street shoes. Socks made especially for hiking boots are available from many suppliers of backpack equipment. A single pair of thick wool socks can be worn; however, most hikers agree that wearing *two* pairs of socks (simultaneously) gives better results than a single pair. These can be two pairs of medium weight wool socks, but the usual preference is for a thin inner sock (next to your foot) of wool or cotton, and a thick outer wool sock. Wool socks have the advantage that when they get wet they do not feel wet in the way that cotton socks do. Also, the moisture in wool socks will more readily evaporate than with cotton socks. Try different combinations of socks on your hikes and see which provides the most comfort. Always carry a duplicate set of socks, in whatever combination you prefer, on your backpack trips. At the end of each day it is a good idea to rinse out the socks you have worn that day and dry them overnight.

If your feet sweat a great deal, it is advisable to carry more than one extra change of socks. Stop and change them during the day when they

SOCKS. Two pairs are recommended, a lightweight inner sock of cotton or wool, and a thick, outer wool sock. Photo by Lou Clemmons.

become sweat soaked. Pin or tie the sweat-soaked socks to the outside of your pack so that they will dry as you hike along. The use of a good foot powder is usually a help to persons whose feet perspire a lot.

When you take off your socks run your hand carefully over the outside to detect and remove any tiny stones, twigs, burrs, balls of thread, and so forth. Then turn the sock inside out and repeat the process. Also check the inside of your boots for such tiny particles, which can easily cause a blister or tender spot on your foot.

HANDKERCHIEF

A handkerchief is not generally essential. This is usually used for blowing your nose, and it is hoped that you won't start a backpack trip with a cold. A handkerchief will soon get dirty and carrying dirty laundry in your pack is not recommended. A small package of Kleenex or some toilet tissue will do the same job. If you usually use your handkerchief or bandana for wiping your hands and face, as many hikers do, a 10-inch square of old, thin toweling carried in your hip pocket will do a better job.

If you use disposable tissues, put them in your pocket after use and burn them later if you have a fire available, or carry them in your litter bag. *Don't* litter the trail with them. To those persons who cannot resist the temptation to nonchalantly toss paper tissues down along the trail after each use, we implore you to please stay with the handkerchief.

A bandana or very large handkerchief is frequently useful when worn as an item of clothing. When placed around the neck it will help keep out dust. The neck, particularly the back and sides, is very susceptible to sunburn. A bandana, worn as a neckerchief, will protect this sensitive area. It will also feel comfortable in a cold wind. To a degree, it provides protection from insects in the neck area.

UNDERCLOTHES

On a backpack trip you can wear the same underclothes that you normally wear. However, in warm weather, after a period of strenuous hiking, the undershirt (in particular) will usually become sweat soaked. It will cling to your skin and wick the moisture into your clothing. A *fishnet* style of undershirt (and drawers also) is available which will prevent this. These fishnet underclothes are cooler and drier in summer and warmer in winter. In warm weather when wearing fishnet underwear you loosen up your shirt at the neck and sleeves, and maybe open the front and also allow the shirttail to hang outside the trousers (if it is really warm). This allows free circulation of air. The skin will "breathe" and your perspiration will evaporate. In cool weather you button up the neck of your shirt and the sleeves. The small pockets of dead air space in the fishnet underwear are heated and you will then be warmer.

PAJAMAS

Under the discussion of sleeping bags it was pointed out that some persons use a liner in their bag to help keep it clean. There is no question that it is desirable to keep a sleeping bag clean. However, pajamas can do essentially the same job as a liner in keeping the sleeping bag clean and they will generally be more comfortable than sleeping with a liner. During the night a liner will often get completely twisted about the body. By sewing "booties" onto an old pair of pajamas you can prevent your feet from soiling the foot end of the bag. By wearing a small cap, similar to a stocking cap, in the sleeping bag, you can prevent the head end from being soiled.

Pajamas can also increase the effective temperature range of a sleeping bag, depending on the material from which they are made. In an emergency, an extra shirt, vest, or jacket can be worn in the sleeping bag at night if needed for warmth. This should not be done, however, if the article is dirty or damp (especially if damp). Determine the expected maximum and minimum temperature, humidity, and possibility of rain or snow for the area in which you will be backpacking. This is very important for proper planning of protective clothing. In the spring and fall, temperatures in the high mountains can change rapidly. In a damp climate you will need more clothing to keep you warm at a specific temperature than in a dry climate at the same temperature.

RAIN GEAR

A discussion of rain gear involves the familiar problem of *waterproofness* versus *breatheability*. Just as in tent design, you cannot make a rain suit which will "breathe," yet have absolute protection from rain.

Ponchos were briefly discussed under Chapter 4 on shelter. A full-size poncho, about 54" x 90", can be used for rain protection on the trail and will serve as an emergency shelter. Ponchos are not formfitting. They are loose and floppy. In a strong wind you will probably have difficulty keeping your poncho from blowing about and you will usually end up with wet legs (unless you wear rain chaps). If the trail goes through

terrain that is thick and brushy the poncho will frequently catch on bushes. The disadvantage of a poncho (being loose and floppy) is also its advantage. Air circulates much more freely under it and you will not become so wet from your own body moisture as you will in a form-fitting rain suit. The poncho is probably the most widely used of all the various garments designed for emergency rain protection. The larger sizes are designed to cover the pack as well as the hiker, while hiking. Inexpensive vinyl plastic ponchos are available for $1 or $2. However, they snag and tear easily. A good nylon poncho is much more durable and will cost from $12 to $16.

On brushy trails rain pants are sometimes carried and worn to protect the trousers from being continually showered by wet brush and grass (even after the rain stops). However, the

Poncho being used as "tent" shelter. Photo by Lou Clemmons.

Rain Gear

Coated nylon poncho, covering both pack and hiker. Photo by Lou Clemmons.

problem of condensation inside the rain pants is great. Rain chaps are two separate waterproof "legs" that fit over the trouser legs and hook to the belt. In combination with a hip-length rain parka, they are preferred by some hikers.

A plastic raincoat can be carried for possible protection against infrequent rain. However, they are not very popular with most back-packers. Ordinary rubber slickers are much too heavy for backpacking.

If the weather is warm and it starts to rain, one way to keep your clothes dry (from perspiration) is to take off all clothes except shoes, socks, and underclothes. You can then put your outer clothes in your pack where they will stay dry until the rain is over. Put your poncho or other rain gear on over your shorts and continue hiking. Admittedly, the company you are in will have a bearing on whether this procedure is practical.

SWIMSUIT

On some backpack trips a swimsuit may be desired. For those persons backpacking in the high mountains, swimming can usually be ruled out. If swimming is not actually forbidden, the cold temperature of the water in many high mountain lakes makes it a dangerous practice. However, there may be some backpack routes at relatively low elevations, where swimming would be allowed and would be enjoyable. On a very few routes it may be advisable to carry a swimsuit for use in the crossing of deep rivers. The latter would probably also call for the use of an air mattress to float the pack across the river.

GAITERS

In traveling through wet grass or snow, the exposed part of your sock will usually get wet very quickly. This will be followed by moisture wicking down to the lower foot and you will soon be walking in wet (and cold) boots. On a trail covered with deep dust, the dust can usually be counted on to find its way into your boots. A water-repellent nylon gaiter covers the gap at the top of the boot and extends up over the trouser bottoms. It will be very helpful in keeping out water, snow, and dust. For most hikers, a gaiter about 6 to 8 inches high and weighing about 4 ounces is very adequate. Long gaiters, up to about 18 inches high, are available.

SHOPPING FOR CLOTHING

As stressed earlier, very little special clothing is needed for mild weather backpacking. If you cannot find the required articles of clothing among clothes you already own, don't overlook the possibility of buying secondhand clothing. Other backpackers, who may have passed on to more sophisticated or special clothing, may be a source. Sweaters, wool shirts and trousers, and other items can often be found at rummage sales at greatly reduced prices.

Sooner or later you will probably want a down vest or jacket. It is suggested that you seriously consider making your own, from kits which are now available from a number of sources (see Appendix A). In deciding on a vest versus a jacket, don't overlook the fact that the addition of sleeves to the vest (making it a jacket) greatly increases its temperature range. There is an extra cost but it is not great in comparison with the extended temperature range which results.

The "do-it-yourself" kits are also available for making wind shell parkas, rain pants, ponchos and other items of clothing.

DUPLICATE CLOTHING

On trips lasting up to a week or ten days, the only duplicate clothing recommended is an extra set of socks (duplicates of whatever combination of socks you hike in). Some hikers may want more spare clothing, but the added weight and the nuisance of carrying around dirty laundry in your pack is seldom justified. You can rinse out underclothes or any other item of clothing in the evening and dry it overnight or by the campfire if you have a fire. You won't get them completely clean with cold stream water and a bar of soap, but it will help a little bit. Your shirt and trousers are going to get soiled with dirt, soot from the campfire, and many other things. However, it is not "dirty dirt" and it is surprising how you hardly notice it after a few days. It is recommended that you have a complete change of clothes, along with soap, towel, and washbasin, to leave in your vehicle at the roadhead, so you can clean up at the end of the trip before starting home. Otherwise, when you stop at a restaurant on the way home, you may get a cool reception.

Incidentally, when you dry articles of clothing near an open fire don't get them too close to the fire, and *watch them* almost continuously. Many hikers have "lost their shirt" (damp shirt) by attempting to dry it near the fire while going about other camp jobs. A slight, momentary shift in wind and you may be without that article of clothing for the rest of the trip. If a fire is not available damp articles can be hung on your pack to dry as you hike.

A large group may find it desirable to carry (as common equipment) a washbasin or bucket of the folding plastic type while on the trail. This will facilitate personal bathing and washing of clothes, as desired. If much washing of clothes is anticipated you may want to carry a special soap for the purpose. Local stores carry a number of cold water soaps that will do a fairly good job of getting your clothes clean.

TRY OUT CLOTHING

The clothing that you wear on a backpack trip is not normally the clothing that you would wear in everyday use. For example, on a backpack trip your preference for clothing may be fishnet underwear, a lightweight wool shirt worn over a thin cotton shirt, and wool trousers. If the weather turns windy you may take a nylon shell jacket from your pack and put it on. In the mornings and evenings when it is quite cool you may add a down jacket (under the nylon wind shell jacket). To have confidence that your clothing is going to do the job you want it to you should try out your clothing and combinations of clothing on short weekend trips near home, or even on day hikes. Carry a thermometer with you and you will gain additional confidence as to just how effective your chosen clothing combinations are for various temperature and weather conditions. This will give you assurance when planning a week-long backpack trip that the clothing you select is going to do the job. Get out your pack and rain gear occasionally and go hiking in the rain near your home. You may want to take along your chosen shelter, tarp or tent, and practice putting it up in the rain. There is nothing like practice to give you confidence when you are deep in the backwoods and faced with adverse weather and other unfavorable conditions.

CLOTHING SUMMARY

By *extra* clothing is meant that clothing which is normally carried in your pack for additional warmth on cool mornings (and evenings) and for protection against adverse weather. A sweater, wind shell jacket, extra wool shirt, and down vest or jacket would be extra clothing. By duplicate clothing is meant that which duplicates an item of clothing that is normally worn and is carried so as to have a change to clean clothes while on the trail. Socks and underwear would be examples of duplicate clothing. The following tables set forth recommended and optional duplicate and extra clothing.

TABLE 5.1 RECOMMENDED DUPLICATE CLOTHING

Item	Approximate Weight (Ounces)
Socks (duplicate of the combination of socks that you wear while hiking)	5

TABLE 5.2 OPTIONAL DUPLICATE CLOTHING

Item	Approximate Weight (Ounces)
Underclothes (duplicate of underclothes worn while hiking)	6 to 18
Bandana	1½

TABLE 5.3 RECOMMENDED EXTRA CLOTHING

Item	Approximate Weight (Ounces)
Nylon wind shell jacket	4
Down jacket	18
Nylon poncho	12

TABLE 5.4 OPTIONAL EXTRA CLOTHING

Item	Approximate Weight (Ounces)
Hiking shorts	12
Canvas (tennis) shoes for crossing streams, or rubber-soled shower slipper	6½ to 22
Stocking cap	2
Gloves	4
Pajamas	11
Moccasins	15
Rain hat	5
Rain chaps	5
Gaiters	4
Swimsuit	3

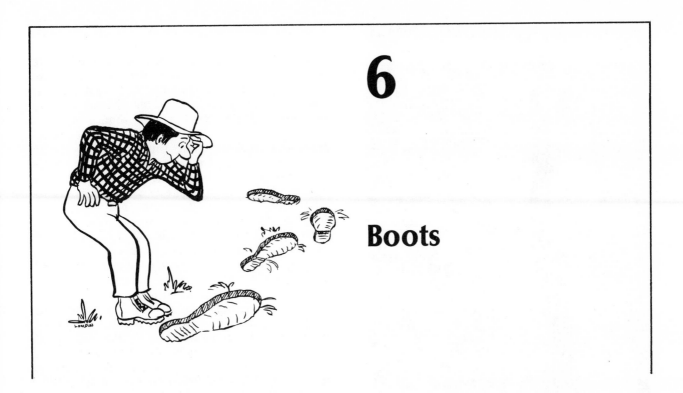

6

Boots

The boots and socks that you wear on a backpack trip are your most important items of clothing. Choose them carefully. Tender and sore feet can make you thoroughly miserable. Blisters or a bruised Achilles tendon (the tendon at the rear of the heel of your foot) can put you completely out of business. Problems with your feet and shoes that never occur in the walking required by your usual daily routine will show up on a backpack trip. If you take the matter of footwear too lightly you can easily ruin a trip for both yourself and your companions.

TYPES

There are several types of boots. Trail shoes are intended for use where the trails are good or for city walking. They are not intended for carrying heavy loads over rough trails. Kletterschues are a lightweight shoe, mostly foreign made, which are intended for technical rock climbing. They are not intended for trail use and are generally unsatisfactory for hiking except for certain brands that may be satisfactory for light duty trail walking. Mountaineering boots are heavy-duty, heavy weight boots, weighing 5 to 6 pounds per pair or more. They are intended for use on very rugged terrain, in ice, snow, and rock. A hiking boot, for typical backpacking use, generally falls between a trail shoe and a mountaineering boot as far as general characteristics are concerned and may have some of the features of both. In general this represents the

best all-purpose boot for general trail usage. Hiking boots are heavier and tougher than trail shoes but lighter and less stiff than a mountaineering boot. Most hiking boots for general backpacking use fall in the weight range of 4 to 5 pounds per pair for men and 3¼ to 4¼ pounds for women. There are many boots, varying in style and construction, that fall in this category. It is important to choose a hiking boot that will be tough enough to stand up to the most rigorous terrain you expect to encounter in your backpacking. Rubber footwear and canvas footwear are not recommended for hiking or backpacking. A good boot for normal backpacking use will range in price from about $25 to $55.

The *weight* of the boot should receive very careful consideration. Carrying one extra pound on the foot is equivalent to carrying 4 or 5 extra pounds on your back. Providing they have good construction and sufficient cushion for the feet, your boots for hiking should not be one ounce heavier than necessary. If you have an average stride, you lift each boot and set it down again about 1100 times in traveling one mile. If your boots are a few ounces heavier than necessary, this represents a lot of useful energy going to waste. For example, if each boot is 4 ounces heavier than necessary, this amounts (energy-wise) to walking one-quarter of the distance traveled with a 1-pound weight strapped to each ankle (as compared to using a proper weight boot).

Typical boots used for backpacking. The upper boot is a fairly heavy duty boot, with padded tongue, padding at ankle, scree collar, etc. The boots weigh about 4½ pounds per pair for size 9½. The lower boot is a lightweight boot, lacking some of the features of the heavier boot, weighing about 3¼ pounds per pair for size 9½. Both boots have the Vibram lug sole.

UPPER BOOT CONSTRUCTION

"Top grain" leather is high quality leather and is used in quality boots. A tanned cowhide in its original form is too thick to use. It is therefore split into sheets. The outside or top layer is called "top grain." It is most used for construction of boot uppers in quality boots.

A hiking boot may be made with either the smooth side of the leather on the outside of the boot, or with the smooth side inside the boot. The latter type is generally referred to as a *rough-out* boot and has a suedelike appearance. "Rough-outs" are not necessarily made of suede leather, which is split leather with the cut surface on the outside. On the contrary, the rough-out construction may simply mean that the leather grain is reversed (smooth side in, rough side out). High quality boots are available in both "smooth side out" and "rough-out" construction. A true suede leather is generally satisfactory only for light boots. It is not normally satisfactory for rough usage and wet trails.

Minor imperfections in the leather are most readily apparent in boots having smooth finish leather on the outside. Such imperfections are frequently found in good quality boots, and are not necessarily a detriment. Smooth leather is also somewhat more susceptible to scratches and abrasions, during trail usage, than rough-out leather. If these scratches and abrasions penetrate the relatively thin, tough outer layer the boots become less water-repellent. Some persons feel that if the leather grain is reversed in boot construction, the rough-out side offers somewhat more resistance to scratches and abrasions. Incidentally, rough-out boots *can* be treated with waterproofing compound as easily and effectively as smooth finish leather.

In quality boots there will be a minimum of seams in the upper boot. That is, ideally, they should be made from one whole piece of leather. This is possible but from an economy standpoint may be impractical. Seams are a potential source of leakage and separation of leather, but good workmanship will usually obviate this problem. A moccasin style construction in the toe area is seldom found in quality hiking boots. This style is particularly susceptible to wear and leakage. In general there should be as few seams as possible in the boot construction. An extra piece of leather on the outside, at the heel, should cover the heel seam. There should be no rough surfaces or edges inside the boot. Careful examination of the inside of the boot and feeling the inside surfaces with your hand is important in your initial examination of a new boot that you are planning to buy.

A boot may be lined, with a thin sheet of leather, or unlined. Many quality boots are lined, to provide a smooth surface for the foot and ankle. Boots should *not* be insulated. If insulated they cannot "breathe" and they are too hot for normal hiking use. The insulation would soon become sweat soaked and you would be hiking with wet socks and feet.

A scree top will be found on many quality boots. This is a piece of leather, with padding, sewn around the top of the boots. It is normally a good addition to the boot, since it helps to keep dirt and small rocks (scree) from entering the boot. A properly installed scree top also aids in preventing chafing of the lower leg in this area. Boots may also be padded (with foam or felt) in the ankle area, and sometimes other areas of the boot. Many hikers feel that too much padding makes a boot uncomfortably hot. Fully padded boots are not recommended.

A good quality boot should have a heel counter. This will cup the heel in such a manner that it helps anchor the foot to the sole. When boots are being fitted they should be snugly laced. With the shoe salesman "anchoring" the boot to the floor, try to lift the heel within the boot. There should be no significant lifting of the heel (not more than $1/8$ inch). There should also be a boxed toe or toe cap. A soft toe construction in the boot will not provide sufficient protection for your toes. In rough terrain your toes will take a beating from rocks, etc., if there is no hard toe cap. An arch support should be neither excessive nor absent because in either case pain and damage to the foot (and maybe the lower back) could develop. High quality boots will provide "shanks" in the sole to support the arch and protect the instep. These shanks may be made of steel, plastic, or laminated wood.

Some of the quality boots will have a double tongue, sewn to either side of the boot, essentially all the way to the top. This tongue keeps water (to some extent), small sticks, stones, dirt, etc., out of the boot. The extra leather folds inward when laced. Under the outer tongue will be found a separate, padded inner tongue. This padded tongue keeps shoe laces from cutting into your sock and foot, when snugly laced, and prevents chafing of the foot in that area. There are also boots with split outer tongues to facilitate getting in and out of the boot, and other variations.

Hiking boots vary in height from about 6 inches to 8 or 9 inches. For normal usage 6 or 7 inches is high enough. An 8 inch boot may be satisfactory, but the higher the boot the more tendency toward sagging of the leather at the ankles and the greater possibility of a tender or bruised Achilles tendon. Also, the higher the boot the more tendency to restrict the calf muscles of the leg.

LACING

The most common arrangement for lacing of boots is eyelets or holes in the leather reinforced with grommets. This is the type of eyelet usually found on street shoes. The eyelets are strong and seldom pull out. There is some disadvantage in that it takes longer to lace up your boots than with some of the other lacing arrangements. Some boots have eyelets part way up the boot with a hook system the remainder of the way. This combination of eyelets and hooks is common in many boots. Sticks and small debris will sometimes catch on the hooks but unless you are doing a lot of cross-country travel in rough terrain this is not usually of consequence. Still another lacing combination is "D" rings or speed lacing. Some boots use a combination of "D" rings on approximately the bottom half of the boot and hooks the remaining distance. In cold weather, if fingers are somewhat stiff, this arrangement is more convenient than eyelets.

Braided nylon laces are very strong and durable, and are commonly used in hiking boots. They do not rot, nor do they absorb water and freeze when they become wet and cold. Porcupines and other rodents do not eat nylon laces, as they sometimes do leather laces. The leather laces will absorb water and stretch. Even when fairly new they are subject to occasional breakage. If your boot laces are too long, it is recommended that you cut them off and seal the end by holding it in a match flame. Tying extra long laces in big bow knots or wrapping around the leg is not recommended. In lacing boots for *downhill* travel, some hikers lace the boot snugly in the *lower* part, tie a square knot there, then continue to lace the upper part, but more loosely than the lower. This is to keep the toes from jamming into the front of the boot in downhill travel. When you are traveling in other terrain, if your feet and toes feel cramped, the procedure can be reversed, with the lacing being somewhat loose in the lower part of the boot and tighter in the upper part. If the knot at the top of the boot is uncomfortable and causes chafing and discomfort at that point, try lacing the boot to the top, then back down again a couple of rows, before tying the knot. Before you start on a backpack trip, take the laces out of your shoes and give them a hard yank. If they break, or appear weak, replace them.

SOLE

All hiking boots have an inner sole and an outer sole, with a layer of material between the two called the midsole. The midsole generally consists of one or two layers of leather. In some boot construction the layer nearest the outer sole is made from wood or fiberglass, plus the addition of a steel shank for arch support and rigidity. A hiking boot should have some flexibility in the sole. Otherwise it will be uncomfortable and blisters will be a problem. The steel shank does not affect the longitudinal movement as much as the "twisting" of the sides of the boot.

The outer sole of a hiking boot should be of the rubber lug type. The yellow label Vibram sole with Montagna lugs is generally used. The Vibram sole is made of rubber of intermediate hardness which does not chip off in large chunks and has excellent wear characteristics. It has thick rubber and deep lugs. A lighter sole, commonly used on climbing boots, is the Roccia. There are harder and softer rubbers used for hiking boot soles. However, again, the Vibram is considered to be the best for an all-purpose hiking boot.

Several methods are used to fasten the soles to the upper boot. The two most common methods are (1) inside-stitched and (2) welted construction. On inside-stitched boots the upper boot is turned under and sandwiched between an inner sole and the midsole. It is fastened in place with a double row of stitching, concealed within the boot. It is thus protected from abrasions and moisture. The soles can be trimmed and the boot can (from this standpoint) be used for rock climbing.

The most common method of fastening the soles to the upper boot uses *welt construction*. Over the years it has proven to be both durable and functional. In this construction the upper boot is turned outward. It is sewn to a lip on the bottom of the innersole by stitching running diagonally inward. A second line of stitching runs straight down to fasten the upper, or welt, directly to the midsole. Some heavy-duty boots have a storm welt, which is an extra piece of leather sewn on top of the normal welt for added protection. The sole usually extends beyond the outside edge of the boot about ¼ inch or more. A welted construction permits easier flexing of the sole and also conforms to the shape of the foot, thus resulting in greater foot comfort. A majority of the quality hiking boots which are made today have welted construction. Both midsole and outer sole are easily replaced on boots having welted construction.

FITTING

A good pair of hiking boots is a substantial investment, not only in money but in hours of foot comfort on the trail. The preferable way to buy your boots is to visit reliable shops that sell hiking boots, try on various boots, and also discuss the boot construction and fit with a knowledgeable boot salesman.

When shopping for boots you should wear the socks, or combination of socks, that you plan to wear while hiking. The size of your street shoes will serve only as a rough guide, at best, as to the size of hiking boot which you will need for a comfortable fit. No one has two identical feet. One foot will usually be larger than the other. Be sure there is adequate room in the boot for your larger foot. Carrying a heavy pack over mountain trails causes the feet to expand. Blood and body fluid tend to collect in the feet during the day, making the feet somewhat larger in the afternoon. It is therefore recommended that you shop for your boots in the afternoon and also try to be on your feet for a significant period, and do some walking, in the morning of the day you do your shopping.

When you are trying on the boots you should lace them tightly. You should also note whether there is sufficient gap between the eyelets to allow space for further tightening as the boots are broken in and conform to your foot. In general, the length of boots should be generous enough so that you can wiggle your toes without having them touch the front end of the boot. If your boots are a bit too short you will suffer real agony in downhill travel and your toes may become so sore that you are essentially "out of business." You should not be able to press your toes against the front of the boot when the boots are laced tight and you are standing on a slope. (Carry a short board and improvise a slope in the salesroom.) When the boot is unlaced and the toe is pushed against the front of the boot, you should be able to slide a forefinger down into the gap remaining at the heel.

When you finally decide on a style and fit of boot that suits you there is another important step to be accomplished before you leave the store. Arrange an understanding with the salesman that you can try out your new boots within your home for several days, and return them if you are not satisfied. Then wear your boots as much as possible in your home for a few days to see if they fit as well as they should. Also find out from the store where you buy your boots how the boot leather was *tanned*. This will be very important later on.

You may not have access to a shop which has quality hiking boots and may find it necessary to order your boots through the mail. If you do so, *always send along an outline of your foot* (the larger foot if one is larger than the other). Better yet, send an outline of both feet. This should be made with your hiking socks on, and by tracing onto a piece of paper with a pencil held vertically (preferably by a helper). Make the outline in the evening, in a standing position, with your full weight on the foot. It is a good idea to state your street shoe size and width, but stress in your order that the foot outline is to govern the size of hiking boot, not your street shoe size. Incidentally, you should purchase only boots which have been made on American lasts. Boots made on European lasts may be too narrow in the toe and too broad in the heel. Women should purchase boots that have been made on lasts for women's boots, rather than purchasing men's boots. Again, have an understanding with the firm from which you order that the boots can be returned, for replacement or refund, if they are not satisfactory. When you receive them, wear them around the house for a few days to be sure you have a boot that you will be satisfied with. Once they are worn out-of-doors they are yours.

CARE OF BOOTS

Most leather boots are water-repellent and will stay that way with reasonable care and periodic treatment. You should be able to wade wet grass and water puddles in the trail, but wading streams is something else. If you are going to be wading streams it is recommended that you carry a pair of tennis (canvas) shoes for this purpose. Some hikers wade across streams by removing their socks and crossing while wearing their hiking boots. When the crossing is accomplished they then dump the excess water from their boots, put their dry socks back on, and the wet boots, and continue on their way. They're your boots. Suit yourself. Wet feet also soften the skin and lead to blisters. Wading of streams is discussed more fully in Part 11, page 111.

Heat can do a lot of damage to leather boots and many good boots are permanently damaged by artificial heat. Forced drying of wet boots by an open fire is an excellent way to ruin them. Using dry socks, and a change of socks, you can walk the dampness out of your boots, with much better results than from forced drying. If you like to sit in front of a campfire and toast your outstretched feet, fine. However, do this only after you have removed your boots.

At home, after a trip, dirt can be cleaned from boots by washing with a scrub brush and cool water. If mud is left to dry on boots it will dry out the leather. It will also dry out the cement holding the boot together and it may come apart. It is a good idea to stuff the boots with crumpled paper towels, or newspaper, which will absorb the excess moisture. Boots

Areas like this in the trail are not uncommon at certain seasons of the year. Well-made boots and good care of the boots are required. When your boots fail you are "out of business." Photo by Lou Clemmons.

Leath-R-Seal is applied to the welt area of the boot and to the seams of the upper boots. Photo by Lou Clemmons.

Sno-Seal and Leath-R-Seal are good products for treating boots, to maintain water repellency and to preserve the leather. Photo by Lou Clemmons.

Sno-Seal is applied to all parts of the upper boot. The Sno-Seal is rubbed into the boot by hand. The process should not be hastened by heating the boot. About 24 hours should elapse between successive coats. Photo by Lou Clemmons.

should be stored at room temperature or below, and *never* near a source of artificial heat.

From time to time boots will require treatment in order to retain their water-repellency and preserve the leather. This is the point at which you will need the information on how the leather in the boot was tanned. In general, for an *oil-tanned* boot treat lightly with oil or a grease, keeping the oil away from the sole. For *chrome-tanned* leather, treat lightly with wax or silicone, again keeping away from the sole. Sno-Seal is a commonly available wax and silicone mixture. Use any shoe preservative in moderation and not too often. Using too much waterproofing compound, or too frequent applications, will soften the leather too much. It is important that the leather be able to breathe, otherwise your feet will sweat and you will be walking with waterlogged boots. Leather-R-Seal is a good liquid compound for keeping soles and seams waterproof.

BREAKING IN BOOTS

Never start a hike with new boots. Boots should always be well broken in. They should not be so old that there is any doubt about their lasting for the trip, however. Don't take any pair of boots on a hike with the thought of getting just "a few more miles" out of them and then throwing them away.

There is more than one way of breaking in a new pair of hiking boots. However, the best way is to simply start wearing them around home for brief periods. To start with you probably won't want to wear them for more than five or ten minutes. Increase this period for five to ten minutes each day until you can wear them comfortably for an hour or more. Then start taking short hikes. After a few short hikes, do some hiking on trails, carrying a light pack load. Gradually increase the distance and load. It will take a month to six weeks to break in a pair of new boots by this method, but it is time well spent.

If you must break in your new boots quickly, one approach is to soak the boots by filling each boot with warm water. When they are thoroughly soaked put the boots on and go hiking until they dry on your feet. I have never tried this method but it reportedly works.

In breaking in new boots always wear the socks and combination of socks that you normally wear when backpacking.

7

Food and Recipes

WATCH THE WEIGHT

There are a number of books available on camp cooking. It may be interesting to learn to cook a variety of foods using different types of fires and equipment. In this book it is assumed that the backpack trip you are about to take will be for the purpose of exploring, rock hunting, wildlife observing, photography, fishing, or some similar objective and that you won't want to spend any more time than is necessary to prepare and cook your meals and still have good nourishing food to eat. Food and cooking equipment, more than anything else you will pack, will have a tendency to get out of hand by leaps and bounds, as far as weight and bulk are concerned. Yet it is certainly important that you eat well. Therefore, some skillful planning and preparation are needed in this area. That is why three parts of this book are devoted to this general subject.

The above remarks are not intended to discourage those persons who like to do "gourmet" type cooking on the trail. If that is your "cup of tea," take along your reflector oven, or whatever else you need and "go to it." Your pack will be heavier and such cooking should generally be pursued only on relatively short trips.

DRIED AND DEHYDRATED FOODS

On a backpack trip the use of dried and dehydrated foods is important. Water is heavy,

about 1 pound per pint. It should be added to the foods after you get to the camp site, rather than carried in with the food. Macaroni, spaghetti, rice, flour, oatmeal, etc., are dry foods by the nature of the product. *Dried* prunes, peaches, apricots, raisins, etc., are foods that have been dried to remove much of the water that is present in their natural form but not all of it. *Dehydrated* and *freeze-dried* fruits, meats, vegetables, etc., are foods that have been specially processed to remove substantially all of the water. The longer the trip the more important it is that meals be planned around dehydrated or freeze-dried foods. A number 2 size can of peaches, for example, will weigh about 1 pound and will serve four persons. If freeze-dried peaches were used, about 1½ or 2 ounces would serve four persons. In general the freeze-dried foods are more expensive but also more tasty than conventional dehydrated foods.

TRY FOODS AT HOME

As with every product, there are good dehydrated foods and there are poor dehydrated foods. If you were to start experimenting with various dehydrated foods and brands of dehydrated foods, it would probably take a long while and you would run up quite a bill before you settled on a full line of foods that you liked. This book therefore suggests particular foods and brands for your guidance; I have tested these on the trail, and most backpackers find them to be satisfactory. There are quite a number of producers and suppliers of dehydrated foods and, if you wish to experiment a bit, order some of their foods and go ahead. Appendix B lists some manufacturers of special foods for backpacking. Many of the firms in Appendix A, as well as some local sporting goods stores, carry the products of those manufacturers. One word of caution. You should not take any food on a backpack trip that you have not cooked at home, in your own kitchen, to prove to yourself that you like it Then you can hit the trail with confidence that you are going to enjoy good food. Also, the experience of cooking the food at home will provide better assurance that you will cook it properly when you are on the trail and cooking under somewhat less than ideal conditions.

KEEP REQUIREMENTS SIMPLE

Cooking can be done with a Dutch oven, over a grill, with a reflector oven, etc. These all have a place in general outdoor cooking. However, in backpacking it is desirable to keep cooking gear and other equipment to a minimum. The food recipes listed in this part are therefore chosen for light weight, for simplicity of preparation, and have been proven on the trail to appeal to most hikers' appetites. Every food recipe listed here can be suitably cooked in one of two basic utensils, either a pan or a skillet. It is possible and practical to plan an entire backpack trip around foods that require only pans for cooking—no skillet. In general the cooking periods listed are for altitudes of 6000 to 8000 feet. For a higher or lower altitude the cooking time will need to be adjusted accordingly.

MEAT

BACON. All bacon should be cooked by starting in a cold skillet and cooking over a medium fire. Do not grease the skillet. The fat on the bacon provides more than enough grease for cooking.

1. Store Bacon. One pound of store bacon will serve from three to five persons, depending upon how much other food you have with it. The bacon you buy in the store will have considerable fat on it. Unless this fat is saved and used for other cooking, it must be looked upon as excess weight in backpacking. Take a small can along, with a tight-fitting lid, to save the grease in. As the bacon cooks, pour off the excess grease into the can. About ten to twelve minutes of cooking is usually sufficient, depending upon how crisp you like it.

Ordinary bacon, in addition to being heavy, is difficult to pack. It should be carefully wrapped and carried in a double thickness of heavy poly bags. Otherwise the grease in it will usually soil adjacent items in your pack.

2. Canned Bacon. A convenient bacon for backpacking is Swift's canned bacon. It requires no refrigeration. It is precooked and only requires heating over a low fire for five to eight minutes. The can weighs 7 ounces (gross) and it contains the equivalent of 1 pound of regular store bacon. The bacon is packed in a roll inside the can, with the layers separated by a heavy paper. The entire contents can be put into the skillet, including the paper. When the bacon starts to warm, the paper can be easily separated and thrown away. There is not much excess grease on this bacon but you should save what there is. Although this bacon is very tasty, it will be too heavy and bulky for all but short backpack trips.

3. Bacon Bar. Many suppliers in Appendix A stock a bacon bar which is a concentrated prefried bacon. A 3-ounce bar is equivalent to about 12 to 14 ounces of uncooked bacon. It can be eaten hot or cold. This is the favorite form of bacon to many backpackers and these bacon bars are widely used.

4. Other Bacon. There are other canned bacons available, including Canadian bacon. Some suppliers listed in Appendix A carry a Canadian type of canned bacon. Several varieties of canned bacon are also available in some of the local stores. Most of these are too heavy and bulky except for very short backpack trips, however.

SAUSAGE. Most local stores carry small cans of sausage links, with a gross weight of about 10 ounces. The Libby brand is good. One can is usually sufficient for three persons for one meal (medium servings), with other food. Canned sausages which are packed in natural juices have better flavor than those packed in water. Dried sausage sticks, which do not require refrigeration, are available from some suppliers of trail foods and occasionally from local confectionery stores. About 1 or 2 ounces per person per meal is a sufficient ration.

SALAMI. This is available in most local stores. It will keep for several days if the weather is not too hot. *Summer Sausage* is sometimes available from local stores and will keep better than salami.

FISH. On many backpack trips trout will be caught. They should be eaten soon after catching, preferably within several hours or less. There are special drying processes and other means of keeping fish without refrigeration, but they are not recommended for the usual backpack trip. Soon after catching fish should be rough-cleaned by removing the contents of the body cavity and bleeding the fish. *Never* soak cleaned fish in water. After cleaning, keep them dry until time to cook. Salt and pepper them lightly, inside and out, before cooking. Trout are very good without being floured before frying. However, if you must flour them a mixture of half flour and half cornmeal is good. Put the flour and fish together in a large plastic bag, using just enough of the flouring mixture for one meal. Shake the bag vigorously and the flouring job is done. The simplest method of cooking trout is to fry them. Bacon grease, cooking oil, peanut oil, or margarine (least satisfactory) can be used for frying. Have the grease medium hot before putting the fish in. Cook over a medium hot fire. During frying they may be basted with a mixture of melted butter and lemon juice, but this is not essential. About fifteen minutes of frying is sufficient for medium-size fish.

Some cooks prefer to prepare trout of 10 to 12 inches long by cutting into the body cavity from alongside the backbone, rather than splitting the belly side. When this is done, the belly acts as a hinge and the thick back section is reduced to a better size for more uniform frying. Removing the bones before eating is a bit more difficult with this method, but the faster and more uniform frying improves the taste so much that it is well worth the effort. Trout which are 13 or 14 inches long or more, as well as many other fish of this size, should be prepared for the frying pan by filleting.

It is frequently difficult to maintain a firm grip on fish while you are cleaning them. Trout, especially, are hard to hold on to. One method that helps to hold the fish is to put salt on your fingers before handling them. However, if you have any small nicks in your fingers or hands, then getting salt in these cuts will probably send you into orbit. A better method is to carry a 6-inch square of wet sandpaper for this purpose. Hold the sandpaper in the palm of your hand, rough side up. Now lay the trout on the sandpaper, close your grip, and you have him. Wearing an old cotton glove on the left hand (if you are right-handed) will also help to hold the fish while cleaning.

If you are going to be cleaning a lot of fish at once, say for a large group, an old toothbrush is handy for cleaning out the "mud vein" (dorsal aorta) that lies along the inside of the backbone. Break this up with your knife or thumb to start; then it can be quickly removed with the toothbrush.

When fish are cleaned, it is frequently a problem to find something to put them in until you are ready to fry them. A spare pan is not always available, and if you use a pan it must be washed before it can be used for another pur-

pose. A good solution to the problem is to make a small bag, about 8 inches by 14 inches in size, out of ordinary muslin or percale. Mark the bag plainly on the outside with the word "FISH," using a felt tip marker, before leaving home. After cleaning, the fish can be kept in this bag until you are ready to fry them. Rinse this bag out after each use, and dry on a rope line. The wet sandpaper and the toothbrush (for fish cleaning) can be carried in this bag between meals. Fold the whole business into a small compact package, and carry it in a pint- or quart-size plastic bag, so that you will not have a fish smell on other items in your pack.

CHICKEN. Most local groceries carry small cans of boned chicken in a number of brands, such as Swanson, Richardson, etc. These are convenient to use as a meat base in a number of dishes, such as explained later in this part. Most of these small cans have a gross weight of about 7 ounces and a net weight of about 5 ounces. Some suppliers in Appendix A carry dehydrated chicken which can be used and will have considerably less weight for the same food value.

BEEF

1. Canned Hamburger. Small cans of hamburger, usually containing five or six small patties, are available in some local stores. The Libby brand is good. Gross weight is about 14 ounces (net weight 12 ounces). These can be heated and eaten separately, or used as a base for a main dish, like spaghetti and hamburger.

2. Dehydrated Ground Beef. A dehydrated ground beef will save weight, and some of the brands are very good. Follow the directions for cooking, which are usually very simple. One method is to put the meat in a skillet, barely cover with water and simmer about fifteen minutes, until the water is gone. Then add a small amount of butter to the skillet and fry very slowly for about five to eight minutes. Do not try to fry it to the point of crispness. It can also be added directly to soups or stews before cooking.

3. Beef Stick. A good beef product for trail usage is the Beef Stick manufactured and sold by the Hickory Farms of Toledo, Ohio. It is tasty when eaten cold. It can also be heated in a skillet, or cut into bite size pieces and added to soups or stews. This beef product will keep well without any refrigeration, even in warm weather.

BEEF JERKY. This is a dehydrated form of beef that will keep almost indefinitely without refrigeration It is usually eaten cold and is good food for lunch or as a trail snack. Most of the suppliers listed in Appendix A carry beef jerky, but it is relatively easy to make yourself and it is recommended that you try this.

TABLE 7.1 INFORMATION ON SOME FOODS FOR BACKPACKING

Item No.	Item	Brand	Weight (Ounces)	No. of Servings
1	Bacon, canned	Swift	7	3 to 4
2	Bacon, bar	Wilson	3	2 to 3
3	Beef, dried	Peacock	2	2 to 3
4	Beef, dehyd. ground	Perma-Pak	1	1 to 2
5	Beef, stick	*Hickory Farms	(4 lb)	—
6	Beef, jerky	—	2	2 or 3
7	Egg, dehyd.	**Durkee	1¼	1 or 2
8	Turkey Tetrazzini	Tea Kettle	3	1 or 2
9	Carrots, puff dried	Richmoor	3½	3 to 4
10	Peas, freeze-dried	Richmoor	2¼	3 to 4
11	Beans, green, freeze-dried	Richmoor	1	3 to 4
12	Beans, Boston style	Seidel	12	3 to 4
13	Salad, dehyd. vegetable	Perma-Pak	1½	3 to 4
14	Chicken stew	Mountain House	3½	1 or 2
15	Applesauce	Perma-Pak	5¾	3 to 4
16	Apples, freeze-dried	Mountain House	1	2 to 3
17	Peaches, freeze-dried	Mountain House	1	2 to 3
18	Pears, freeze-dried	Mountain House	1	2 to 3
19	Fruit mix, dehyd.	Seidel	3½	3 to 4
20	Pineapple Waikiki	Richmoor	5¾	4 to 5
21	Banana Chips	Richmoor	4	2 to 3
22	Nuts and fruit	Richmoor	5	2 to 3
23	Pancake syrup	Seidel	9	3 to 4
24	Trail Candy	Traubenzucker	2	8 pieces
25	"Gorp" (Trail Snack)	Richmoor	6	3 to 4
26	Cookie, enriched	Turblokken	8	6 pieces
27	Chocolate, tropical	Hershey	1	1
28	Pem fruit bar	—	1	1
29	Kendall Mint Cake	Wilson's	6	3 to 4
30	Lemonade mix	Wylers (with sugar)	7½	3 to 4
31	Cocoa	Swiss Miss	1	1
32	Wafer, whole wheat	Nabisco "Wheat Thins"	9¾	7 to 9
33	Wafer, whole wheat	Nabisco "Triscuit"	9¾	7 to 9
34	Ice cream, freeze-dried	Mountain House	2½	3 to 4
35	Cottage Cheese, freeze-dried	Mountain House	2	3 to 4
36	Lemon crystals	Lemon Queen	2½	3 to 4
37	Lime crystals	Lime Queen	2½	3 to 4
38	Pan-coating oil	***Vegalene	1	—

*Hickory Farms of Ohio, Western Division, P.O. Box 3306, Van Nuys, California 91401.

**Many brands of dehydrated eggs taste terrible. However, the Durkee brand is unusually good. If your local store doesn't carry Durkee brands, you might write to Durkee Famous Foods, 900 Union Commerce Bldg., Cleveland, Ohio 44101, and inquire as to a source in your area.

***Vegalene is used for coating all pans prior to cooking. It prevents food from sticking to pan and makes the dishwashing job much easier.

Note: The above foods and brands are those with which the writer is familiar from personal experience and which he can recommend. This list represents a lot of "trial and error" testing of many dehydrated foods over a period of years. No aspect of backpacking is more important than having good, tasty foods. Yet, to find a full range of appetizing foods—meats, vegetables, salad, beverages, etc.—requires more time and expense than many backpackers can afford. With a few exceptions, this list is primarily concerned with foods for which no equivalent is available in local stores.

Beef jerky, drying on clothesline

Top round steak, with very little or no fat, is recommended for making beef jerky. With a sharp knife cut the round steaks into slices about ⅛ to ¼ inch thick, about ½ to ¾ inch wide (thickness of steak), and 6 to 10 inches long. Using the blunt edge of a cup or similar tool, pound the strips as thin as possible, being careful not to tear them apart. Salt and pepper these strips quite heavily. Using a wire basket strainer like those used for making french fries, lower the strips into a pan of heavily salted, boiling water. Leave the strips in the water about fifteen seconds, just enough to blanch the meat, then take out and place on paper towels to drain.

Make a tube or cylinder out of cheesecloth, about 3 or 5 feet long and 8 inches in diameter. You will also need a piece of stout clean cord about 6 feet long. Using a large needle and strong white cotton thread, pierce the cord near one end, then pierce a piece of jerky 1 inch away from the first point, and so on. In this manner, "sew" the jerky to the cord. Now slip the cheesecloth cylinder over the sewed jerky and snap a rubber band or clothespin over each end of the cylinder to keep out flies.

Holding on to the two ends of the cord which protrude from the cheesecloth cylinder, carry the line of jerky outside and fasten it between two tree limbs or to a clothesline (safest place) where cats and other animals cannot reach it. Select a place in the sunlight where there will be free circulation of air. If it rains, cover the jerky or take it inside. Leave it in the open for about five days, and you will have finished jerky. It will get stiff and brittle, and very dark, but it is good to eat and very nourishing. It will keep practically indefinitely. Store it in plastic bags, which in turn can be kept in a closed container such as a coffee can.

Sixteen ounces of fresh meat will provide about 4 ounces of jerky when the process is completed. A good way to eat jerky is to spread mustard on it and eat it cold. A tangy mustard, such as a horseradish mustard, is particularly good.

OTHER CANNED MEATS. Some other meats which are suitable for short backpack trips are available in canned form from local groceries. Some of these are Swift's Prem, Hormel Chopped Beef, Spam, etc. Most of these only require to be cut into thin slices, placed in a skillet with a little shortening, and thoroughly heated. Gross weight of cans is usually about 14 ounces (net weight 12 ounces).

EGGS

FRESH EGGS. It is not safe to keep fresh eggs for more than a couple of hours without refrigeration, and at high temperatures (70° F and up) even this exposure may be too long. For an overnight camp with temperatures below 50° they may be satisfactory. They must be carefully packed as they make a fine mess if they are broken in your pack. Aluminum egg carriers are available from several of the suppliers in Appendix A. Another way to carry eggs is to use a small can with a tight-fitting lid, about the size of a baking powder can. Push a pint plastic bag down into the can as a "liner." Now break the eggs out of their shells and into the can. Close the bag and seal the top with a small rubber band. Then put the lid on the can and seal it with tape. As soon as you get to camp, put the can in a stream or other place where it will be kept at below 50° F until ready to use.

DEHYDRATED EGGS. There is a wide difference in the taste of dehydrated eggs. Whatever brand you choose, you should by all means try it out thoroughly *at home* to be sure you are going to like it. One of the best tasting brands of dehydrated eggs that I have found is "Durkee," available in some local stores. It is also one of the least expensive brands.

Dehydrated eggs are very easy to fix. You simply mix with water into a paste (instructions are on the package) and add to a greased prewarmed skillet. Cook over a low fire for two or three minutes. Be careful not to overcook. When they are a nice golden brown, they are overcooked. Throw them out and start over. Stir the egg in the skillet almost continuously while it is cooking. One very good way to cook these eggs is to first crumble part of a bacon bar into a greased skillet and cook for several minutes over a low flame. Then add the scrambled egg mixture and continue to cook for about two minutes longer, stirring continuously. Remove from fire and add plenty of salt and pepper. Omelets made from dehydrated eggs frequently end up tough and rubbery (and tasteless). Most cooks prefer the scrambled version. A good addition to scrambled eggs is dehydrated onions, which can be put to soak the evening before (for breakfast), if desired.

Most freeze-dried dehydrated eggs are rather good. They are more expensive than ordinary dehydrated eggs, but some backpackers will consider them worthwhile.

CEREALS

OATMEAL. Many persons who wouldn't think of eating oatmeal for breakfast at home find it very much to their liking on a backpack trip. A number of brands of "minute" oats are available, such as Mother's Oats. For each person you will need: ½ cup oats, ¼ tsp. salt, and about one cup of water. You can start the oats in cold, warm, or boiling water. If creamy oatmeal is desired, start it in cold water. For a thicker, less creamy oatmeal, start it in boiling water. Cook for a minimum of three to five minutes, even for one-minute oats. At high altitudes, ten minutes on the fire is not too much. Eat with sugar and milk or cream.

There are some instant oatmeals available, such as Quaker, that are quite popular with some backpackers. Individual serving size packages are available, if desired. About ¾ cup of boiling water is added to the individual serving; stir, and the oatmeal is ready to eat.

Good additions to oatmeal are raisins, banana chips, brown sugar, and nuts (such as almonds). You can put any or all of these items right in the plastic bag with the oatmeal when it is packaged. Some margarine can also be added to the oatmeal during preparation. It will improve the taste and it is a good way to get additional calories.

OTHER COOKED CEREALS. You may prefer some other type of cooked cereal, such as Wheatena. There are a number of such cereals. Most of them have a relatively short cooking time.

COLD CEREAL. Most of the cold cereals which are commonly eaten for breakfast at home are too bulky and too low in calories to be suitable for backpacking. However, there are some exceptions. Grapenuts and Heartland (made by Pet Co.) cereals are good for backpacking use and are available in many local stores. Familia and Bircher Muesli are very good and are available from some of the suppliers listed in Appendix A.

PANCAKES

A traditional camp food is pancakes with butter and syrup. A number of prepared pan-cake flours are available, such as Aunt Jemima brand, and they are very satisfactory. Add water or milk to the flour (not vice versa). Stir the mixture just enough to get the lumps out. A fork is a good stirring tool. Do not beat the batter. Hold back a little flour just in case you should get the batter *too thin* to start with. There is nothing worse than using up all of your flour in one grand start and then having the batter come out too thin.

Dip out 3 or 4 tablespoons of batter onto a hot greased skillet and cook over a medium hot fire. Turn only once, when bubbles have appeared over the top surface of the uncooked side. It is much easier to make one large pancake in an average size skillet than to make two or more small ones. Cut the large pancake into two or more pieces as soon as it is removed from the skillet and divide it among several persons who are eating so that each will have a hot piece. One large pancake will get partly cold just while it is being eaten.

A satisfactory pancake syrup can be made from brown sugar and water. Good prepared syrup mixtures are also available. In making syrup from brown sugar, use about 1 cup of sugar to ½ cup of water. Bring to a boil and stir until dissolved. Be very careful not to use too much water or the syrup will be too thin.

There are several disadvantages to having pancakes as a food item in backpacking. First, the pancake flour and the sugar from which to make the syrup are relatively heavy, compared to other suitable breakfast items. Also, not all backpackers will be carrying a skillet, which is necessary. A wood fire is also desirable. A pancake breakfast takes considerable time in preparation, eating, and getting the dishes washed. If you are trying to get an early start down the trail, better skip the pancake breakfast. For short backpack trips and for layover days in camp it may be entirely satisfactory.

FRUIT

At least one meal each day should include fruit. If you plan to have fruit for breakfast, it is a good idea to cook it in the evening. Dried fruits such as prunes, peaches, apricots, etc., are available. There are several types, as described in the following paragraphs.

ORDINARY DRIED FRUITS. Most grocery stores carry dried fruits. These have had much of the water removed, but not so much as to make them hard or brittle. Prunes usually come in a 1-pound box, apricots and peaches in a 10- or 12-ounce box. Pitted prunes are available from suppliers of trail foods, and the pits do represent extra weight. However, on many backpack trips the weight will not be that critical. About 2½ ounces of prunes per person per meal and 2 ounces of apricots or peaches per person per meal is the right amount. Put the fruit in a saucepan, cover with cold water, and simmer for about twenty minutes. During the last five minutes on the fire, add 2 level teaspoons of sugar for each 2 ounces of fruit. These fruits are also good to munch on while on the trail, just as they come from the box.

VACUUM-DRIED FRUITS. The vacuum-dried fruits are available from most of the suppliers of trail foods. They have had most of the water removed, to the point where they are hard and brittle (before cooking). Removing this extra water saves weight, however. About 1 ounce per person per meal provides an ample serving. The vacuum-dried fruits are cooked in the same manner as ordinary dried fruits. Cover the fruit with cold water in a saucepan and simmer for fifteen to twenty minutes. Add sugar during the last few minutes of cooking.

Vacuum-dried apple bits make a good side dish for lunch and supper. Two ounces provide servings for two or three persons and can be cooked in five to seven minutes.

FREEZE-DRIED FRUITS. The freeze-dried foods are a relatively new product. Some of the freeze-dried fruits are quite tasty. They are very light, about 1½ ounces providing servings for three persons. Another advantage is that they are *quickly* and *easily prepared.* After removing from package, soaking for about five minutes in cold water makes them ready to eat. *No cooking is necessary.* They also make a good snack while traveling along the trail. You can pop a piece of freeze-dried fruit into your mouth, suck on it until it softens, and it is quite good. The freeze-dried fruits (and other freeze-dried foods) are more expensive than the vacuum-dried fruits, but they have a place in some backpack food lists.

BEVERAGES

What you drink on a backpack trip, and especially *how much* you drink, is important. You will be exerting and perspiring and your body will lose a lot of fluid which needs to be replaced if you are to feel well. If you were to drink only water you would probably not take in as much liquid as if you drank a few beverages. Therefore, some variety of beverages and a beverage with every meal is important.

COFFEE. The best coffee for backpack use is the instant or freeze-dried kind. No coffee pot is required (it would mean added weight) and instant coffee is light in weight compared to the regular kind. Two ounces of instant coffee will make about thirty cups. It can be made in either of two ways. One way is to simply bring water to boiling in a pan, pour the hot water into cups, add a rounded teaspoon of instant coffee to each cup, and stir. Another way is to put the desired number of cups (of water) into a pan, bring to a boil, and add the instant coffee directly to the boiling water in the pan. Let the water (with the coffee in it) boil for several minutes on the fire before removing and pouring into cups. Add cream substitute or sugar to taste.

TEA. The instant variety of tea is also recommended. Bring water to a boil in a pan and then pour into cups. Then add 1 level or rounded teaspoon of instant tea per cup (depending on the strength desired). Sweeten to taste. Never add tea to boiling water. The water must always be removed from the fire before adding the tea. Tea is very light in weight. One and one-half ounces will make thirty-five to forty cups. If you prefer to use tea bags rather than instant tea, you will find that two cups of tea can usually be made from one tea bag.

It is interesting to note that many persons who are strongly in favor of coffee as a drink at home often revert to tea as a mealtime drink in the woods. It somehow seems to "fill the bill" better.

Many persons add a teaspoon or more of margarine (or butter) to their tea. This gives it an interesting flavor and it also provides some calories in the form of fat, which is an important consideration.

BOUILLON, INSTANT SOUPS. Bouillon is carried in most local food stores. The instant broth and instant soups carried by many of the suppliers of trail foods are much more flavorful and satisfying, however. Instant beef broth, chicken broth, pea soup, and potato soup are common. Several good brands are conveniently packaged in individual size foil envelopes, providing for some variety at the same meal. All that is required is to add the contents of the package to a cup of freshly boiled hot water and stir. These soups and broths will have a place on most backpack food lists. While hikers are setting up camp or preparing other food items and waiting for them to cook, it is convenient and most satisfying to sip a cup of hot soup or broth. Bouillon may also be used to flavor rice and noodle dishes, giving a gourmet touch to meals in the woods. As with tea, adding a bit of margarine to the bouillon or soup will add to the flavor and also provide more calories.

HOT GELATIN. Most persons are surprised to find that they like hot gelatin for a drink. The Royal and Jell-O brands are good. These drinks are rich in protein and sugar, and the Royal brand also contains Vitamin C. About ¾ ounce of gelatin powder is required for a 1-cup serving. Simply heat water to boiling point and dissolve the gelatin in the hot water. Drink it at the same temperature that you would drink hot tea or coffee. Any flavors are satisfactory, but *orange* and *lemon* flavors are particularly recommended as a hot trail drink.

COCOA. The instant variety of cocoa is recommended for its convenience. Place about 3 heaping teaspoons of cocoa in a cup, add hot water, and stir. One of the most tasty cocoa products is the Swiss Miss instant cocoa. In your menu planning it should be noted that a serving of cocoa is relatively heavy, compared to tea or coffee. However, it does provide some nourishment (with the milk that is included in the instant products), whereas tea or coffee has no nourishment.

LEMONADE. Hikers will frequently develop a craving for something tart and sour while on a backpack trip. There will be times when you would "give your kingdom" for a dill pickle. It is not convenient or practical to carry dill pickles on a backpack trip. However, you will find that a lemon drink, strongly on the tart side, will satisfy your craving for something sour, as well as help make for a balanced diet.

Many persons, myself included, prefer to use the pure lemon powder, without sugar or other additives, in making a lemon drink. For each cup of lemonade about 1 level teaspoon of lemon powder is required. A small amount of water is added at first and mixed thoroughly with the powder to make a paste. Then fill the cup with water, sweeten only very slightly and you will have a very tart drink. If you prefer the "ready to use" type of lemonade (with sugar already added), the Wyler brand is good. It is available in many local stores.

SOUPS

Most soups are an ideal backpack food. They are easily and quickly prepared and readily digested. They supplement beverages in replacing fluids lost from the body. Lipton, Knorr Swiss, Wyler's, and Campbell are most commonly found in local stores. The directions will be found on the package and should be followed carefully, since they vary. For example, for some soups the contents of the package are added to hot water and for others to cold water (which is then heated).

VEGETABLE SALAD

Some of the dehydrated vegetable salads require boiling in hot water for a short period. Others (such as the Perma-Pak brand) only require *soaking* in cold water, and this latter type is recommended, since most persons prefer their salads cool. One ounce of salad provides ample servings for three persons. Before you break camp in the morning you can put your salad to soak in a tight jar. When you stop for lunch (or supper) your salad is ready. Most salad dressings which are purchased in the store require refrigeration after they are once opened. A good salad dressing, which does *not* require any refrigeration, is made from the following ingredients. (It can be made at home and carried in a small plastic bottle.)

¼ cup   wine vinegar
⅛ cup   salad oil
½ tsp.   salt
½ tsp.   black pepper
several cloves of garlic

Simply put the ingredients in the plastic bottle, shake well, and it is ready for use. If the garlic cloves are left in the bottle for a trip of several days or a week, the garlic flavor will gradually get stronger, but this spicy flavor tastes good in the out-of-doors, even to most persons who do not eat highly seasoned foods at home. The salad oil and the vinegar will quickly separate in the bottle, so shake well each time before using.

Another salad dressing which does not require refrigeration is made from the following:

1½ tsp. lemon powder
6 tsp.   water
1½ tsp. sugar
3 tsp.   Pream or other cream substitute
½ tsp.   salt
6 or 8   shakes black pepper

Mix the above ingredients together, first making a paste of the lemon powder and water, making sure to get all the lumps out. Because of the nature of the ingredients, this salad dressing can easily be made up fresh at each meal where you use it.

BREAD

The bread which you normally buy in the store is not suitable for backpacking. It is bulky, if carried it usually ends up in crumbs, and it molds easily. It is therefore recommended that you use a bread substitute that does not have these undesirable properties. If you want to sacrifice some trip time that could be spent in other pursuits, you can of course bake bread or biscuits in camp. To bake consistently good camp bread or biscuits with an open fire usually requires the use of a reflector oven or similar device. A reflector oven will weigh about 2 to 3 pounds. In addition to the added weight that a reflector oven makes in the pack, there is some problem in keeping it clean enough to pack from place to place. This means extra time required during the dishwashing operation. Additional utensils are usually required for the mixing of ingredients and for the baking process in the oven. Assuming that all of the cooking in the oven turns out perfectly and that none of the "results" are thrown away (that would be rare), there is still a considerable investment in *weight*. For a lesser total weight you can probably provide an ample "bread" ration for each person by using canned bread and cakes, hard crackers, wafers, or other bread substitutes. The most food value per unit weight will result if you use a fortified biscuit, fruit cake, nut bread, or similar product.

For those persons who feel they must have bread, some pumpernickel, rye, and black breads are sufficiently durable that they will last for several days. They must be carefully packed, however.

APPLESAUCE

A good side dish for many meals is provided with applesauce. There are several "instant" types of applesauce available. To make applesauce you simply mix the applesauce granules with cold water and let it stand for ten to fifteen minutes. No cooking is required. A number of suppliers also carry apple nuggets or diced apples (vacuum dried) which require a short cooking time (usually about ten minutes). Most persons find these cooked apples to be somewhat superior in taste to the instant applesauces. A bit of cinnamon is a good addition to applesauce and can be put into the poly bag when the applesauce is packaged at home.

VEGETABLES

Many backpackers seldom bother with a side dish of vegetables. Beans and potatoes are sometimes an exception. Beans, with the addition of a meat bar, can be a main dish. Potatoes, corn, peas, and string beans can be a good addition to a stew which you concoct yourself. Dehydrated spinach, in my experience, is better left at home (or in the store).

Potatoes. Dehydrated potatoes are now a common item in most local food stores. In cooking, the potatoes are covered with salted water and boiled for about fifteen minutes or until soft. Presoaking will reduce the cooking time to just a few minutes. About 4 ounces of dehydrated potatoes are sufficient for three persons. A tasty addition to boiled potatoes is to add ½ cup of powdered milk (or equivalent cream substitute) and about 3 ounces of cheese during the last five minutes of cooking. Cut the cheese into thin slices and stir these and the powdered milk into the potatoes after most of the water has boiled off (or pour it off).

Dehydrated *instant* white potatoes are available in local food stores. In preparation of most of the instant potatoes, a measured amount of water is first brought to a boil. It is then removed from the fire and a measured amount of milk is added. (Dehydrated milk or cream substitute can be used to make the required milk.) The instant potato granules or flakes are then quickly added and stirred so as to obtain a uniform "mashed" potato. Instant sweet potatoes are also available. It is very important to *carefully measure* the amount of liquid used. Otherwise the potatoes will turn out too soupy or too gummy.

There are some very good prepared gravies available in local stores, such as the French's gravies, that are an excellent addition to the instant mashed potatoes. They can also be used on the dehydrated potato "buds," etc.

BEANS. Precooked dehydrated beans are available in some local stores. Many firms listed in Appendix A carry one or more brands of dehydrated bean dishes. The Seidel brand of Boston Baked Beans is good. With the addition of a bacon bar or other meat bar, a pan of beans can become the main dish for supper. As with most dehydrated foods, presoaking will reduce the cooking time.

CORN. Some local stores stock dehydrated corn. The John Cope brand is quite tasty. It is desirable that the corn be soaked all day, however, so that it will cook in about twenty minutes for the evening meal. Freeze-dried corn, available from some of the suppliers of trail foods, can be cooked in about ten minutes, without presoaking. Corn makes a good side dish for a main meal, or it can be added to soups and stews. About ½ ounce of freeze-dried corn per person is ample.

PEAS, STRING BEANS. The freeze-dried peas and string beans, available from some of the suppliers in Appendix A, are much more tasty than the ordinary dehydrated variety. About ½ ounce (before cooking) of freeze-dried peas or string beans is sufficient for one person, and they will usually cook in about fifteen minutes.

MAIN DISHES

Some meals, especially supper in the evening, are frequently planned around a main dish. A main dish should not be complicated to cook, and it should be filling. Unless you have fish or other meat with the meal, the main dish preferably should contain some meat or meat substitute. A few main dishes will be discussed in the following paragraphs.

SPAGHETTI AND HAMBURGER. The following ingredients will provide a main dish sufficient for three persons:

```
7 oz.   elbow spaghetti
1 pkg.  spaghetti sauce mix
1 can   cooked hamburger (about 10 oz.)
             or
2 oz.   dehyd. ground beef
```

Put 1 quart of water in a saucepan, add ½ tsp. of salt, and bring to a boil. Then add the spaghetti and cook for about twenty minutes. While this is cooking, take the hamburger, chop into small bite size lumps, and heat thoroughly in a skillet. Do *not* fry it brown or crisp. If you use dehydrated ground beef, put it in a skillet, barely cover with water and simmer about fifteen minutes.

At the same time the above is cooking, have another person put the package of spaghetti sauce mix in a saucepan, add 2 cups of water and bring to a boil. Then remove to low heat and simmer for fifteen to twenty minutes. Watch this mix very closely and stir frequently. The Chef Boy-Ar-Dee brand is a good spaghetti sauce.

When the spaghetti is cooked (taste it to see if it is soft), drain off the excess water, add the hamburger and the sauce mix, then mix the contents thoroughly and simmer five to ten minutes longer.

CHICKEN AND NOODLES. The following ingredients will provide a main dish for three persons:

```
5 oz. noodles (short pieces, break if necessary)
1 pkg. dehyd. chicken noodle soup (such as
    Wyler's or Lipton)
1 — 7 oz. can cooked chicken, or 2 oz. dehyd.
    chicken
```

Put 1 quart of water in a saucepan, add ½ tsp. salt, and bring to a boil. Add the noodles, cook seven to ten minutes, or until soft. Pour just enough water off the noodles so that about 2 cups of water still remain in the pan. Then add the package of chicken noodle soup and the can of chicken (or dehydrated) to the pot and cook about five minutes longer.

One of the little problems in wilderness cooking is to avoid a bland taste in certain foods. A "chicken and noodles" dish can be improved upon by adding two tablespoons of

dehydrated onions and/or bell peppers. These can be added to the poly bag with the noodles when they are packed at home. If you use dehydrated chicken it can be put in the same bag.

MACARONI AND CHEESE. You will need the following, to serve three persons:

```
6 oz. elbow macaroni
4 oz. mild or sharp cheese, as preferred
some dehydrated milk or cream substitute
```

Place a little over 1 quart of water in a pan, add 1 teaspoon of salt, and bring to a boil. Add the macaroni and cook about fifteen to twenty minutes, or until soft. Now pour off practically all of the water, leaving not more than ½ cup on the pan. Add several tablespoons of dehydrated milk or equivalent cream substitute. Cut the cheese into thin slices and add this. Stir the mixture thoroughly. Now place back on the fire, over low heat, for about five minutes, stirring frequently.

CHOW MEIN. Several of the suppliers of dehydrated foods carry a dehydrated form of chow mein. Most are satisfactory to use just as they are purchased. With a few additions, however, they can be made even better. The additions are indicated below. This will make a sufficient dish for three or four persons:

```
1 pkg. dehyd. chow mein, about 6 oz.
3 oz. dry chow mein noodles (available local
    stores)
1 — 7 oz. can chicken, or 2 oz. dehyd. chicken
```

Empty the contents of the package of chow mein into a pan containing 4½ cups of warm water and soak for fifteen minutes. Then put the pan on the fire, bring the contents to a boil, and cook for about five minutes. Then add the chicken to the pan, mix thoroughly, and cook for five to ten minutes. When the mixture is finished cooking, remove from the fire and pour over the chow mein noodles, which have been divided up and placed on the individual plates. (Note: The chow mein noodles, purchased from a local store, usually come in a can. Repackage them in a plastic bag. They are a little bulky, but light.)

CHICKEN AND RICE. You will need the following ingredients to provide a main dish for three or four persons:

```
3 oz.   Minute Rice
2 oz.   peas (dehyd.)
2 oz.   chicken (dehyd.)
3 oz.   chicken rice soup (dehyd.)
```

Cook the peas separately, according to directions on the package. When the peas are about done (taste to see if soft), add the chicken, chicken rice soup mix, 5 cups of water and ½ teaspoon of salt. Bring the mixture to a boil and continue to cook over a medium fire for about ten minutes. During the last few minutes of cooking, add the Minute Rice and stir frequently. (Dehydrated chicken noodle soup can be used in place of chicken rice soup.)

SPANISH RICE. Several brands of Spanish rice which make a good main dish are available in many local stores. One brand is Betty Crocker Rice Milanese. A 5-ounce package makes sufficient servings for several persons. Another is the General Foods Minute Spanish Rice. Cooking time is about ten to fifteen minutes. Mushrooms, peas, diced chicken, meat bar, etc., can be added to these Spanish rice mixes to provide a complete meal. Follow instructions on the package.

RICE AND GRAVY. This is an inexpensive dish, quickly prepared and very tasty. For three persons you will need the following:

5 oz.   Minute Rice
1 or 2 pkg. French's Gravy Makins chicken
              gravy mix

Heat water to a boil. Add salt and a chunk of margarine. Stir in the rice and remove from heat. Let stand for three to five minutes. Fluff with spoon.

Another person can make the chicken gravy. Add 1 pkg. Gravy Makins to 1 cup of boiling water, stirring constantly.

Spread the gravy over the rice and eat immediately.

HASH. The following ingredients will provide a main dish for three persons:

4 oz.   dehyd. potatoes
2 oz.   dehyd. onions
3 oz.   bacon bar

If the dehydrated potatoes are the kind consisting of small hard cubes, they should be soaked at least an hour, or even all day. The onions can be soaked with them, but this is not essential. (The dehydrated potatoes that are in the form of small thin slices need not be presoaked.) Put a quart of water in a saucepan, add ½ teaspoon of salt, and bring to a boil. Add potatoes and cook them for about fifteen minutes, or until they are soft (taste them). During this time, put the bacon bar in another pan, or on a dish, and shred it into small bits. Now put a heaping tablespoon (or equivalent) of margarine, bacon grease, or cooking oil in a skillet and heat it until it is very hot. Then ladle the potatoes and onions from the pan into the skillet, using a pancake turner so as to drain off

the water in the process. Fry about half of the potatoes at once and they will fry faster. After they are in the skillet, add half of the shredded bacon bar to the potatoes and onions, mix thoroughly, and fry over a medium hot fire about ten minutes, stirring frequently.

Hash makes a good dish for breakfast. Soak the onions and potatoes (together) all night, and they will quickly fry to a finish in the morning. No boiling will be required. With other food for breakfast, the amount of ingredients recommended for three persons is as follows:

2½ oz. dehyd. potatoes
1 oz.   dehyd. onions
3 oz.   bacon bar

CHILI. Dehydrated chili beans are now found in many local stores. A good chili (sufficient for three persons) is made as follows:

5½ oz. chili beans (presoaked)
½ oz.   onions
2 oz.   dehyd. beef
¼ oz.   dehyd. tomatoes

The beans should be soaked from four to eight hours before cooking. After they have cooked about fifteen minutes, add the dehydrated beef, onions, and tomatoes. Continue cooking for another fifteen minutes or until tender. About ¼ to ½ ounce of dehydrated bell peppers, available in local stores, can be added to give the chili a more spicy flavor, if desired. The onions, dehydrated beef, tomatoes, and bell peppers can all be put in the poly bag with the chili beans when they are packaged.

If you want to cut down the preparation time, try the Mountain House brand of freeze-dried chili and beans. It is quite good. All that is required is to add boiling water to the contents of the package.

DESSERTS

Your appetite for ordinary food will usually be sufficient that you won't need to pamper it with elaborate desserts. Most hikers do develop a yearning for some sweets, however, so it is a good idea to include some. Following are a few suggestions for desserts:

CANDY. In normal backpacking a lot of physical energy is expended. To sustain your energy at a high level, it is recommended that your *protein* and *fat* intake be increased over what you would eat at home, through use of such lightweight, nonperishable meats as beef jerky and hard dried sausages. Cheese, nuts, gelatin and eggs are good energy sources and are also recommended. *Quick* energy (but not long lasting) can be supplied by increasing your *sugar*

TABLE 7.2 MEASURING UNITS (APPROXIMATE) FOR FOODS USED IN BACKPACKING

Food		Volume		Weight (ounces)
Cocoa, instant		3 heaping tsp.		1
Coffee, instant		6 rounded tsp.		½
Cornmeal		1 cup		4
Flour		1 cup		4
Lemon powder		3 level tbs.		1
Macaroni, small elbow		1 cup		4
Margarine		1 cup		8
Noodles, fine, short		1 cup		3
Oatmeal		1 cup		3
Pepper		8 level tsp.		1
Pream (cream substitute)	(a)	3 rounded tbs.	(a)	1
	(b)	1 cup	(b)	4½
Popcorn		1 cup		6
Raisins, store variety		1 cup		5
Rice, instant		1 cup		4
Salt	(a)	3 level tsp.	(a)	1
	(b)	2 level tbs.	(b)	2
	(c)	small cardboard shaker, 1¾″ x 3¾″	(c)	4
Sugar, white	(a)	4 level tsp.	(a)	1
	(b)	1 cup	(b)	8
	(c)	2 tbs.	(c)	1¼
Sugar, brown		1¼		8
Shortening, liquid	(a)	3 level tbs.	(a)	1
	(b)	1 cup	(b)	7
Tea, instant	(a)	11 rounded tbs.	(a)	1
	(b)	1¼ cup	(b)	1
Wheatena		1 cup		5
Hickory Beef Stick		2⅝″ x 5″ cylinder		16

Note: One cup refers to 1 standard measuring cup. If you do not have a standard measuring cup, take a glass or other container, set it on a kitchen scale and fill with 8 ounces of water. Draw a line on the container at the level of the liquid and you have approximately 1 standard cup.

3 level teaspoons (tsp.) = 1 level tablespoon (tbs.)
2 level tablespoons of water = 1 ounce
16 tablespoons of liquid = 1 cup

intake. You can use bulk sugar, but a somewhat more pleasant way to increase your sugar is in the form of various candies. Even though you don't normally eat much candy at home, you will probably find it welcome and beneficial on a backpack trip. You will find candy in many lunch menus which follow in Part 8. When the cook rations out the candy at lunchtime, slip it in your pocket. When you are on a steep climb in midafternoon, or simply beginning to feel "dragged out" after severe exertion, eat your candy then. It will give you a quick pick up.

Specially prepared, quick-acting candies are available from some of the suppliers listed in Appendix A, for example, the Tex-Schmeltz Traubenzucker. Each 2-ounce package contains eight individually wrapped squares of lemon-flavored, quickly absorbed, high energy candy. Other special candies, including high melting point chocolate such as Hershey's tropical chocolate, are also available from some of the suppliers listed. The M & M chocolate-covered peanuts have a fairly high melting point. Peanut bars are also good. These come in packages with a gross weight of about 1 ounce each, which is about right for one person (one ration). Peanuts are also available in cellophane bags having a gross weight of about 1 ounce, or you can buy them in bulk and package your own. Glucose tablets are also good for quick energy.

"Gorp" is an arbitrary name given to a mixture of about equal parts of nuts, raisins, and chocolate. Many backpackers carry it as a trail snack. It is available from some suppliers listed in Appendix A, or you can make your own.

For a hot day on the trail, sour hard candies can be very refreshing. It is best to get individually wrapped candies, whether for hot weather use or otherwise.

PUDDINGS. Instant puddings, such as the Jell-O instant brand, are found in many local stores. Many are fairly good and make a good dessert for supper, or a good evening snack. They are very easily prepared. Many of the suppliers listed in Appendix A carry various brands of instant puddings and cobblers. I have found also that most backpackers like fruit and that a ration of fruit, either in the pudding, or separate, is readily accepted as a dessert or as a trail snack.

POPCORN. As an evening snack, popcorn is a real favorite. To cook the popcorn, take an aluminum saucepan and fasten an extension handle to it as described for the skillet in Part 9. You will need a piece of aluminum foil slightly larger than the pan opening (make it about 10 inches square) for a lid. By repeated folding you can work this foil into a 2-inch square, and put it right in the bag with the popcorn when you pack the food. For several persons use about $2/3$ cup of popcorn. Place the foil lid over the top of the pan, making slits where it meets the wire bail, and bend over at the edges. Add a rounded tablespoon of shortening to the pan and one or two grains of popcorn. A piece of stove wire around the pan, just below the top edge of the rim, will help hold the foil "lid" in place. When the grains pop, lift the edge of the foil cover, dump in about $1/3$ cup of popcorn (I recommend popping in two batches), and bend the edge of the cover over again. Hold over a medium hot part of the fire, shaking frequently but gently, and you will have popcorn in four or five minutes. Don't leave it on the fire too long, and as soon as you remove it dump it *quickly* into another utensil (such as a skillet) or it will burn. Sprinkle it liberally with salt, and then get back so you don't get stepped on in the rush.

If you don't have an open fire you can try making the popcorn on your backpack stove. In such case you will need two rags or towels, or heavy gloves, for holding onto the pan. Remove the pan from the stove momentarily when you shake it.

OTHER FOOD ITEMS REQUIRED

A few other food items and condiments are going to be required for your cooking. The basic items that are needed in the foregoing recipes will be briefly discussed.

SUGAR. If you use sugar in coffee or in other drinks, as well as on cereal and for cooking, it can add up to considerable weight for a week-long backpack trip. If you use candy liberally in your backpack diet it is recommended that you be a bit conservative in the use of sugar in various foods where it is called for. Use of foods containing *fat* will better supply your requirements for energy than an overuse of sugar.

SHORTENING. Margarine can be used as shortening in most recipes. If you want a spread for bread or pancakes, margarine is usually acceptable. Butter will turn rancid much more quickly in hot weather than margarine. Margarine can also be used for frying, although it has a lower burning point than Crisco or a similar product. If you are frying fish regularly, much more shortening will be required than if you are not. Analyze your menus to determine your requirements. Running out of shortening can be a real inconvenience. Several shortening products such as Vegalene and Golden Clear are packaged specifically for backpackers in convenient nonbreakable dispenser bottles. Coating the *entire* inside surface of a cooking pan with one of these products before cooking a food such as oatmeal, spaghetti, or chili will reduce the tendency of the food to stick to the pan.

It should be emphasized that margarine (or butter) is an *excellent* source of fat, high in calories (about 200 calories per ounce). It is recommended that it be used fairly liberally as a spread for crackers or bread, in oatmeal, soups, stews, main dishes, etc.

MILK OR CREAM. Many brands of dehydrated milk and cream substitutes are available from local stores. The cream substitutes will weigh a bit less and are a little richer when used in recipes that call for milk. If you like milk to drink, Carnation, Pet, and Lucerne are good brands, found in many local stores. There are many others. If you have cool water at hand for mixing, they can be mixed in a poly bottle and will taste almost as good as the real thing.

CONDIMENTS. Don't take too many condiments. On many backpack trips, salt will be the only condiment, or possibly salt and pepper. Catsup, mustard, fruit preserves, and various spices may be desired in some cases, but be prepared for a real mess if they are not packaged properly. Also, rummaging through a lot of small bags, or other small containers in which condiments are packaged can be pretty exasperating when the cook is trying to find something he really needs. With all foods being grouped together in a few large bags it is far different from the situation at home when you are trying to find a certain food in a neatly arranged pantry.

The salt requirement is roughly ¼ ounce per person per day.

PREPACKAGED MEALS

Completely prepackaged meals are available from some of the firms that sell dehydrated foods. You can buy a variety of breakfasts, lunches, and suppers which contain everything from beverage to dessert. These prepackaged meals are *not* particularly recommended, however, unless you are short on time for putting together your own menus.

Many of the prepackaged meals are fairly expensive, considering the food items that they contain. They will also frequently weigh more than a similar meal that you would put together yourself. There will be too much of some foods and too little of others. There will probably also be some foods that you do not like. In general you cannot rely on a package labeled "Dinner for Four" feeding four people. For healthy appetites the number of people that a package of dehydrated food will feed is frequently overstated. Experience with certain foods and brands of foods, and keeping records, is the solution.

I strongly recommend making up your own menus, along the lines of the menus given in Part 8. It is hard to predict in advance how your appetite is going to be when it comes time for a certain meal on the trail. Also, weather, a strenuous climb ahead, or other factors may influence the amount and nature of the foods desired when it comes time to eat. It is therefore recommended that in making up your own menus all *breakfast* items be packaged together in a large poly bag (about 9″ x 18″), *lunch* items together in another bag, *supper* items together, and finally a bag of *extra* foods. Then if you do not feel up to eating all the food called for on a certain "breakfast menu," the food not opened will be in the proper bag and can be eaten at another breakfast. Also, the cook can quickly tell just how much food remains for breakfasts, lunches, suppers, and trail snacks.

FOODS FOR STOVE COOKING

For those persons who plan to do all or most of their trail cooking on a backpack stove, and possibly for wood fires as well, one brand of foods deserves special mention. These are the Mountain House freeze-dried foods made by Oregon Freeze Dry Foods. Most of their foods are quite tasty and are especially easy to pre-pare. All that is required in preparation is to bring a specified amount of water to a boil, add to the food, and let stand about five minutes, stirring occasionally. The food is then ready to eat. Thus the preparation time is short and the dishwashing job is much easier than with many other foods.

Some backpackers may object to the relatively high cost of freeze-dried foods. However, the philosophy of many is that backpacking is a relatively inexpensive sport in itself and even if you use all freeze-dried foods you will spend considerably less for food than if you were on a vacation where you ate all meals in restaurants. Most freeze-dried foods are lighter in weight than other dehydrated foods. This, and the fact that preparation time is generally short (less fuel to be carried) means a lighter pack load. Additionally, less time spent in cooking and dishwashing means more time available for other aspects of the trip.

FOOD SHOPPING

Many foods suitable for backpacking can be found in the supermarket and other local stores. Some of these are:

beans, precooked
bouillon
bread, pumpernickel, rye and
    other hard breads
candies, hard, nonmelting
cereal, Grape Nuts, Granola, Heartland (Pet Co.),
    oatmeal (instant and regular)
cheese, Gouda or Cheddar
chicken (canned, boneless)
chocolate, Baker's semisweet
cocoa, instant
coconut
coffee, instant
condiments: salt, pepper, sugar, catsup, mustard,
    margarine
cookies, hard
dates
fish, tuna
fruit, dried
fruit drinks: Start, Tang, Wyler's
gelatin desserts
gravy mixes
jam
Lipton dinners
macaroni
meats, canned bacon
meats: salami, summer sausage
milk, dehydrated
mushroom slices, freeze-dried
noodles
nuts: peanuts, filberts, cashews

onions, dehydrated
peanut butter
peppers, dehydrated bell
potatoes, dehydrated (cubed,
    sliced, and mashed)
puddings, instant
raisins
rice, Minute
sardines
soups, Lipton and other instant
spaghetti
tea, instant
wafers, Ry Krisp & Triscuits

In addition to shopping in conventional supermarkets and food stores, try *specialty food stores*. These include health food stores, Japanese and Chinese food stores, gourmet shops, etc. You will find numerous food items that are satisfactory for backpack trips.

If there are some mountaineering and backpacking equipment shops in your area, you will want to include these in your shopping for foods for backpack trips. Although generally more expensive than similar foods which you will find in conventional food stores, such shops will usually have many specially prepared backpacking foods which cannot be found elsewhere. You may also need to purchase some of your foods from the mail order firms that carry mountaineering and backpacking equipment. If you do, allow plenty of lead time for ordering and receiving merchandise.

8

Menus and Food Lists

GENERAL PLANNING

Whether you are to be on the trail for one day, one week, or more, you should have a written menu plan for every meal that you expect to eat. There is certainly no rigid rule that you must eat each and every meal in the exact order and amount as planned, but you should have a plan. With the menu plan you can then make up the food list, adding some extra food for an emergency. The amount of extra food will depend upon the length of trip, the distance from the roadhead, and your experience and skill in planning food lists. Some important factors to be considered in your planning are discussed below.

Whether you are going to do most or all of your cooking on a portable stove will have a definite effect on the planning of menus. Many backpackers are accustomed to cooking on a backpack stove and they will probably continue to do so even though there may be a sufficient wood supply for cooking. Others prefer to cook over a wood fire, if there is a sufficient wood supply and wood fires are not prohibited. However, even though wood fires are normally allowed, they may be prohibited at certain times because of forest fire hazard.

To avoid long cooking time and carrying an unnecessarily large supply of stove fuel, many adherents to stove cooking have learned to plan their meals so that a minimum of cooking time is required. It is true that cooked food supplies no more *calories* than cold food. A few backpackers plan an entire trip with no hot food whatever. However, most backpackers prefer some hot food and drink for breakfast and supper, if not for lunch.

The type of activity which is to follow the meal is frequently a consideration in the type and amount of food to be eaten at a particular meal. This especially applies to breakfast and lunch. If heavy exertion is to follow a meal, keep the meal *light* and avoid the use of much *fat*, which is not easily digested. Heavy exertion will interfere with digestion of most foods and may actually lead to temporary illness.

There is also the matter of expediency. If a group is trying to get a very early start on the trail so as to reach a certain destination during the day, at a certain hour, then breakfast should be very simple. The larger the group, the more important this becomes, if the leader has such an objective in mind. A large group can literally "fritter away" hours in preparing a substantial cooked breakfast, packing up their gear, and cleaning up the camp.

Whether you expect to supplement the plan with game or fish should be considered. Even if you expect to, you should still take enough food so that you will have enough to eat in the event you do not get the game or fish you are after.

On trips into a wilderness area (and many other areas) you are completely on your own after you leave the roadhead. There is no chance to pick up food along the way. On some trail routes, however, there may be an opportunity to add supplies along the way every few days, and this will affect your plan.

Weather may be a factor. If rain is to be expected, it may be desirable to include a number of foods that can be eaten cold in the event you are caught in the rain at mealtime.

The type of trip and daily routine has its effect. If you are to camp in the same spot after you reach a certain destination, the meals will be somewhat different than if you are hiking most of each day and making camp at a new spot each night. Some backpackers who hike most of each day prefer a hot breakfast and hot supper and a light, cold lunch at noon.

A FUNDAMENTAL RULE

Regardless of the type of backpack trip, however, a fundamental rule is to count the ounces and keep the pack light. When the sun is bearing down and the pack is starting to feel heavy, you will thank yourself for the extra time you took in planning and packing to enable you to keep your pack weight down. Insofar as possible, leave the cans at home. This does not mean you should not have a single can in your pack. Certain meats, especially, are best carried in canned form, since no refrigeration is available. It does mean that you should give very careful thought to each can you put in your pack and ask yourself it if is really necessary. On many backpack trips excess food is carried deep into a remote area, lugged around for a few days, and then packed out again. Carrying too much food is just as bad as too little. This is the result of poor planning, and it represents a lot of useful energy to waste.

OTHER FACTORS INFLUENCING MENUS

Some other considerations that should go into your menu planning are:

1. Include in your menus only foods that you have had experience in cooking on previous trips or at home and which you have found that you liked. Also, the saying "If everything else fails, try reading the instructions" had best not be applied to cooking of foods on a backpack trip. If the cook wants to stay popular he had better know his recipes—but good—and follow them.

2. Leave out the food dishes that are complicated to prepare and those that take long cooking time. If you use a portable stove for cooking, concentrate on *one-dish meals*, especially for supper.

3. Foods should ordinarily not require special cooking equipment. Any cooking gear other than two aluminum pans and a skillet is con-

sidered special. (Some menus will not require a skillet.) The packing and use of a reflector oven, Dutch oven, broiler, etc., may be justified in a large group, but seldom for the average small group of backpackers.

However, the fact should not be overlooked that some groups particularly enjoy cooking on the trail. If they are in an area where wood is plentiful they may want to carry a reflector oven for making biscuits, cobblers, and the "works." That is their prerogative, and if it adds to the enjoyment of their trip, they should by all means do it.

4. The menus listed in this part of this book are reasonably well balanced, as they should be. However, unless you are going to be on the trail for two weeks or more, don't worry too much about how the proteins, carbohydrates, etc., balance out. Assuming that you are on a good day-to-day diet before you start the trip, and that you will return to the same when the trip is over, then a week or two of diet which is not perfectly balanced will not hurt you. You will probably feel better, and have more energy, if you substantially increase your protein and fat (particularly fat) intake over what you would normally eat at home. Sugar will provide *quick* energy, but proteins and fats will provide more *lasting* energy. Proteins are also needed for tissue and cell building. Proteins and fats are not readily digested. They should be eaten *frequently*, and in relatively *small amounts* at any one time. They should not be eaten just before or during strenuous exercise.

5. Lunch is the meal most likely to be skipped over lightly, and sometimes this is justified. However, a hot drink or some hot soup is quickly prepared. Lunch does not have to be a big meal, but fixing something substantial to eat will help avoid the physical "letdown" that frequently comes along about midafternoon. It will also eliminate the necessity for an extra big meal at supper, when you may be too tired to fix it or to appreciate it after it is fixed. Further, your body does not digest food well when it is overfatigued.

6. Where unusually strenuous activity is required, such as a climb up a very steep trail for a considerable distance, it is best not to eat just prior to the climb, even though it occurs at meal time. Delay the meal (or any food) until the worst part of the climb is behind. After the strenuous climbing is accomplished, eat lightly on cold snacks before continuing the trip.

7. To some degree, your cooking gear influences your menus. For example, it is not too convenient to have fried fish and fried potatoes for supper when you only have one skillet because excessive time would be required.

Boiled potatoes, creamed potatoes, or potatoes with cheese would be a better choice to have with your fried fish, since they would be cooked in a pan.

8. Don't hesitate to repeat certain foods in day to day menus. If you are hungry, and the food is good, then the fact that you ate the same food dish two days ago (or even yesterday) won't be any problem. It is much better to do this than to start out with a large variety of foods that you are not familiar with. Also, it generally makes for easier packing if you hold to a reasonable variety.

9. The *length* of the backpack trip is a factor. On a trip of over three or four days you will want to use the most concentrated, light-weight foods, and mostly dehydrated foods. On a short backpack trip you may prefer to use many and perhaps all foods that are locally available. Some backpackers keep a good stock of dehydrated and freeze-dried foods on hand and use them on every trip, regardless of duration.

10. In some groups, particularly large and formally organized groups, *religious practices* may influence the menu planning.

EXPERIMENTING WITH FOOD

If the cook likes to experiment with new food dishes, that is fine, but he should do his experimenting *at home*, not on the trail. Most hikers will not appreciate a cook who experiments with food that has been carried deep into a remote area on their backs, over many miles of rugged trails. Cooking any food dish for the first time is an experiment. Neither will hikers appreciate waiting an hour or more for more exotic dishes to cook when adequate, tasty, and nourishing food can be cooked in much shorter time, with proper planning and selection of menus.

"FILLER UPPERS"

One of the important factors in keeping the food load light is to eat *all*, or substantially all, of the food that is cooked at any one meal. Food that is thrown out represents wasted energy of the hikers in carrying it. It isn't very convenient to pack a plateful of leftover spaghetti and beef and eat it at the next meal. In fact it just isn't feasible, from several standpoints, to try to save leftover cooked food from one meal to another while backpacking. The secret of eliminating the problem of leftover food lies first in proper selection of the amount and combinations of food, and in careful planning and weighing of food at home. Secondly, an important factor is to plan some "filler

uppers" on many menus, particulary the lunch and supper menus. A "filler upper" is a food that is normally eaten cold and is conveniently packed and rationed out in one man portions. Candy, fortified biscuits, sausage sticks, beef jerky, peanuts, and cheese are examples of good "filler uppers." A wise cook will see that the soup, salad, main dish, and other foods that are cooked for lunch and supper (in particular) are well on the way to being finished up before he rations out the "filler upper" for that meal. Then if it turns out that some appetites are satisfied by the time the cooked foods are completely eaten, those persons can save their ration of "filler upper" until the next meal, or later in the day. A "filler upper" is not usually necessary for breakfast. Hikers will be fresh and rested and appetites keen at breakfast time, and a substantial meal will normally be assimilated with no difficulty.

BREAKFAST

The starting meal of the day should normally be a hearty one and should usually include the following:

FRUIT. Dried or dehydrated prunes, peaches, pears, or apricots.

HOT DRINK. Coffee, tea, or cocoa.

CEREAL. Oatmeal and Wheatena are suitable hot cereals. If you prefer a cold cereal, Granola, Heartland, Bircher Muesli, and Familia are good. Pancakes, with butter and syrup, may be a suitable substitute in some instances, particularly on a short backpack trip. A pancake breakfast takes relatively long cooking time, however.

MEAT. Bacon or sausage is a good meat for breakfast. A good way to fix it is mixed with potatoes and onions for hash, or mixed with dehydrated eggs.

HASH. This may not appeal to you as a suitable dish for breakfast at home, but your viewpoint (and appetite) will probably change on a backpack trip.

EGGS. An important item on the breakfast menus of any backpack trip is eggs. They contain a lot of concentrated nourishment. On a trip of over a few days, alternating dehydrated eggs with hash works out well. Choose your brand carefully and try them out at home before depending upon them on the trail.

LUNCH

A cold lunch may be entirely satisfactory.

However, it is suggested that you occasionally include some hot food along the following lines.

HOT OR COLD DRINK. On cool days, a cup or two of hot tea, coffee, or gelatin is good. On a warm day a pan of lemonade will hit the spot. If it is a bit on the sour side, so much the better. Orange or other fruit drinks may be substituted if you prefer, but will mean more weight in the pack.

HOT SOUP. The use of dehydrated soup in many lunch menus is recommended. It is easy to fix, nourishing, and readily digested. It will replace some of the liquid in your body that you have lost through perspiration.

SALAD. A vegetable salad, applesauce, or cooked apple nuggets goes well with lunch. It is refreshing, tasty, and helps make for a balanced diet. Instant potatoes are quickly fixed and make a good alternate for salad, if you feel the need for something a bit more filling.

FISH OR MEAT. If you have caught fish in the morning, they should be eaten while they are *fresh.* They will be most tasty if they are eaten within two or three hours after they are caught. If you do not have fish, some sausage sticks, beef jerky, beef stick, or cheese will supply some protein and fat and help round out the meal.

DESSERT. If you feel you are still hungry, a ration of candy, peanuts, or raisins will probably fill the gap.

SUPPER

Although this is usually the big meal of the day, don't try to eat too much if you are excessively tired. That is one reason why both breakfast and lunch are planned as substantial meals, to avoid the necessity for heavy eating at any single meal. It is also the reason why main dishes have been used which are easily prepared, yet filling and nourishing. There is no need to wear yourself out with a lot of complicated cooking at supper time.

HOT DRINK. While you are getting ready to start the rest of the supper, it is easy to heat water for tea, coffee, bouillon, or a drink of hot gelatin. It will pick you up, and will again help to replace the water in your body that you lost during the day through perspiration. It is a good idea, while waiting for the water to boil, to drink a tall cup of cool water with some salt in it.

SOUP. A cup of soup will help to whet your appetite. If you don't feel very hungry, choose a thin soup, like onion soup or tomato soup.

MEAT. In many remote areas you will be able to catch some trout. If you caught some in the afternoon, this is the time to have them. If not, you will probably want some other meat, either small separate portions or mixed in with the main dish which follows.

MAIN DISH. A good main dish is a meal in itself. If you do not feel up to tackling a main dish, along with fish or other meat, try corn, peas, string beans, or potatoes in its place.

EVENING SNACK

If you haven't worn yourself out during the day, so that you need to hit the sleeping bag soon after supper dishes are washed, you may want something more to eat or drink. Tea or coffee are *not* recommended just before bedtime. If you still feel thirsty, fix a cup of soup or hot chocolate to drink. Popcorn usually goes over well and is easy to fix. It also has substantial food value and is good for you. When you plan to have popcorn in the evening, the evening meal for that day should be a bit lighter than usual.

If the night is cold and you feel you may be a bit cool in your sleeping bag, make it a point to eat something before going to bed. A cup of soup, a bar of candy, etc., will help you to sleep warmer.

If you plan to have stewed fruit for breakfast, cook it in the *evening,* after supper. Then it will be ready to eat and save time in the morning. If you plan hash for breakfast, put the potatoes and onions to soak in the evening. They can then be quickly cooked (by frying) in the morning.

COLD MEALS

There will be occasions when a cold lunch or other cold meal will be advisable. Foul weather may necessitate a cold meal. Some hikers prefer a cold lunch at all times. During a long and strenuous climb, a series of very light, cold snacks along the trail will be found better than a single, heavier meal. The following are some foods that are especially good for making up a cold meal or for cold snacks. As a substitute for a hot meal, a total of about 6 to 8 ounces per person of several of the following foods will usually be found to be sufficient:

beef jerky or beef stick	fruit cake
candy	fruit, dried
cheese	"gorp"
chocolate	pemmican
coconut	raisins
cookies, hard	sausage, hard dried

EATING ON THE TRAIL

Many backpackers find it convenient and satisfying to snack frequently along the trail during the day, between meals. An hour or so after breakfast they will pause on the trail to eat some candy and to have a drink of water. Sometime later in the morning, as they hike, they may be chewing on some dried fruit or beef jerky. This is their pattern of eating more or less throughout the day, to "nibble" often and take a few bites of a cold snack when they stop for a drink or rest. Candy, cheese, jerky, nuts, raisins, etc., are included in many of the menus. These items can be slipped in your pocket at mealtime and eaten later on the trail. In addition to such cold snacks as are included in the menus, about 2 ounces per person per day of additional cold snacks in the same category should be added for further snacking on the trail during the day. Try to avoid the constant use of candy. Include generous amounts of foods that contain some fat and protein, for the purpose of sustained energy. Pemmican, bacon or other meat bar, beef stick, nuts, cheese, jerky, cookies, coconut, etc., are good alternatives to candy. Generous use of such foods will keep your energy at a high level. These between-meal snacks are not listed separately in the following detailed menus. Nibble when you stop for a drink, or during a rest stop. With a little practice your general feeling of well-being and your energy level will

tell you whether you are getting the most value out of the foods you eat. It isn't necessary to stuff yourself and it is very undesirable to do so, especially when exerting a great deal. You will feel better if you undereat a bit rather than overeat. Stuffing yourself at any one sitting, with foods that are concentrated to begin with, can lead to problems. As long as your energy stays at a good level, the fact that you lose a few pounds on a backpack trip is of no consequence. Forget about trying to eat (and digest) a certain number of calories each day.

OVERNIGHT HIKE

Now that we have discussed foods and menu planning, let's see what we can put together for an overnight hike requiring three meals to be cooked. The quantities given are for three persons, which is the minimum recommended for a trip into a remote area (for safety reasons). You can easily figure the food requirements for any other size group from the quantities given. Obviously, with a little ingenuity, there are many possible variations in these menus. The recipes for various food dishes are given in Part 7. Since an overnight hike will probably be your first experience in backpacking, these menus are planned around foods which are available in most local groceries. It is assumed that the trip will start after breakfast and that each hiker will take his own lunch.

SUPPER

Item Number	Food		Requirement For Three Persons
1.	Tea	½ oz.	(3 tea bags makes 6 cups)
2.	Pea soup	4 oz.	(dehyd.)
3.	Spaghetti and hamburger	14 oz.	hamburger (canned)
		7 oz.	elbow spaghetti
		3 oz.	spaghetti sauce
4.	Candy	3 oz.	
		31 ½ oz.	

Note: Cook fruit for breakfast.

BREAKFAST

5.	Coffee	½ oz.	(6 tsp. instant makes 6 cups)
6.	Stewed apricots	6 oz.	(dried, local store variety)
7.	Pancakes	10 oz.	prepared pancake flour
	Syrup	6 oz.	syrup mix or brown sugar
8.	Bacon	12 oz.	(local store variety)
		34 ½ oz.	

LUNCH

9.	Hot gelatin or cold fruit drink	3	oz.
10.	Salami or cheese	8	oz.
11.	Hard crackers or cookies	6	oz.
12.	Vegetable beef soup	2 ½	oz. (dehyd.)
13.	Candy	3	oz.
		22 ½	oz.

TRAIL SNACKS

14.	Cheese, cookies, nuts, pemmican, etc.	6	oz.

OTHER FOOD ITEMS. In addition to the above foods, you will need the following, for preparing the food dishes listed:

Food	Amount		Needed for Item No.
sugar	3	oz.	1, 6
salt	¼	oz.	3
margarine	3	oz.	7
cream substitute	½	oz.	5
	6 ¾	oz.	

TOTAL FOOD WEIGHT. All of the food adds up to a total of about 102 ounces, or about 34 ounces per person. This weight could be cut down by using dehydrated beef in item 3 (save about 11 ounces), vacuum-dried apricots in item 6 (save about 3 ounces), and cooked canned bacon or bacon bar instead of store variety "fresh" bacon (save 5 to 8 ounces). Pancakes are also a fairly heavy food item, compared, for example, to dehydrated eggs or cooked cereal. This "fine" planning is not considered essential for an overnight trip where the food load is not a major item. However, on extended backpack trips it becomes very important.

THREE-DAY BACKPACK TRIP

For a three-day backpack trip the food weight will become a larger portion of the total pack load and more attention to the weight of the individual food items is necessary. However, some persons will not plan a three-day trip sufficiently far in advance to allow time to obtain such special foods as dehydrated meat, vacuum- or freeze-dried fruits and vegetables, dehydrated eggs, etc. Therefore, the menus for this three-day trip have again been planned around foods which are available in most local stores. If you want minimum weight in your pack, plan your trips far enough in advance that you will have time to obtain some dehydrated foods. Or, simply keep an advance supply of such foods on hand, if you do sufficient backpacking. For minimum weight, select your menus even for short trips from those given for the week-long trip that follows the three-day trip.

SUPPER (First day)

Item Number	Food		Requirement For Three Persons
1.	Tea	½ oz.	(3 tea bags makes 6 cups)
2.	Vegetable soup	2 ½ oz.	(dehydrated)
3.	Potatoes and gravy	4 oz.	instant mashed potatoes
		4 oz.	dried beef (for gravy)
4.	Raisins or candy	6 oz.	
		17 oz.	

Note: Cook fruit for breakfast.

BREAKFAST (Second day)

5.	Coffee	½	oz.	(instant; makes 6 cups)
6.	Stewed prunes	7 ½	oz.	(dried; local store variety)
7.	Oatmeal	4 ½	oz.	
8.	Bacon and eggs	12	oz.	bacon (local store variety)
		7	oz.	eggs (3 fresh eggs)
		31 ½	oz.	

LUNCH (Second day)

9.	Fruit drink (cold)	3	oz.	(makes 1 qt.)
10.	Beef soup	2 ½	oz.	(dehydrated)
11.	Sweet potatoes	3 ¼	oz.	(dehyd., instant)
12.	Salami or cheese	8	oz.	
13.	Ry Krisp or Triscuits	6	oz.	
		22 ¾	oz.	

SUPPER (Second day)

14.	Hot gelatin	3	oz.	(makes 3 cups)
15.	Onion soup	2	oz.	(dehyd.)
16.	Chicken and noodles	5	oz.	noodles
		3	oz.	noodle soup (dehyd.)
		7	oz.	can boned chicken
17.	Mixed nuts	3	oz.	
		23	oz.	

Note: Cook fruit; soak potatoes and onions for breakfast.

BREAKFAST (Third day)

18.	Coffee	½	oz.	(instant; makes 6 cups)
19.	Stewed apricots	6	oz.	(dried, local store variety)
20.	Grapenuts	5	oz.	
21.	Hash	2 ½	oz.	potatoes (dehyd.)
		1	oz.	onions (dehyd.)
		10	oz.	can pork sausages
		25	oz.	

LUNCH (Third day)

22.	Fruit drink (cold)	3	oz.	(makes 1 qt.)
23.	Tomato soup	2 ½	oz.	(dehyd.)
24.	Hard crackers or cookies	6	oz.	
25.	Summer sausage or cheese	8	oz.	
26.	Candy	3	oz.	
		22 ½	oz.	

TRAIL SNACKS

27.	Coconut, "gorp," cheese, pemmican, etc.	12	oz.

OTHER FOOD ITEMS. In addition to the foods given above, you will need the following, for preparing the food dishes listed:

Food	Amount		Needed for Item No.
sugar	9	oz.	1, 6, 7, 19, 20
salt	1 ¼	oz.	3, 7, 8, 16, 21
pepper	¼	oz.	8, 11, 21
margarine	5	oz.	3, 11, 21
cream substitute	4	oz.	3, 5, 7, 18, 20
flour	½	oz.	3
	20	oz.	

TOTAL FOOD WEIGHT. All of the food adds up to a total of about 174 ounces. This amounts to about 29 ounces per person per day. Compare these menus with those for the overnight hike and note where the differences occur. Note the weight for the second meal, Breakfast, second day, and penalty in weight for carrying store bacon and fresh eggs (19 ounces) compared with the weight for a bacon bar and dehydrated eggs (6 ounces).

ONE-WEEK BACKPACK TRIP

For a one-week backpack trip the food weight will become a very significant part of the total pack load, and some skillful planning is required to keep it from getting out of hand. Some of the foods listed may need to be mail ordered. In general you should allow a minimum of two weeks from the time you send in your order (preferably by air mail) until the order is received. We will again assume that the trip starts in the morning (after breakfast) and that the first lunch will be a cold lunch, each hiker providing his own. On the trail some hot food for lunch is suggested. However, two cold lunches are included in these menus, to illustrate suitable foods and quantities for those occasions where a completely cold lunch is desired.

SUPPER (First day)

Item Number	Food			Requirement For Three Persons
1.	Tea	¼	oz.	(instant; makes 6 cups)
2.	Onion soup	2	oz.	(dehyd. for 3 cups)
3.	Spaghetti and Beef	7	oz.	elbow spaghetti
		3	oz.	dehyd. ground beef
		2 ½	oz.	spaghetti sauce
4.	Ry Krisp or Triscuits	3	oz.	
5.	Candy or raisins	3	oz.	
		20 ¾	oz.	

Note: Cook fruit for breakfast.

BREAKFAST (Second day)

6.	Coffee	½	oz.	(instant; makes 6 cups)
7.	Stewed apricots	3	oz.	(vacuum-dried)
8.	Oatmeal	4 ½	oz.	
9.	Eggs and bacon	3	oz.	dehyd. eggs
		3	oz.	bacon bar (mixed with eggs)
		14	oz.	

LUNCH (Second day)

10.	Lemonade	1	oz.	lemon powder (6 cups)
11.	Chicken noodle soup	2 ½	oz.	(dehyd.)
12.	Cooked apple nuggets	3	oz.	(vacuum-dried)
13.	Dried beef or sausage	6	oz.	
14.	Ry Krisp or Triscuits	3	oz.	
15.	Candy	3	oz.	
		18 ½	oz.	

Note: Soak salad for supper.

SUPPER (Second day)

16.	Hot gelatin	3	oz.	(makes 3 cups)
17.	Tomato soup	4	oz.	(dehyd.)
18.	Macaroni and cheese	7	oz.	macaroni
		4	oz.	cheese
19.	Vegetable salad	1	oz.	salad (dehyd.)
		1	oz.	salad dressing
20.	Peanuts or other nuts	3	oz.	
		23	oz.	

Note: Soak potatoes and onions, cook fruit for breakfast.

BREAKFAST (Third day)

21.	Coffee	½ oz.	(instant; makes 6 cups)
22.	Stewed peaches	3 oz.	(vacuum-dried)
23.	Wheatena	4 oz.	
24.	Hash	2 ½ oz.	potatoes (dehyd.)
		1 oz.	onions (dehyd.)
		3 oz.	bacon bar
		14 oz.	

Note: Soak chili beans for supper.

LUNCH (Third day)

25.	Gouda cheese	4 oz.
26.	Beef stick	5 oz.
27.	Ry Krisp or Triscuits	5 oz.
28.	Candy	3 oz.
29.	Raisins	3 oz.
		20 oz.

SUPPER (Third day)

30.	Tea	¼ oz.	(instant; makes 6 cups)
31.	Pea soup	4 oz.	(dehyd.)
32.	Chili	5 ½ oz.	dehyd. chili beans
		½ oz.	dehyd. onions
		2 oz.	dehyd. beef.
		¼ oz.	dehyd. tomatoes
33.	Ry Krisp or Triscuits	4 oz.	
34.	Mixed nuts	3 oz.	
		19 ½ oz.	

EVENING SNACK (Third day)

35.	Popcorn	4 oz.

Note: Cook prunes for breakfast.

BREAKFAST (Fourth day)

36.	Coffee	½ oz.	(instant; makes 6 cups)
37.	Stewed prunes	3 oz.	(vacuum-dried)
38.	Oatmeal	4 ½ oz.	
39.	Eggs and bacon	3 oz.	dehyd. eggs
		3 oz.	bacon bar (mixed with eggs)
		14 oz.	

LUNCH (Fourth day)

40.	Lemonade	1 oz.	lemon powder (6 cups)
41.	Vegetable beef soup	3 oz.	
42.	Beef jerky or sausage sticks	3 oz.	
43.	Instant potatoes	5 oz.	(dehyd., instant)
44.	Candy or raisins	6 oz.	
		18 oz.	

SUPPER (Fourth day)

45.	Hot gelatin	3 oz.	(makes 3 cups)
46.	Potato soup	3 oz.	dehyd.
47.	Chow mein	5 oz.	dehyd. chow mein
		3 oz.	dry chow mein noodles
		3 oz.	dehyd. chicken
48.	Ry Krisp or Triscuits	3 oz.	
		20 oz.	

Note: Soak potatoes and onions, cook fruit for breakfast.

BREAKFAST (Fifth day)

49.	Coffee	½	oz.	(instant; makes 6 cups)
50.	Apricots	3	oz.	(vacuum-dried)
51.	Wheatena	4	oz.	
52.	Hash	2 ½	oz.	potatoes (dehyd.)
		1	oz.	onions (dehyd.)
		3	oz.	bacon bar
		14	oz.	

LUNCH (Fifth day)

53.	Lemonade	1	oz.	lemon powder (6 cups)
54.	Vegetable soup	3	oz.	(dehyd.)
55.	Apple slices	2	oz.	(freeze-dried)
56.	Ry Krisp or Triscuits	3	oz.	
57.	Candy	9	oz.	
		18	oz.	

SUPPER (Fifth day)

58.	Tea	¼	oz.	(for 6 cups)
59.	Tomato soup	4	oz.	
60.	Potatoes with cheese	4	oz.	potatoes (dehyd.)
		3	oz.	cheese
61.	String beans	1 ½	oz.	(freeze-dried)
		1	oz.	sour cream sauce
62.	Beef stick	3	oz.	
		16 ¾	oz.	

EVENING SNACK (Fifth day)

63.	Pudding	4	oz.	

Note: Cook fruit for breakfast.

BREAKFAST (Sixth day)

64.	Coffee	½	oz.	(instant; makes 6 cups)
65.	Stewed peaches	3	oz.	
66.	Oatmeal	4 ½	oz.	
67.	Eggs and bacon	3	oz.	dehyd. eggs
		3	oz.	bacon bar (mixed with eggs)
		14	oz.	

LUNCH (Sixth day)

68.	Lemonade	1	oz.	lemon powder (for 6 cups)
69.	Pea soup	4	oz.	(dehyd.)
70.	Rice and gravy	4	oz.	Minute rice
		2	oz.	prepared gravy mix
71.	Gouda cheese	3	oz.	
72.	Candy	3	oz.	
		17	oz.	

Note: Soak salad for supper.

SUPPER (Sixth day)

73.	Tea	¼	oz.	(for 6 cups)
74.	Vegetable beef soup	4	oz.	
75.	Rice Milanese	5	oz.	(rice, flavoring, etc.)
		2	oz.	dehyd. beef (added to rice)
76.	Vegetable salad	1	oz.	salad (dehyd.)
		1	oz.	salad dressing
77.	Mixed nuts	6	oz.	
		19 ¼	oz.	

Note: Soak potatoes and onions, cook fruit for breakfast.

BREAKFAST (Seventh day)

78.	Coffee	½	oz.	(instant; makes 6 cups)
79.	Stewed prunes	3	oz.	(dehyd.)
80.	Wheatena	4	oz.	
81.	Hash	2 ½	oz.	potatoes (dehyd.)
		1	oz.	onions (dehyd.)
		3	oz.	bacon bar
		14	oz.	

LUNCH (Seventh day)

82.	Lemonade	1	oz.	lemon powder (for 6 cups)
83.	Mixed fruit	1	oz.	freeze-dried
84.	Turblokken	7	oz.	
85.	Beef jerky	3	oz.	
86.	Candy	3	oz.	
		15	oz.	

TRAIL SNACKS

| 87. | Hard candy, raisins, nuts, dates, etc. | 36 | oz. | |

OTHER FOOD ITEMS. In addition to the foregoing foods, you will need the following items, in preparing those foods:

Food	Amount		Needed for Item No.
sugar	28	oz.	1, 7, 8, 10, 12, 22, 23, 30, 37, 38, 40, 50, 51, 53, 55, 58, 65, 66, 68, 73, 79, 80, 82, 83
salt	4 ½	oz.	3, 8, 9, 18, 19, 23, 24, 35, 38, 39, 43, 46, 51, 52, 60, 61, 63, 66, 67, 70, 75, 80, 81
shortening (including at least 8 oz. margarine)	14	oz.	4, 9, 14, 24, 27, 33, 35, 39, 43, 48, 52, 56, 67, 81
cream substitute	9	oz.	6, 8, 18, 21, 23, 36, 38, 49, 51, 60, 64, 66, 78, 80
pepper	½	oz.	9, 19, 24, 39, 52, 67, 76, 81
mustard	4	oz.	13, 26, 42, 62, 85
	60	oz.	

TOTAL FOOD WEIGHT. All of the food adds up to a total of 414 ounces. There are eighteen meals, two evening snacks, and 36 ounces of trail snacks. Also, at least two of the food items used in every lunch menu are suitable for saving, to be eaten on the trail later in the day. The total food weight amounts to 23 ounces per person per day. Compare these menus with those for the overnight hike and for the three-day hike and note where the differences occur. These meals provide generous portions and in a large group there will be some food wasted. Experienced backpackers, who have learned to plan food menus and cook without waste, will be able to cut quantities on some items so as to reduce the overall food weight by about 10 to 15 percent. This particularly applies to small groups of experienced adult backpackers. In general, the larger the group and the more teenagers in the group (if any), the more wasted food. Fish have been omitted from these menus. However, on many trips into wilderness areas, and other remote regions, trout would be caught and this would make some further reduction in the food weight.

FOOD LIST

The total food list and total weight of the separate food items is easily arrived at. Simply go through the menus, writing down the name and weight of the food the first time it occurs on the menu, and adding the necessary weight for each repetition of the item.

9

Cooking

PLANNING

One member of your backpack group should be designated to be the cook.

One of the most important jobs to be done on any backpack trip is the cooking. Choose your cook carefully. He should not only be interested in outdoor cooking (on the trail) but he should have had significant experience in cooking dehydrated and other trail foods on actual backpack trips. Prior to the trip the cook will be responsible for preparing the menu, getting the food and cooking gear together, ensuring that it is properly packed, and distributing an equal load to each hiker. He should call on the other hikers for help in these preparations, but it is important that some one individual, a leader, have the overall supervision of the job. The cook should know how to properly prepare every item of food on the menu. He should have note cards, or a small notebook, showing each menu and the recipe for each food item on the menu, if it is not already on or with the food package. Then there will be no need for guessing on the amount of food, seasoning, cooking time, etc.

Many of the foods listed in Part 7 may be purchased from local food stores or perhaps sporting goods stores. Depending on the length of the backpack trip, a few will probably need to be ordered by mail. In mail ordering it is desirable that the order be sent approximately one month prior to the takeoff date. Allowing two weeks until mail order foods are received, an additional two weeks is available prior to takeoff; this is none

too long when the packing is done in your spare time. An alternative is to keep a supply of certain dehydrated foods (those not available from local stores) on hand at all times.

PACKING FOOD

Most of the individual foods carried on a backpack trip are suitable for packing in plastic (polyethylene) bags and should be so packed. Most of the plastic bags (pint and quart size) sold by local stores for home use in packing foods for deep freezers are not suitable for this purpose. They are too light in weight and will not stand up under trail usage. Some of the suppliers listed in Appendix A carry plastic bags for packaging of trail foods. (Recreational Equipment has a good variety.) A common weight is 2 mils, which means the plastic material is .002 inches in thickness. Depending upon the size of the party, the pint size bags will do for many of the food items. When the food is used the bag is burned. All dry foods should be repackaged in these bags, except for certain dehydrated foods that should not be opened until ready for use. Double bags, one inside the other, should be used for fine particle foods like flour and sugar. When repackaging food that comes in boxes, cut the recipe from the box and put it in the bag with the food (or copy onto a small note card and put that in the bag).

Small rubber bands can be used for closing the bags at the top, after they are filled with food. These are not as readily installed and removed, however, as a wire "twister" type of closure. The wire "twister" closures with paper cover, that are furnished with the plastic bags sold in most local stores, are generally unsatisfactory for trail usage. The paper cover is not sufficient protection for the wire. Some of the wire ends will poke into adjacent bags, puncture them, and you then have spilled food (and a mess). A good solution is to use ordinary tobacco pipe cleaners, cut in half. After cutting in half with pliers, the ends of the pipe cleaner should be doubled back and crimped with pliers so that no sharp ends protrude to puncture other bags. These pieces of pipe cleaner, or "twisters," are simply twisted around the top of the bag after putting in the food.

It is particularly recommended that such "twisters" be used on bags which hold sugar, tea, coffee, dehydrated milk, and other food items wherein the bag is opened and closed repeatedly during the trip. A rubber-band closure is usually adequate for bags which hold one-meal portions of such foods as macaroni, spaghetti, noodles, etc., and which are destroyed after one use. (When I use rubber bands I generally use bands of ½-inch diameter, purchased at an office supply store.)

OTHER CONTAINERS. For packaging of certain foods, you may want some durable plastic or lightweight metal containers. Such containers should be kept to a minimum. I have made many trips where only one such container, a lightweight aluminum can for margarine, was taken. Some of the suppliers listed in Appendix A carry suitable containers. *Glass* containers should *not* be carried on a backpack trip. They are not needed, and they are not suitable. They are too heavy and they are subject to breakage. If you want to take some food that comes packaged in a glass container, you should repackage it. If for some unusual reason a glass container is carried on a backpack trip, it should be carried home again after the contents are used (just as all metal containers should be carried out). For all practical purposes they are nondestructible. Wherever you leave them they will be there for the next hundred years. Under certain circumstances sunlight shining through glass may start a forest fire.

Experienced backpackers will be on the lookout throughout the year for various plastic and lightweight metal containers that will serve their needs when it comes time to go backpacking. A baking powder can may make a suitable container for margarine or fresh eggs. A large plastic pill bottle, with screw top lid, is suitable for carrying lemon powder.

Shortening, store bacon, sausage sticks, and other foods that tend to be greasy should be packaged with particular care. Don't depend on the thin cellophane wrapper on store bacon to provide adequate protection in backpacking. Repackage the bacon in a heavy plastic bag, tightly sealed. The plastic or metal container in which shortening is carried should, in turn, be carried inside a heavy plastic bag also. In warm weather the outside of the container will become greasy and soil other articles if not properly protected.

WEIGH OR MEASURE FOOD

All foods should be weighed with a scale reading in ounces or measured (by "standard" cups) before placing in the individual plastic bags. An ordinary kitchen scale, which measures in ounces, is good for this purpose. Do not guess at the amounts. This can be disastrous.

A postage scale, calibrated in ½-ounce increments (up to 2 pounds), is particularly useful for weighing food items. When on the trail a small spring scale can be used for weighing equal loads of food, cooking gear, and other common equipment for distribution to hikers at the start of each day.

LABEL THE FOOD BAGS

Label all bags before putting the food into them. A felt tip marker is good for this purpose. You can write directly on the bag. It is desirable to mark each bag with the name of the food and the weight. For those bags that are used repeat-

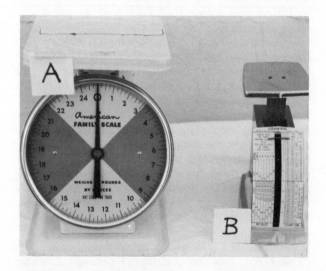

WEIGHING SCALES. The kitchen scale (A) will weigh quantities up to 25 pounds, in one ounce increments. It is useful for weighing large food items and some items of equipment. The postage scale (B) will weigh items up to two pounds, in fraction ounce increments. It is particularly useful for weighing small quantities of food and small equipment items.

edly during a trip, like bags for sugar, tea, coffee, milk substitute, etc., an ink marking on a polyethlene bag will gradually wear and become faint. Protect the marking by an overlay of transparent tape, or use gummed white paper labels for those bags.

FINAL FOOD PACKING

For final packing of the individual bags it is recommended that large, heavy plastic (polyethylene) bags be used. Bags measuring approximately 8 by 4 by 20 inches, with a material thickness of 2 or 3 mils, are most suitable for this purpose.

There are several approaches to packing food so you can find the particular foods for a given meal when you want them. Rummaging through all of the food bags looking for one or two food items can be quite exasperating and time-consuming. You can package foods so that all meats, cheese, shortening, etc., are grouped together in a large bag; products such as macaroni, noodles, soups, etc., in another; sugar, salt, tea, coffee in another, and so forth. You can put all foods for a given day in one bag, with three

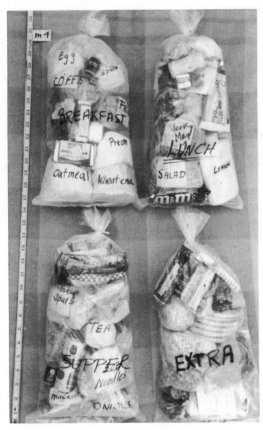

FOOD READY FOR TRAIL. Four plastic bags, each 8″ x 4″ x 19″ x .002″, contain all the food for three adults for a week-long backpack trip, except for some of the trail snacks.

bags within that bag being labelled "Breakfast," "Lunch," and "Supper."

However, the recommended method is for all foods for breakfast to be together in one large bag(s); lunch foods in another bag; supper foods in a third bag; and a last bag to be labelled "Extra." The "Extra" bag will contain sugar, salt, candy, tea, coffee, shortening, and similar food items that are either common to many meals or planned as surplus. This latter method has been found to be satisfactory on most backpack trips.

It is important that only one person, the cook, be responsible for packaging the foods into the various large bags and for repacking them after each meal. Unless this is done you will have a situation like a housewife trying to get a meal, with some other person rearranging the contents of the cupboard each time just before she starts.

Try to put the foods into the proper bag for the meal for which they will be used but, in order to make the weight of the bags balance out evenly (for distribution to the hikers), it may be necessary to put a food used for supper into the breakfast bag, etc., when you first start the trip. As you use the food from the bags you will soon be able to pack all of them in the right bag.

A pipe cleaner type of "twister," as described under "PACKING FOOD," is also recommended as a closure for these large food bags. You will be opening and closing these bags repeatedly during the trip and a "twister" will be least time-consuming and most effective.

Pint size plastic food bags, suitable for packaging of many of the individual foods, weigh about 1 ounce for each ten bags. Plastic bags, suitable for holding a quantity of the pint (or quart) size bags, bacon bars, and other food items, weigh about ½ ounce each (9″ x 20″ size). Use only plastic bags which are absolutely new.

COOKING UTENSILS

KEEP THEM SIMPLE. The recipes listed in Part 7 were chosen not only for light weight of the foods required and simplicity of preparation, but also because they require a minimum of cooking gear. All of the menus for the meals given in Part 8 can be prepared with the following cooking utensils. The capacity and number of utensils is ample for a group of three or four hikers. For a larger group, simply use the same type of cooking pans but of greater capacity, and a skillet of greater diameter, or more units. These are the cooking utensils required:

1. Two aluminum cooking pans, capacity 2 quarts each. If they do not have lids this is not

generally any great problem. In cooking back-pack foods having relatively short cooking time, over a hot flame, most foods need to be watched almost continuously and stirred very frequently. If you had a lid it would probably be off the pan as much as on.

2. Teflon skillet, about 10 inches in diameter. If you do not plan to be frying fish you can readily make up menus for a one-week (or more) backpack trip where no frying is required. Thus a skillet may be an optional item of equipment.

3. Plastic jar (pint or quart size) for soaking dehydrated foods. Not required if you do not plan to have food soaking in your pack while hiking.

4. Two tablespoons, aluminum.

5. Small wood or plastic turner (not required if no frying is to be done).

6. Can opener (not required if no cans are carried).

7. Pan-gripping tool.

The weight of the above items is about 29 ounces. Now let's discuss them a bit.

Cooking Pans. These can be bought in most department and variety stores for about $1 each. A two-quart size is recommended for a group of three or four persons. If you are to be cooking over a wood fire it is recommended that the pans be adapted for hanging from a pole (dingle stick) by drilling three small holes (about $1/_{16}$-inch diameter) at equal points on the circumference of the rim, just below the top edge. Through these holes run three flexible wires and twist together at the top to form a bail. When pans are suspended from a pole by a three-wire bail (using light gauge, easily bent wire) they are much more stable than when using a conventional bail (one heavy wire), running from one side of the pan to the opposite side. Cut off the handles of the pans so that only about a 2-inch stub remains (for gripping with needle nose pliers) and they will be lighter. After the pots are well blackened on the outside by the cooking fire they will do the job better. Cooking pots should be packed in a *pan bag*, as discussed later, to keep them from blackening up other equipment in your pack.

Cutting off the handles of the pans also serves a purpose from a safety standpoint. If there is no handle you are not likely to grab the pan with your hand and possibly get a good burn in the process if it has been on or near the fire.

In packing the cooking pans, simply push the wire bails down into the pan. Unless you put a very sharp kink in the wire (bending it back on itself) it can be repeatedly bent and it will not break. Replace the bails at the start of each backpack trip and carry about 2 feet of spare

stove wire with which to replace a bail during a trip if it becomes necessary.

If you are certain that all of your cooking on a particular trip will be done on a backpack stove, then the wire bails and pan handle stubs are not necessary. However, don't overlook the fact that on some trips some of your cooking may be done on a wood fire.

In selecting a pan for use on a backpack stove, the diameter of the pan may be important. Some models of backpack stoves are prone to overheat if too large a pan is used. The critical aspect is that the pan not be allowed to hang over the fuel tank and overheat it.

Skillet. There are a wide variety of shapes, sizes, and weights of *teflon-coated* skillets available in local stores and many are not expensive. With some searching you can find a 10-inch diameter teflon skillet, weighing about 12 ounces, that will be suitable for backpacking. A teflon skillet is recommended over aluminum or plain steel because it will fry your food more evenly with less shortening and the result will be more tasty. Aluminum skillets may be used but the food will burn quite easily and much more shortening will be required. There are certain precautions that should be observed in using a teflon skillet. The cook will want to instruct others, who are helping with the cooking operation, rather carefully in regard to the following precautions:

1. Although the instructions for many teflon skillets say it is not necessary to use shortening after the skillet is once "broken in," it is recommended in cooking over an open fire that you use a small amount of shortening *each* time. Coat the entire inside surface with shortening, right up to the rim of the skillet. Put a small spoonful of additional shortening in the bottom.

2. Don't thrust a cold teflon skillet into a hot flame and hold it there. Heat it up somewhat gradually.

3. Use only a wood or plastic turner for handling food in the skillet, *never* a metal utensil.* A metal turner will mar the inside teflon surface and the skillet will soon become burnt and useless.

4. A teflon skillet can usually be satisfactorily cleaned with cold water. Use warm water or warm soapy water if necessary. Rinse in water that has been boiled.

5. Never use a metal cleaning pad or pot scratcher in cleaning a teflon skillet. Use only a rag or a plastic scrub pad. There are teflon skillets available that do not require this pre-

---

*Teflon II cookware, now obtainable, does not require these precautions. However, see (5) above.

caution. However, they are generally heavy and also expensive, and are not recommended for backpacking.

6. In packing the skillet be sure that metal objects are not next to it which may rub the inside surface and mar it. A separate lightweight bag is recommended as a cover.

Soaking Jar. If you want to be soaking dehydrated food while you are hiking, then a leakproof, unbreakable plastic jar is recommended. If you are staying at the same camp after you reach a certain destination then such a jar may not be essential. You can have dehydrated food soaking in camp by placing it in a strong plastic bag and hanging it from a tree limb. It can also be put to soak in an open pan which has been tied to a tree limb by its wire bail. (The purpose in hanging from a tree limb is to keep the food out of reach of animals.)

Tablespoons. These are needed for measuring and stirring food while cooking and for serving. Aluminum tablespoons are lighter than steel. The difference will not be important on a short backpack trip but on a long trip it will be.

Plastic or Wood Turner. This is needed in frying, and a wood or plastic turner must be used with a teflon skillet.*

Can Opener. The "GI" baby can opener, listed by suppliers in Appendix A, will save weight (weighs about ¼ ounce), and it will do the job. It just takes a little longer than most can openers. It is so small that it can easily become lost. Tie it to the handle of the turner (drill a hole if there is none there) or other utensil with a stout cord or leather thong so you will know where to find it.

Pan-Gripping Tool. If you have a pair of needle nose pliers these will serve very adequately to handle the pans mentioned and they will also be useful for other camp and trail jobs. Grip the pans by the stub of the handle, by the wire bail, or at the pan edge. Aluminum tools which grip the pan edge are available in a variety of styles. Some have a unit weight of about 1 ounce.

Carrying Bag. All cooking utensils should be carried in a bag which you can easily make at home out of ordinary muslin or percale. This will keep the utensils together and will keep the soot on the pans from getting onto other items in your pack. Make the bag of generous size, with a tie string at the top. You should use new material so the bag will be strong. *Don't* try to use a *paper* or *plastic* bag for this purpose. The bag will split open and the inside of your good pack bag will get coated with soot from the

pans. The inside of the carrying bag will be thoroughly blackened during each trip and should be washed at home before the next trip. Plates, cups, and materials for dish washing can be carried in another cloth bag.

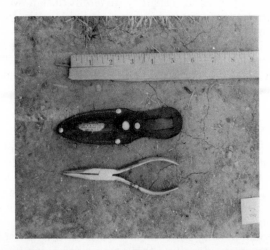

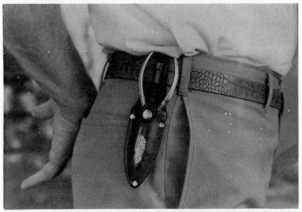

A pair of needle-nose pliers is one of the most useful camp tools. You cannot grab a pan, or the bail on a pan, with your bare hand after it has been on the fire. I frequently use needle-nose pliers when working around an open fire, and also in working with my backpack stove.

*See footnote on page 78.

Cook Kits. Some backpackers will prefer to buy a cook kit, but it takes some shopping to find a good one. Quite frequently cook kits are heavier than necessary. They also often contain one or more items that you either don't need or would prefer in a slightly different design. Many varieties of cook kits are available. It's your choice.

It is possible to buy a backpack stove that has a cook kit designed especially for the stove. The Sigg Tourist cook kit and Svea 123 stove is such a combination.

EATING UTENSILS

PLATES. In general a plate is *not* considered necessary in backpacking. The usual procedure, especially with a backpack stove, is to cook and eat one food item at a time. Also, many menus are planned around a main dish, or a couple of cooked foods, rather than a variety of cooked foods at any one meal. Quite a few persons manage to do all of their eating (and drinking), including fish or what have you, from a single cup. Others find that a lightweight plastic or aluminum plate, or a plastic bowl, makes for greater convenience in eating and is worth the small additional weight. Foil plates are very light in weight, about ¾ ounce, and will usually last for a week or ten-day backpack trip if treated with reasonable care.

CUPS. Plastic cups are good. They will take considerable rough treatment, are light in weight, and can be used for either hot or cold liquids. Such cups are available in many local stores. One such cup weighs 1 $\frac{1}{3}$ ounce, holds about 1 ½ "standard" cups, stacks easily, and costs about thirty cents. *Numbering* the cups on the outside with a felt tip ink marker will help each hiker to know which cup is his when he sets it down some place during a meal. Cereals such as oatmeal, stewed fruit, and soups are

The Sierra cup. Photo by Lou Clemmons.

Eating utensils: Plastic cup and bowl, and large spoon. Weight, 5½ ounces.

most conveniently and efficiently eaten from cups rather than plates.

Some backpackers favor a stainless steel cup, with wire handle. One such cup is the famed Sierra cup. It holds about 10 ounces, weighs 3 ounces, and costs about $1.

SILVERWARE. Each person needs one large spoon for eating. A lightweight fork is permissible (barely) but most foods can be eaten without difficulty with just the spoon. For the foods that require use of a knife while eating, you can use your pocketknife. Do not carry the common silverware knives that you use on the table at home. They are much too heavy and they are not needed. Silverware can be carried in a small lightweight bag with other eating utensils.

WOOD FIRE COOKING

The use of wood fires for cooking in wilderness areas is becoming more and more obsolete, particularly in the well-used areas. As greater numbers of backpackers take to the woods, areas that once had a sufficient supply of dead wood for cooking are being rapidly depleted of such wood. However, there are still some areas where dead wood is available and, if forest conditions permit, a cooking fire is in order if that is the way you wish to cook. A fire-building permit may be required in some government-controlled areas.

THE COOKING FIRE. Sticks lying on the ground should be the source of wood for your cooking fire. Limbs, either dead or alive, should not be broken off trees. The same applies to limbs on logs lying on the ground. These are part of the landscape and to break off limbs is to mar the natural scenery of the area. If you cannot find an adequate supply of wood lying on the

Two automobile radiator hose clamps, used as shown here, will hold the skillet securely to the extension handle.

An extension handle for your skillet, five or six feet long, supported on a rock, will keep the cook from getting uncomfortably hot during the relatively short period that is required for most frying.

DINGLE STICK. This is a good method for suspending pans over an open fire and is quickly rigged. Note the three wire flexible bails on the pans; this is more spillproof than a single heavy wire bail.

One of the problems of wood fire cooking is to find some lightweight devices for holding or suspending pots, pans, and skillets over the open fire. Shown here are some recommended devices and methods.

ground, a cold meal is in order (unless you have a backpack stove).

If there have been recent rains you may need to look under cliff overhangs, under large trees lying on the ground, or in similar protected places in order to find a dry wood supply for starting your fire. Once a good fire is going you can dry out fairly wet wood by laying it very near or on the fire, then removing it (for later use) before it starts to burn.

Have a good wood supply *before* you start to cook. Nothing is worse than having the fire die down when you are halfway through with your cooking and then having to stop everything and go look for more wood.

If you are building your fire near a stream, try to pick out a spot of sand or dirt in the stream bed, free from small rocks, or a large, flat, solid stone area on which to build your fire. When a fire is laid on shale, porous rock, or wet stones some of the stones may explode and cause injury.

If your fire is to be built away from a stream, take every precaution to build the fire on sand, dirt, or solid rock. It should be away from brush, dead grass, and overhanging tree limbs. *Never* build the fire against a log or tree stump or between two parallel logs. Such a fire is next to impossible to put out, if you are to be absolutely sure that it is out. It may require considerable time, if you are away from a stream, to find a suitable place for a fire and to exercise the necessary precautions so that there is no fire hazard. If you are not willing to take that time, or if such a place just isn't available, then eat cold food for that meal.

Many times you can start your fire simply by gathering twigs, pine needles, etc., holding a country match under a few until they ignite, and then adding larger twigs and sticks. Frequently, however, the match will go out just when the twigs are about to get started to burn. That is where *fire-starting aids* are useful. Fire cubes, fire-starting jelly, or a candle will save time. Have your supply of small dry twigs handy. A good handful of these should be about the diameter of a wood pencil and some of them only half as big. Using two short, parallel sticks about 1 inch in diameter as a platform, lay a few pencil size sticks on top. Use these as a base for fire-starting cubes or jelly. Light the fire aid and then very slowly add additional twigs, one at a time, placed very carefully on the flame until the fire is started. In using a candle, simply hold the lighted candle under the platform until the material is burning well, then withdraw it for future use.

If you expect rain a plastic sheet about 6 or 8 feet square can be a big help. Gather some dry twigs and small sticks in the evening, put under this sheet, and weight the corners with rocks. Then if it rains you will have some dry wood to start the fire in the morning.

For a group of three or four persons cooking together at least one person's job should be to help the cook with the food that is cooking and to feed the fire so that it burns steadily. A small wood fire will burn down quickly if not constantly attended to. Feed the fire one or two sticks (about 1 to 3 inches in diameter) at a time. Do not build it up into a big fire. It will

FIRE STARTING AIDS

waste wood and it will be uncomfortable to cook with. When using a dingle stick build your fire "long" rather than "round."

As soon as your fire is going well you are ready to cook. Cooking over coals may be a bit more romantic (and necessary for some cooking), but heat is heat and it doesn't matter to food inside a utensil whether the heat is coming from coals or an open flame. You are going to waste a lot of time and have some very hungry people getting restless for food if you wait for coals. It is important that you have a controlled flame, however. Don't have it blazing all around the pans one minute and almost going out ten minutes later.

When you are finished cooking put the fire out with water, dirt, or sand, and take every precaution to see that it is completely out. More than one wood fire that was supposed to be out has blazed up again after the campers' departure, especially with the aid of a little wind. This is one way of starting a forest fire. If you carry water in one of your cooking pans for putting out the fire, use a minimum of three full pans to put out a small cooking fire. When you are sure it is out make one more trip to the stream. Poke around in the ashes with a stick (or your hand) to be sure they are all well doused with water. Never leave a cooking fire or any other fire unattended in the woods, even for short periods. When you go to bed at night put the fire out just as completely as though you were leaving the area. Any party that "had" to keep a fire going all night for warmth should best keep the story to themselves. This is simply admitting that they were not properly prepared. It is a very poor practice.

THE DINGLE STICK. There are numerous ways of suspending pans over the fire while cooking. They can be set on two parallel stones or suspended from a tripod or ridge pole (supported by forked stakes). Another way, which can usually be quickly rigged and will not be likely to dump the cooking pots into the fire, is the dingle stick.

The dingle stick is a pole about 8 to 10 feet long, 3 to 4 inches in diameter at the base, and 1 or 2 inches in diameter at the tip.

The dingle stick is rigged so that the large end is on the ground (away from the fire) and the other end is suspended about 18 to 20 inches above the ground, over the fire. Laying the dingle stick over a rock or short log, at about its midpoint, will elevate the tip end. The base end is weighted with several rocks to hold it in place.

If you use a three-wire flexible bail on your cooking pans, as discussed earlier, they can be easily suspended on a dingle stick so that they will not tip. If you keep your fire at the right size for a cooking fire there will be no danger of burning the dingle stick.

GRILL. For a short backpack trip, or for a fairly large group where the additional weight is justified, the use of a wire grill with folding legs may be desirable. Many grills are too heavy to be suitable for backpacking. (Why don't "they" make a grill to last one or two seasons instead of five?) A wire tray from a stove oven may be suitable. It has the disadvantage of being somewhat unstable unless you can find two or three good size rocks for "legs," of roughly equal height, flat on the top and "tip proof" (not an easy job—try it sometime!).

Grills with folding legs are available. They provide a surface area of about 10 by 15 inches and have a total weight of about 1 pound. Some backpackers may consider these satisfactory. Grills with folding legs should be examined carefully before buying. The type and strength

A backpacker's grill is another method of supporting pans over an open fire.

The backpacker's grill in use. It will get very black and must be carried in a substantial cloth cover, in being packed from place to place.

of attachment of the legs to the grill top frequently leave something to be desired. Many are designed so that there is a "bump" in the grill surface at each point where a leg is attached. This effectively reduces the usable surface area. If a flush mounting is used an additional cooking utensil can be set on the grill, as contrasted to the same size grill that does not have the legs flush mounted.

As with cooking utensils, a grill (if you use one) will become thoroughly covered with soot after each use. You will need a sturdy cloth bag in which to carry it between meal stops.

It should be pointed out that, from an ecology standpoint, a grill without legs is undesirable. This means that you will need to support your grill with rocks. Those rocks are going to get very black from the cooking fire. Unless you can find a fire ring and suitable rocks that have already been blackened by previous backpackers, then blackening "new" rocks is going to deface the landscape a bit. I have not yet met backpackers in the wilderness who were scrubbing rocks to remove the soot caused by their cooking fire.

EXTENSION HANDLES. Even a small wood cooking fire can be uncomfortably hot when you are continuously close to it while cooking. Since a skillet will usually be held while it is being used it is a good idea to use an extension handle with it. Find a piece of stout wood about 1½ inches in diameter and break it to a length of about 24 to 30 inches. Place one end alongside the skillet handle. Wrap the two handles together at several places with tape or wire. You can also use two automobile radiator hose clamps instead of tape or wire and get a more positive fastening. Use the type of radiator hose clamps that have a screw thread adjustment. For special purpose cooking (such as popcorn) an extension handle can also be used with the cooking pans in the same manner, placing the hose clamps very close together on the stub of the pan handle. The handle of a spoon will usually fit the screw head for adjusting the hose clamps. If not, a little modification of the end of the handle with a file (before leaving home) will make it fit.

When a skillet is being held while cooking, the least tiring way is to find a log or stone on which to rest the extension handle (at the end nearest the skillet).

USING COOKING PANS. Dishwashing is frequently a chore, especially the job of washing out the cooking pan(s). Remains of oatmeal, macaroni, stew, or whatever else you cooked in the pan will cling stubbornly to the sides and bottom. However, this problem can be essentially eliminated. Carry a small bottle of *cooking oil* and about a square foot or two of ordinary paper towels. Before you start to cook use a very small piece of paper towel soaked in cooking oil to thoroughly coat the entire inside surface of each cooking pan. Several special products are also available for this purpose. One goes under the name of Vegalene. After thoroughly coating the inside of your pans with the oil, add water and go ahead with your cooking process in the normal manner. When it is dishwashing time you will find that pans "prepared" in this manner clean very easily.

If you want to keep cooking pans clean on the outside, you can rub *soap* over the outside surface before using. Some backpackers have used *shaving cream* for this purpose.

COOKING STOVES

More and more backpackers are coming to rely on *portable stoves* for cooking and are making such stoves a regular part of their backpacking gear. There are a number of reasons for this. First, wood for cooking fires is simply not available in many of the heavily used backwoods areas. Some of the National Parks and Forests prohibit the use of wood fires for cooking or any other purpose. Others allow wood fires providing you obtain a permit for such use. At certain seasons forest conditions (high fire hazard) may preclude the use of wood fires, even though a wood supply may be available. Possible foul weather, the time required to gather wood, cook over a wood fire, and clean cooking pans, and convenience also favor the use of a portable stove.

Some persons cook substantial and even elaborate meals on the trail, over a wood fire where possible. They consider cooking part of the overall "fun package" of backpacking. Others want to spend minimum time in food preparation, cooking, and clean up.

Some dehydrated foods are now available which only require the addition of boiling water, thorough stirring, and the food is ready to eat. Other foods, with short cooking time, are also conveniently prepared over a stove. A bowl of hot soup at lunchtime, or a cup of hot tea at a rest break are easily and quickly prepared.

On the debit side, only one food can be prepared at one time on a one-burner stove. However, eating food in "courses," rather than the "home style" of eating several foods simultaneously, is acceptable to most backpackers. The many "one-pot" meals which are available and can be concocted make one-burner cooking and meal planning relatively easy. Frying is somewhat difficult on many backpack stoves,

since the heat is concentrated in a relatively small area. If you intend to be fishing and want to fry fish for some meals, you may want to get a fire-building permit, to supplement your backpack stove for those meals where frying is to be done.

GASOLINE STOVES. One-burner stoves are most commonly used for backpacking and they can be roughly categorized by the type of fuel they use. Gasoline stoves are probably used by the majority of backpackers. This refers to stoves which burn unleaded white gas. Such gas is often sold in bulk at gasoline service stations but in purchasing white gas from such a source considerable caution should be exercised to ensure that it is clean and uncontaminated. If there is any doubt about the purity of the gasoline, it should be *strained.* A little dirt or foreign material can quickly put your backpacking stove out of business and require taking it apart for cleaning. Considering the quantity of gas normally used on a backpack trip it is recommended that you buy Coleman fuel, Blazo, or a similar product sold in 1-gallon cans at many sporting goods stores. Most of the stoves described in the following paragraphs are dependable if given reasonable care. As with other equipment, you should become thoroughly familiar with them in your backyard at home before taking them on a backpack trip.

The Optimus and Primus stoves are well-known brands to most backpackers. Both of these brands of stoves are made by the same company. To avoid confusion the Optimus Company discontinued using the Primus label on stoves marketed in the United States, as of January 1973.

The Optimus 8R is quite a popular stove among backpackers. It is contained in a box that

has dimensions of about 5″ x 5″ x 3″. The weight is 1½ pounds. The fuel tank contains ⅓ pint of fuel, which will burn 1¼ hours. It will boil 1 quart of water in six or seven minutes. No wind screen is provided. It is somewhat difficult to get a simmer heat, which is true of many backpack stoves. It has a built-in cleaning device. The stove burns by self-pressure. A very large pot should not be used on the stove, since it may cause the fuel tank to overheat and blow the safety valve. Also, in hot weather, at low altitudes, the fuel tank may have a tendency to overheat. Cost is about $16.

The Optimus 80 stove is of the same basic design as the 8R. The rectangular box container provides its own wind screen. It does not appear to have any tendency to overheat. Cleaning is accomplished by first removing burner head and tip. The stove burns by self-pressure. The burner can be turned down to a simmer heat. This stove has a rather high profile and some care must be exercised so that it does not tip. In general this is a good stove. Cost is about $12.

Another popular stove among backpackers is the Svea 123 (also made by Optimus). This stove also burns by self-pressure. The burner head and tip should be removed for cleaning. It is available with built-in wind screen and two stacking pots (combination referred to as Sigg Tourist). The stove kit has a wide base and is essentially tip proof. Cost is about $24 (Sigg Tourist Kit with stove).

In using a gasoline stove it is important to protect it from wind as much as possible, to keep the flame from blowing out. Even for those stoves that have built-in wind screens it is a good idea to cook on the lee side of a boulder, log, or other natural wind barrier. You can also purchase a separate wind screen, or you can make one, if you feel it is necessary (very windy) in the areas where you will be cooking. The fuel tank on the stove should be filled only about ¾ full, to allow room for vapor pressure to build up. Unless the stove has a built-in cleaning mechanism, a separate cleaning wire will be furnished which must be used regularly, to obtain proper operation. The burner head and tip should be removed before plunging the cleaning wire through the gas vent in the burner tip. (Otherwise small bits of soot which are loosened by the wire will fall into the gas tank, where they may cause a clogging problem later on.) Most of the small gasoline stoves have no pumps. Heat from the burning stove causes the volatile fuel to expand and forces it into the burner. The stove must be preheated by some method to force a small amount of fuel into the burner head so that the stove can be started (lit). If conditions are just right this can sometimes be done by cupping the fuel bowl with warm hands, or by setting the stove in the sun, or on a hot rock. One soon learns that these methods are somewhat unreliable, however.

Most backpackers who regularly use stoves carry a plastic eyedropper or a short length of transparent plastic tubing as part of their stove kit. Either of these can be dipped into the fuel tank to extract a very small quantity of fuel. This fuel is placed in the bowl at the base of the vaporizing tube, the fuel tank cap is then closed, and the control valve is also turned to the closed position. The fuel in the bowl or spirit cup is then ignited. Within a few seconds, just as the flame in the spirit cup is about to go out, the

Optimus 80 Backpack Stove. Photo courtesy of AB Optimus, Inc.

The Svea Stove

Spare parts for stove. Clockwise from left: Wick, tank lid, burner plate, cleaning needle, gasket for tank lid (center). The cleaning needle should always be carried. Photo by Lou Clemmons.

control valve is opened. The stove should start burning at this point, and should soon be burning with a roar. If the stove fails to start on the first try the procedure will need to be repeated.

Some important precautions must be taken in operating these stoves. If they must be operated inside a tent, snow cave, or other closed space, adequate ventilation and other factors require careful consideration, as discussed in Chapter 11 on "Safety." Better to have a cold meal in your tent than no tent. After the stove has cooled, and before it is packed away, the fuel tank cap should be momentarily loosened to relieve the vacuum in the tank. The fuel supply should be checked before starting to cook. If the fuel is used up during the cooking, the stove should be allowed to cool before it is refilled. When the stove is not to be used for some time it should be drained of fuel. Aluminium fuel bottles with tight-fitting caps (and pouring caps) are available from equipment suppliers and should always be used for carrying gasoline. When packing, keep gasoline supply and stove as far apart from food supplies as possible, preferably in separate packs.

KEROSENE STOVES. Kerosene stoves must be primed prior to lighting, so as to vaporize the fuel, in a manner similar to the gasoline stoves just described. However, alcohol must be used for priming kerosene stoves. Kerosene will not work as a primer and white gas is dangerous to use for this purpose. A kerosene stove is smellier than most other stoves. However, kerosene is less volatile than gasoline. A kerosene stove is therefore generally safer to use. All kerosene stoves have hand pumps on the fuel tank. The flame height is controlled solely by the amount of pressure in the tank; the more pumping (pressure), the hotter the flame. Kerosene stoves

are available with both "roarer" and "silent" burners. Since fuel pressure is maintained by pumping, kerosene stoves are especially suited for very cold weather use, being more reliable in such temperatures than stoves without pumps.

A popular model of kerosene stove is Optimus 00L. Its dimensions are about 7" x 5½" x 3½", weight a little over 2 pounds, and it is equipped with a "roarer" burner. The fuel tank holds 1 pint of fuel. Stove cost is about $16.

The Optimus 96L is a slightly smaller kerosene stove. It has dimensions of 5½" x 5½" x 3½". Weight is about 2 pounds. Fuel capacity is ½ pint. This is a collapsible stove which folds into a metal box. Wind screen, primer can, wrench, and cleaning pins are included. Cost is about $16.

ALCOHOL STOVES. Backpack stoves which burn alcohol for fuel are available (barely). They have essentially disappeared from most backpacking equipment shops. They are not very popular among backpackers. One reason is that alcohol has only about half the BTU rating of white gas and kerosene. On the credit side, they will not explode and they are nontoxic. However, cooking time and extra weight of fuel to be carried are major disadvantages. Persons who carry "canned heat" for making an occasional cup of soup or hot tea might consider them an improvement. However, most backpackers prefer one of the other types of stoves.

BUTANE STOVES. The butane stoves are gaining in popularity among backpackers. For simplicity of operation they are virtually foolproof. Butane fuel is a liquid contained in a thin metal cylinder under low pressure. A control valve allows the fuel to escape from the cylinder to a burner device and upon contact with the air the fuel vaporizes. A lighted match is applied to the burner, the control valve is opened and you are in business. By varying the position of the control valve, you can adjust the flame over a considerable range.

Butane does not have the BTU output per unit weight of gasoline or kerosene. Therefore, butane stoves are best suited for short trips and those where a minimum of cooking is to be done. Cooking time is longer and more fuel must be carried for a given amount of cooking. The empty cartridges are trash which should go into the *litter bag* and be carried out of the back country. At temperatures below freezing, operation is less efficient and stops altogether at 15° F, at which temperature the butane freezes solid. In planning for breakfast on a cold morning, it may be necessary to put the butane cartridge in your sleeping bag at night, to keep it at operating temperature. It is difficult to tell just how much fuel remains in a cartridge. For rough estimating you can record the minutes of operation as the cartridge is used for cooking and thus have a guesstimate of how much cooking time remains.

The Bleuet S 200 is a commonly used butane backpack stove. It weighs 14 ounces by itself and 24 ounces with one fuel cartridge. It is 5½ inches high, 3½ inches in diameter. The butane cartridges are purchased separately, weigh 10 ounces full, and contain about 7 ounces of fuel. When in use the stove is 8½ inches high and tips readily. A base comes with the stove but a broader improvised base is desirable. The stove costs about $8 with one cartridge. It is important in using this stove to place the cartridge on the stove *exactly in accordance with directions.* Otherwise it may blow off and you may end up chasing a burning cartridge through the brush. In a high wind, shielding is required or the flame may blow out. For summertime use, and limited cooking, this stove has proven to be quite popular.

PROPANE STOVES. Propane is bottled at a pressure of 124 psi at 70° F. It is superior to butane for cold weather use, since it freezes at −50° F. The higher pressure requires heavier cylinders than for butane, weight about 1 pound each (empty). The Primus Grasshopper (# 2361) is a good backpack stove in this category. It has dimensions of 11¼″ x 3″ x 3″ and weighs 40

ounces, with fuel cylinder. The cylinders are not reusable. Extra cylinders cost about $1.80. The stove, without fuel cylinder, costs about $9. The empty cylinders may grow heavy in the pack but there is only one answer. Pack them out with other litter! If they were packed in full they can be packed out empty.

GASOLINE AND KEROSENE

Extra gasoline and kerosene should be carried only in tight metal containers specifically designed for the purpose. In a group where common equipment is being shared, only one person should carry the stove and extra fuel in his pack for the entire trip. That person should not carry any food items. Food is easily contaminated by fuel fumes and odor when they are carried together.

In those situations where one person must carry the stove and fuel, as well as food, some special precautions are necessary. It is recommended that the food be carried as high in the pack as possible. The stove and fuel should be carried in a lower compartment and wrapped in double poly bags, or similar precautions taken to see that the fuel does not contaminate other items. The conventional quart fuel bottles will fit nicely in the outside pocket of some packbags.

Keep the extra gasoline well back from the burning stove while cooking. The burning stove

TABLE 9.1 REPRESENTATIVE BACKPACKING STOVES

Stove Model	Type of Fuel	Capacity of Tank or Cartridge in Pints	Minutes to Boil 1 Pint Water at Sea Level	Dimensions (inches)	Weight (without fuel) in Pounds	Approximate Cost
Optimus 8R	white gas	⅓	7 to 8	5 x 5 x 3	1½	$16
Optimus 80	white gas	½	6 to 7	6 x 4 x 4	1¼	$12
Svea 123 and Sigg Tourist Kit	white gas	⅓	6 to 7	8 x 5	2	$24
Optimus 00L	kerosene	1	5 to 6	5½ x 7 x 3½	2⅛	$16
Optimus 96L	kerosene	½	7 to 8	5½ x 5½ x 3½	2	$16
Bleuet S200	butane	¾	10 to 12	5½ x 3½	⅞	$8
Gerry Mini	butane	⅔	10 to 12	1½ x 4½	½	$11
Primus Grasshopper	propane	1¾	8 to 10	11 x 3 x 3	¾	$9

should never be set near an open fire or other intense heat. It may explode! This can happen when pine needles or other material near the stove accidentally catch fire, so keep the stove away from any such material. Plan your cooking operation so that it is not necessary to refill a stove while it is hot. A gasoline stove should be watched just as closely as a wood fire. If the stove goes out it should be relit at once.

DISHWASHING

Heat water for dishwashing in the two cooking pans. As soon as a pan is emptied during a meal, rough-clean it with a rubber scraper or pot scratcher. This will not take too long. Then fill the pan with water, put it back on the fire, and finish your meal while the water is heating.

Use bar soap or a biodegradable detergent in washing dishes. Each person should rough clean his own eating utensils before they are washed with soap and hot water. Use a sponge in washing dishes. Each person should rough-clean is washed, one person should rinse it in a pan of clean, very hot water (that has been boiled for a few minutes), holding on to it with needle nose pliers or a similar tool. Use a cup to dip the hot water and pour over it. Then drop it directly into the carrying bag (cups and plates) or the silverware bag. The use of dishcloths and dishtowels is *not* recommended. They are not needed, drying them is a problem, and after a few meals they will look as though you washed the family car with them.

A teflon-coated skillet is usually easily cleaned in either cold or warm water without soap. An aluminum or steel skillet may require special effort in getting it clean. Cold washing won't help much. Instead, put a small amount of water in the skillet and have one person hold it over the fire until the water is hot. It will heat quickly. Then go to work on it with a pot scratcher and soap.

After all dishes are washed, rinse out the cooking pans that were used for dishwashing. Don't try to scour the cooking fire soot off the outside of the pans. It is beneficial. Take a quick pass over the outside, however, to remove any loose dirt or soot. When the job is finished squeeze out the sponge, rinse out the pot scratcher, and drop them into the pan bag. With coordination and cooperation the dishwashing can usually be done in ten minutes.

RESPONSIBILITY

It is again emphasized that the food, and all matters pertaining to menus, food packaging, and cooking should be the responsibility of one person, the cook. This is one of the most important functions connected with any backpack trip, and it cannot be emphasized too strongly. If you divide the responsibility, or change it from meal to meal or day to day, you will probably have less than satisfactory results. This does not mean that the cook should not get the advice of others on certain matters pertaining to food. He should consult others, especially in planning the menus before leaving home. However, all final decisions pertaining to food, especially after you are on the trail, should be the cook's responsibility. With various people getting into the food and being responsible for the cooking, you are going to run out of certain food items before you had planned to. You will probably also end up with too much or too little of certain foods at some meals, as well as some foods that are either underdone or overcooked. The cook should know or have a record of the recipe of every item of food on the menu. He should give overall supervision to the preparation of every food item at every meal, even though others are preparing it or helping in the preparation. While others are washing dishes, the cook will be repacking the food, getting it ready for the trail again, putting some foods to soak for the next meal, and making up equal food and cooking gear loads for distribution to each backpacker. The cook has an important job. Give him your full support, and it will pay off in the long run with better food, better dispositions, and a more enjoyable trip in general.

TABLE 9.2 RECOMMENDED COOKING GEAR

Item	Approximate Weight (Ounces)
Backpack stove, wind screen, two pans, small frying pan, burner tip cleaner, eye dropper, funnel, match supply, and cloth carrying bag.	39
Hot-pan gripper, two tablespoons, G.I. can opener	3
Fuel for backback stove (1 qt. in aluminum fuel bottle)	30
Dishwashing (small sponge, pot scratcher, biodegradable soap)	4
	76

TABLE 9.3 OPTIONAL COOKING GEAR

Item	Approximate Weight (Ounces)
Grill, with folding legs	28
Reflector oven	42
Frying pan, teflon	12
Food soaking jar, 1 pt.	2
Spatula	1½

COOKING GEAR SUMMARY

The cooking gear and accessories to be carried on your backpack trip will depend considerably on whether you plan to cook on a backpack stove, or an open fire, or perhaps a combination of the two. For arriving at a weight for cooking gear it will be assumed that cooking is to be done on a backpack stove. There are a number of good backpack stoves available. I frequently carry the Sigg Tourist Cook Kit and Svea stove, which is one of the lightest and most compact stove-cook kits available. With proper choice of menus it will serve adequately for three persons. This kit, including stove, wind screen, two pans, small frying pan, burner tip cleaner, eye dropper, funnel, and match supply, all in a light cloth carrying bag (handmade) weighs 39 ounces. (Eye dropper, funnel, and match supply added to kit.)

10

The Complete Pack Load

Previous chapters have discussed packs, sleeping gear, shelter, clothing, cooking gear, and food. The various items of equipment that make up the *completed pack* will now be discussed. This is another area where it is recommended that you proceed cautiously. You can invest a lot of money in nonessential knickknacks. It is quite likely that many of these may be left at home when you become an austere backpacker and start paring away at the ounces in your pack. It is suggested that you make up a list of essential and strongly preferred items of equipment and take few if any other items for your first few backpack trips. As you become more knowledgeable, from experience and discussions with other backpackers, there may be other items that you will want to obtain.

ESSENTIALS

In addition to your basic outfit (pack, sleeping gear, shelter, and clothing) the following items of equipment are considered essential by most backpackers:

Fire-Making Equipment
Canteen
Knife
Flashlight
First Aid Kit
Map and Compass
Extra Protective Clothing
Sunglasses

Nylon Cord or Rope
Litterbag

FIRE-MAKING EQUIPMENT. You may be planning to do all of your cooking over a backpack stove. However, if wood fires are allowed you may want to carry some fire-building equipment for an occasional wood fire. Regardless of whether wood fires are permitted or not, fire-building equipment should be carried for *emergency use.* You may get lost, or soaked in a rainstorm, and require a wood fire for survival. Your stove may possibly break down.

The name "country matches" or "kitchen matches" is usually applied to those matches having a "handle" about 2½ inches in length. You should carry about four country matches for every fire you intend to build, in waterproof containers. To save time a few fire-making aids, such as a plumber's candle, inflammable pellets, fire ribbon, etc., are also recommended. Another fire aid, which is especially good in damp, muggy weather, is a short length of gum rubber hose with a *metal tubing* on the end. With this you can direct a draft to the fire just where you want it. It is usually better than fanning the fire with your hat or a plate or blowing on it in the usual fashion.

In addition to fire-making equipment which is carried for use by the group it is suggested that *each member* carry some such equipment for possible survival use, in the event he should get lost or separated from the group under adverse conditions. As a minimum it is recommended that each person carry about 15 or 20 country matches, in a waterproof container, and a candle stub, for this purpose (weight about 2 ounces).

If fire permits are required for the area you are going into, it is a good plan to get one, even though you may not intend to use it.

CANTEEN. On most backpack trips you should carry a canteen. Admittedly, there are some areas where good drinking water is so plentiful that a canteen may not seem necessary. However, although water is plentiful there will frequently be some doubt as to its *purity*. It isn't very convenient to carry a cooking pan of water along the trail while you are waiting for halazone or iodine tablets placed in the pan to purify the water. A canteen is much better for the purpose. Also you may want to mix a quart of fruit punch to drink on the trail. Again, a canteen or water bottle is most convenient.

Even though you drink water frequently during the day, it is not unusual to wake up during the night feeling very thirsty. A canteen of water near your sleeping bag will be very welcome at such times.

It is extremely important to know the availability of drinking water along the route you will be traveling. It should be remembered that the flow of some springs varies from year to year, and with the season. A spring that was good last year may be dry this year. Unless you are thoroughly familiar with the trail and know positively that there will be good drinking water at frequent intervals along the trail, then by all means carry a canteen. It can save your life! Running out of water can be one of the most serious problems you will encounter in wilderness camping.

A quart of water should last from three to five hours, depending on the weather and your level of exertion. If in doubt, carry 2 quarts.

A good alternative to a conventional canteen is a wide-mouth, unbreakable, 1 quart, plastic bottle. I have found that such a bottle slips in and out of the side pocket on my pack somewhat easier than a canteen. It is also more convenient to use (because of the wide mouth) than a canteen for mixing fruit drinks, powdered milk, etc.

KNIFE. A good pocketknife should be carried. Some prefer a fairly large pocketknife. I have one which is 4¾ inches long, weighs 3½ ounces, and has a large blade which locks in open position. I often carry a smaller two-blade pocketknife. I also have a Swiss Army knife which I sometimes use. I find that I seldom use all the "accessories" on the Swiss Army knife, however.

A sheath knife should not be carried on a backpack trip. It is too large and heavy, and, if carried on the belt, will interfere with the waist strap of your packframe. It is not a good eating tool and this will be one of the primary purposes of your pocketknife—to eat with, taking the place of a conventional table knife.

Depending on the anticipated use of your knife (much cleaning of fish for instance), you may want to carry a small whetstone. On the average backpack trip, however, a whetstone is not usually required.

FLASHLIGHT. A large flashlight is not generally required. With few exceptions, camp should be made, the evening meal prepared, and dishes washed *before dark*. If you start each day at daylight or soon after, you will be ready for your sleeping bag soon after dark. Admittedly, there is usually a "bull session" at night, to review the events of the day and do some planning for the next day. However, you do not need a flashlight for this. The requirement for a flashlight is therefore simple. You need the light to find your way from the "bull session" area to your sleeping bag. You can undress and get ready for the sleeping bag in the dark except for an occasional beam of light to untie a shoe or stow your clothes. If you wake up thirsty during the night you may also need the flashlight to find your canteen (which should be near the head of your sleeping bag). It all adds up to about three to five minutes of intermittent light required each night.

A standard "D" size two-cell flashlight can be used (weight about 10 ounces with batteries). The small "C" size flashlight can also be used and will weigh less (about 5 ounces with batteries). The recommended flashlight, however, is a good two-cell penlight. Many ordinary

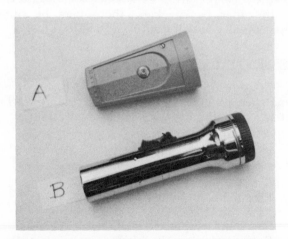

MALLORY FLASHLIGHT. The Mallory flashlight (A) is shown in comparison with an ordinary two cell "C" size flashlight (B).

penlights are so cheaply constructed and unreliable as to be worthless. The Mallory is a good flashlight, using two penlight batteries, with a total weight of about 3½ ounces. It can be held in the mouth while working with both hands, and this is an advantage. Cost is about $2.

To prevent your flashlight from accidentally coming on while in the pack you can reverse *one* of the batteries. (Don't reverse both batteries, because some flashlights will still work with both batteries reversed.) For the Mallory flashlight, simply tape the switch in the "off" position when it is not in use during the daytime.

Two long-life penlight batteries will usually be adequate for a backpack trip of a week's duration. If you use ordinary batteries, rather than the long-life kind, you should carry two extra batteries for each three or four days of the trip. Always carry a spare bulb. Batteries will usually burn out gradually, but a bulb will give no warning. Do not dispose of batteries by throwing them in the fire. They may *explode*.

FIRST AID KIT

Individual Kit. Except for a family group it is recommended that each hiker carry a first aid kit. It need not be elaborate but should contain items for treatment of minor difficulties that frequently occur on the trail. The following items are recommended, as a minimum, for a one-man first aid kit:

Band Aids—about 3 to 6.
Sterile Gauze Pads—3 pads, 3″ x 3″
Adhesive Tape—1 small roll, 1″ wide (Can be rerolled on tongue blade, or stick.)
Aspirin Tablets—6 to 10, depending upon length of trip.
Salt Tablets—6 to 10, depending upon length of trip and weather. (They should be of the coated variety to avoid nausea.)
Needle—for removing splinters, opening blisters.
Razor Blade, single-edge—for cutting tape and moleskin, removing hair.
Moleskin or molefoam—for covering sore areas on toes, etc., before they develop into blisters.
Wash and Treat—a small foil packet containing antiseptic wash cloth.
Matches—3 or 4 for sterilizing needle.
Snakebite kit (suction type)—depending upon region and season.
Milk of Magnesia tablets—6 to 10, to be taken for constipation and upset stomach.
Glycerin Suppositories—2 or 3 for constipation, if individual's past experience indicates a need for such.
Small booklet on first aid, or instruction

sheet. A small first aid booklet, weighing 1 oz, is available from Johnson & Johnson, New Brunswick, N.J. 08903.

If a wound occurs on a part of the body which is thickly covered by hair, it may be desirable to remove some of this hair before dressing the wound. Also, the suction cup on a snakebite kit will not work too well if that part of the skin is covered with hair. Such hair can be readily removed with a sharp single-edge razor blade (no soap or water needed), by holding the blade almost parallel to the skin.

Some persons are highly allergic to bee, wasp, and other insect bites. If you are in this category it is advisable to carry some Benadryl tablets or similar medication, as advised by your physician. If you are regularly taking some prescription medicine then this can be either added to the first aid kit, or placed elsewhere in the pack.

The items listed above can be easily packed into a small aluminum box. My first aid kit is 1⅜ by 3¾ by 5¼ inches and has a weight of about 7½ ounces when filled. An oval aluminum container of similar capacity, readily available at many backpacking equipment supply stores, can also be used.

If the purity of the water in the area is questioned, it is recommended that each hiker carry water purification tablets. Halazone or iodine tablets can be used. *Iodine* tablets are recommended, because halazone tablets lose their strength and effectiveness after a period of storage. It is recommended that the water purification tablets be carried in the same pocket of your pack as your canteen or water bottle, so that they will be readily available.

Group Kit. In a small group of 3 or 4 persons, assuming that the group plans to stay together at all times while on the trail, the items listed above for the individual first aid kit will probably be adequate for the individual. Some additional first aid items should be carried for the benefit of the group. The following items are recommended:

½ oz. tube Antibiotic Ointment.
Codeine, Darvon, or other tablets for severe pain. Consult your doctor.
⅛ oz. Ophthalmic Ointment for eye injuries. Consult your doctor.
1 Elastic Bandage for sprains, 3″ (Ace bandage).
1 Triangle Bandage for sling.
1 Inflatable Leg and Arm Splint
Antidiarrhea pills. Consult your doctor.
4 Butterfly Band Aids (or make your own from adhesive for closing cuts).
1 pair Small Scissors.
1 pair Tweezers.
6 extra Sterile Gauze Pads.

1 Antivenin kit for snakebite—if in snake country.

1 tube Ethyl Chloride—for use in treatment of snakebite.

For the last two items (antivenin kit and ethyl chloride) you should get expert pretrip instruction on their use. For example, you must know the horse serum sensitivity of the patient before using antivenin. Ethyl chloride, if sprayed directly on the skin, can cause "sloughing" of the tissue, with very serious results. It should be sprayed on a cloth, which is then carefully applied to the skin. (Ethyl chloride which is contained in a metal tube with a valve and spray nozzle on top is recommended.) These last two items are recommended *only* if the area has a reputed population of poisonous snakes.

An instruction booklet on first aid is also recommended. One such booklet that is very good is *Mountaineering Medicine* by Fred T. Darvill, Jr., M.D. The booklet measures 4¼" x 6⅝" and weighs 1½ ounces. It is available for $1 from Skagit Mountain Rescue Unit, Inc., P.O. Box 2, Mount Vernon, Washington 98273.

All items listed, except for the antivenin kit and ethyl chloride, have an approximate weight of 10 ounces. The antivenin kit and ethyl chloride weigh 5 ounces and 6 ounces respectively.

MAP AND COMPASS. In a small group a map and compass for the group may ordinarily be sufficient. However, in remote and unfamiliar regions it is recommended that each hiker have a map and compass. To become proficient in their use, practice is important. It is best to practice using map and compass in familiar areas so that you will be capable and confident in their use when they are really needed. For this reason it is recommended that each individual carry a map and compass, and practice using it, even though you are in familiar territory.

To be oriented means to know where you are. On most trips into wilderness areas or other back country you will be following trails which will be marked. *You should stay oriented at all times,* following your progress on a map, and knowing at all times where you are on the map. In the United States the topographic maps put out by the U.S. Geological Survey will be found most helpful to the average backpacker. These maps show all of the important natural features, as well as main trails. Elevations are shown by contour lines and this is an important feature when traveling in rugged terrain. For the Western states an index of the maps, as well as the maps themselves (costing about $.75 each), is available from the U.S. Geological Survey, Denver Federal Center, Denver, Colorado 80225.

Some very useful maps of forest and wilderness areas are available from the U.S. Forest Service and are usually free. They can be obtained at ranger stations or requested by mail from headquarters of National Forests.

It frequently happens that your route will cover only a relatively small portion of the total map. It is often helpful to outline this portion, including some of the surrounding area (peaks, etc.) for orienting purposes, and then have that portion of the map *enlarged.* A litho printer can make such an enlargement, and it will be much easier to read in the field.

Before going into an unfamiliar area try to talk with a Park ranger, rancher, or other person who is familiar with the area, and go over your map with him. *Make a sketch of your route.* Note helpful landmarks, such as abandoned cabins, unusual rock formations, fallen trees across the trail, and other features that will not appear on a topographic map. If water sources are few, ask about water supply, and the flow of springs shown on your map.

You should have a good compass, but it need not be expensive. A liquid-filled compass, having a clear base and attached base plate, is recommended. The base should have a direction-of-travel arrow and grid lines that can be aligned with a map reference line when orienting the map. Satisfactory compasses are available at from $5 to $7. If the end of the needle which points north is not unmistakably marked, then you should make a small note as to which end of the compass needle (such as the "red" end) points north. Use transparent tape and tape this note to the bottom of the compass.

EXTRA PROTECTIVE CLOTHING. The matter of having extra items of protective clothing was discussed in Chapter 5. On the warmest summer day a wind jacket should usually be carried. In wet, cold country wool clothing should be worn and an extra wool shirt or a jacket carried in the pack. In addition a lightweight tarp, with rope and a few ground stakes, should be carried even for a day hike. Unexpected weather or illness may force you to bivouac overnight or longer when you least expect it.

SUNGLASSES. Whether sunglasses are to be considered an essential item of equipment depends primarily on the season, your headgear, and the type of country you will be hiking in. Even with a broad-brimmed hat that shades the face and eyes, sunglasses should normally be worn in desert country, open alpine regions, and *always where snow is expected.* Snow blindness is serious and you should take no chances with it. If your travel is to be primarily in forested areas, and your eyes are protected by a brimmed hat, sunglasses then become an optional rather than essential item of equipment.

I find that if there is much rough hiking or scrambling to be done, sunglasses have a habit of getting knocked out of position and need to be continually pushed back into place. The cure for this is to use an adjustable elastic band that passes around the back of the head and slips over the end of each earpiece on the glasses.

NYLON CORD OR ROPE. A 50- or 75-foot length of $5/16$-inch diameter nylon rope, weighing 1½ to 2 pounds, will sometimes be useful in negotiating very short stretches of steep trail, or possibly river crossings. This depends somewhat on the experience of the hikers and whether women and children are in the group. For the young and inexperienced a rope tied around the waist while negotiating perilous places can mean the difference between a pleasant trip and one where they are occasionally scared half to death.

Braided nylon cord of $1/8$-inch diameter (550 lb. test), usually referred to as parachute cord, is most commonly used by backpackers for rigging tents and tarps, clotheslines, and the like. It is recommended that the cord required to rig your tent or tarp be packed with that equipment. If you are not in bear country, about 25 to 30 feet of cord should be sufficient to suspend your food bag and and other "smellables" from a tree limb so that it is safe from raccoons and other small animals. If you are in bear country the rigging will be a bit more complicated and a minimum of about 100 feet of nylon cord should be carried for that purpose. In throwing a cord over a high tree limb you will need to tie the end to a stone, about fist size or larger. This is no easy job. The rope frequently comes loose from the stone and the flying stone may hit a companion (or yourself). An easier approach is to make a very small cloth bag with drawstring at home and keep this with the "bear-rig" rope. Then place the stone in the bag, fasten the rope to the bag, and the job is much more easily accomplished.

It is a good idea to suspend your packframe from a tree limb or high rope line at night so that a porcupine or deer doesn't chew away on the sweat-soaked straps. Also, you should remember when in bear country that your pack is one of the items that is probably tainted with *food odors.* For night rigging of packframe allow about 25 to 50 feet of parachute cord. Such cord can also be used for boot laces, fish stringers, and similar purposes. You will have to do some thinking on this item to determine whether rope is required, and how much nylon cord to take. It is hard to conceive of a trip where at least 25 to 50 feet of nylon cord would not be required.

LITTERBAG. A stout *cloth* litterbag is recommended. My litterbag is about 9″ x 12″ in size, with a zipper across the top (9″ dimension). It has four tie tapes, one sewn to each corner. The litterbag can be carried inside the pack but I usually carry mine tied into position against the back of my pack, using the tie tapes to fasten the bag to "D" rings on the packbag.

OTHER IMPORTANT EQUIPMENT

TOILET ARTICLES

Soap. There are a number of good bar soaps available, which will lather well in hard water and can be used for your personal bathing as well as washing dishes. Vel brand soap is an example. With frequent bathing, about 2 ounces of soap per person per week is required for personal use. The same bar can be used for dishwashing. Germs are *not* carried by a bar of soap, so don't worry about using the same bar for this dual purpose. Packing of liquids should be avoided in backpacking whenever possible, and this certainly applies to liquid soaps. It is downright disheartening when someone accidentally knocks over an unstoppered bottle of liquid soap and you watch the week's supply of liquid soap soak into the ground.

There are also a few liquid biodegradable soaps available that are packaged so as to be suitable for camp use. One brand is Biosuds, which comes packaged in a plastic bottle that is relatively spill-proof. Another is Coghlan's Plus 50 which is packaged in a plastic tube, similar to a tube of toothpaste.

Towel, Washcloth. One small towel and washcloth per person should be sufficient. A large bath towel is too heavy and bulky. If you don't have a small one, make one from a towel remnant. If it should get too dirty, rinse it out and hang on the line to dry overnight. Some persons get by with just the washcloth, and let the air do the drying. A Curity diaper is lightweight and absorbent and makes a good towel.

Washbasin. I find that some kind of washbasin is almost indispensable for taking a bath or just washing the hands, face, and upper body. Washing in a stream or spring is "against the rules." I like to heat the water, dipped from stream or spring, in one of the cooking pans enough to take the chill off. The washbasin can

Folding plastic washbasin, 10" dia., 4" high, weight 3 oz.

Plastic "homemade" washbasin, 6" dia., 3" deep, weight 1½ oz.

be a coffee can or one of the commercially available plastic or canvas basins. However, I consider many of the commercial plastic washbasins to be too shallow and flimsy and the canvas ones too heavy.

After much experimenting with various washbasins I have finally settled on an unbreakable plastic bowl that some frozen foods, such as ice cream, are now packaged in. (I think my "washbasin" originally contained Cool Whip.) It is flexible and, for all practical purposes, unbreakable. It weighs 1 ½ ounces. It is about 3 ½ inches high and 6 inches in diameter.

I use my washbasin by partially filling it with heated water from one of the cooking utensils. By repeatedly dipping the washcloth into the basin I can take a full-fledged "bath." I sometimes splurge and take two such basins (nesting together), one for soaping and one for rinsing. In addition to other benefits, I find that on the trail a daily washing is a good morale booster.

Toothbrush, Paste. You will want a toothbrush, but toothpaste is not considered essential on a backpack trip. You can satisfactorily brush your teeth with half a teaspoon of salt. Rubbing the bristles of your toothbrush against a cake of soap will also provide a good cleanser for your teeth. This may not sound very appealing, but it works. Try it at home. It will leave your mouth clean and refreshed. If you must carry toothpaste, be sure that it is a very small tube or one which has been mostly used up. A full large-size tube of toothpaste weighs about 8 ounces, and there is no need to carry that much weight just to brush your teeth a few times.

You may have heard of backpackers sawing off the handles of toothbrushes. In case you should get the notion to saw off the handle of your toothbrush in order to save weight, you may be interested to know that a full-size toothbrush, about 6 inches long, weighs only ³⁄₈

to ½ ounce. If you saw off the entire handle, about 4 inches long, you will save only ³⁄₁₆ to ¼ ounce, which isn't much—even to a backpacker. Also, after the handle is sawed off, there would seem to be some doubt as to how useful the toothbrush would be. The plastic holders (carrying cases) for toothbrushes are something else. The usual plastic case toothbrush holder will weigh ¾ to 1 ounce. You can save essentially all of this weight by using a small pint-size plastic bag to contain your toothbrush, or simply wrap the bristle end in a small square of aluminum foil. Folding toothbrushes are available in which the container case unfolds to become part of the handle. Still others, designed for camping, are made so the handle can be filled with toothpaste. Those persons who regularly use *dental floss* may want to take about a yard, wrapped around a matchstick.

Toilet Tissue. This is best carried in *roll form*, just as it comes for household use. It should be packed in a small plastic bag and kept out of the

"Self-contained" toothbrush. Toothpaste is contained in the handle and is propelled into the bristles by twisting the handle. Weight is 1½ oz when "loaded" with sufficient toothpaste for a week.

rain and away from anything damp. This is very important. The requirements are about $\frac{1}{3}$ ounce of toilet tissue per person per day. As bought in the store, a full new roll is about 4½ inches in diameter and weighs 7 ounces. One-third ounce is equivalent to about a 9-foot strip of the common household variety.

Comb. A comb is advisable, but a hairbrush is not. You can usually get along without brushing your hair for the length of a backpack trip. A possible exception is female backpackers, whose taking a hairbrush might be considered justified (barely). Toilet kits should be left at home.

Shaving Gear. On most backpack trips, the usual rule is to "let 'em grow." Shaving gear means added weight. It frequently turns out that even those persons who carry shaving gear don't use it. If some members of the group decide that they· want to carry such gear, it is best to get together on the equipment required so as to save weight. Battery and spring-wound shavers are available. It's your decision.

MIRROR. Polished steel mirrors are available in a 3″ x 4″ size, weighing 2½ ounces. After three or four days on the trail you may prefer not to look at yourself. However, a mirror can be used for signaling and can be considered a good item from a *survival* standpoint. The cost is about $.75.

FOOT CARE. Some persons seem to have naturally "tough" feet that require very little care beyond occasional application of some moleskin to a tender spot, and the wearing of clean socks. Others find that their feet need considerably more attention. If you are in the "tender feet" category, daily application of rubbing alcohol and foot powder will probably be helpful while you are on the trail. At home, going barefoot for short periods as often as possible will help to toughen the feet.

SKIN CARE. Your skin needs protection from the elements, if you are to feel comfortable. Overexposure also frequently leads to severe illness. You will get plenty of sun and wind without purposely exposing yourself. Even though you wear a broad-brimmed hat, long-sleeved shirt, and long trousers, most persons need some protection from strong winds and intense sunlight that are usually encountered in mountain travel. At certain seasons of the year you will also need protection from mosquitoes, black flies, deer flies, and similar insect pests.

Sun and Wind Protection. The degree of protection required varies greatly from person to person. However, almost everyone needs some protection from the sun at high altitudes. Glacier cream, available from most mountaineering shops, gives protection from the sun,

wind, and cold. It is used particularly by mountaineers and skiers. It is not a tanning agent. It is packaged in a tube that will not break or split in your pocket or pack. A-Fil cream, made by the Texas Pharmacal Co., San Antonio, Texas, also prevents sunburn and suntan. It is available from many pharmacies. It too is well packaged in a strong tube. Sea and Ski is not a positive barrier against the sun and permits some tanning. There are many other lotions and creams in this latter category.

Hand Lotion. The backs of your hands can get painfully sunburned, and they can get very rough and uncomfortable, if not protected. Especially if you are fishing and have your hands in and out of the water frequently they can get so they feel like a coarse grade of sandpaper. You can use one of the face creams mentioned above on your hands. Or, you may prefer to use one of the many hand lotions that are available.

Lip Protection. Some persons find that a special lip salve is necessary to keep their lips from getting sunburned and chapped. The higher the altitude, the more likely that special protection will be needed. Labiosan lip cream offers good protection and is available from many mountaineering stores. An ordinary chap stick may also be satisfactory.

INSECT REPELLENT. At certain seasons the only satisfactory protection from insects is a face net, gloves, and long trousers (in other words, *complete coverage*). At other times a liquid or cream repellent, applied to face, neck, and hands will do the job. The most effective repellents have one ingredient in common. That is *N. N.—diethyl metatoluamide.* One rather inexpensive product containing this ingredient is a liquid generally known as Jungle Juice, available in some mountaineering stores and war surplus stores. A more expensive but popular repellent, also containing diethyl metatoluamide, is Cutter Insect Repellent. It is in the form of a cream and is considered by some backpackers somewhat more pleasant and longer lasting than Jungle Juice. Repel is another good insect repellent that uses diethyl metatoluamide as a base. Repellents which come packaged in glass bottles or aerosol cans are generally unsatisfactory for backpacking.

REPAIR KIT. There will be occasions when repairs will need to be made on the trail. You may tear your sleeping bag on a tree branch or a bush. A packframe joint may develop a crack. Perhaps a sharp rock will make a hole in your tent floor. You may rip your shirt or trousers, or lose a shirt button. A small repair kit, for making repairs on the trail, will usually be worthwhile. A single kit to be shared by all members of the group as an item of *common* equipment is recommended. The amount of the various items to be carried will depend upon the number of persons in the party and the length of the trip.

Sewing Repairs—Several needles of various sizes, including one curved needle. Several yards of cotton-covered nylon thread should suffice.

Ripstop Tape—This tape is good for repairing clothing, sleeping bags, tents, and similar cloth articles.

Safety Pins—A few medium-size safety pins are useful. In addition to their ordinary uses they are smaller than clothespins and equally suitable for hanging socks or towels on a line to dry. They can also be used to pin sweat-soaked socks and other items to your pack bag, for drying as you hike along the trail.

Wire—Several yards of light gauge wire, commonly referred to as "stove wire," is frequently useful. This flexible wire can be used for temporary repairs to packframes, spare bails for cooking pots, etc.

Cloth Tape—4 or 5 yards to be used in repairing polyethylene tarps, if you are using such a tarp, rather than a nylon tarp.

Awl—Some parties may want an awl for heavy duty repairs.

PLIERS. A small pair of needle nose pliers is a useful camp tool. They should be kept in a leather sheath, preferably having a belt loop so you can wear them on your belt while working around camp. Or, if you put them in your pocket the sheath will prevent a hole being torn in the pocket. Needle nose pliers are handy in moving pans on and off the fire, unless you have a pan-gripping tool. They can be used in first aid for removing splinters and thorns. In dishwashing they can be used to dunk eating utensils in a pan of hot water for rinsing. If you are fishing, needle nose pliers are almost a necessity for removing fishhooks (preferably from the fish).

Pliers are also useful in making repairs when using wire, or in removing a tight knot from wet (or dry) rope. The cost is about $3.

In servicing your backpack stove, *pliers* or a *wrench* may be required to remove the burner tip from the stove before cleaning (so that loosened soot, etc., does not fall into the fuel tank). They are also useful in bending the tabs on the stove burner plate, to hold it in place on the burner head. If the cap on the fuel tank was tightened too much when the stove was last used, pliers may be necessary to remove the cap.

A HIKING STAFF. Whether to carry a hiking staff or not is a very controversial subject. A hiking staff can be useful in negotiating rough terrain or a steep slope and serve as a "third leg" in helping to steady yourself in some situations. In other places many persons consider a staff to be just so much added weight and more of a nuisance than a help in most hiking. A few consider a hiking staff to be a liability and claim that you have to watch your step to keep from stumbling over it.

Some persons have a "pet" hiking staff of ash or hickory wood, or bamboo, or even aluminum tubing, which automatically goes along whenever they go on a backpack trip. Others acknowledge the usefulness of the staff in certain terrain but depend upon finding a makeshift staff in the form of a stick or pole in the area where they need it.

I have used a hiking staff at different times during my "backpacking career." A photo (see page 5) reminds me that when I hiked the Grand Canyon at age sixteen, I used a wood hiking staff. I have since used other wood staffs and even a rather fancy aluminum one with a few "survival goodies" stuffed inside.

For the last eight or ten years, however, I have not carried a hiking staff. I spent the summer of 1973 hiking in the Canadian Rockies and some of the trails were fairly crowded. I probably met 200 persons on the trail during the summer. I don't believe more than 10 or 12 of these hikers were carrying a staff. I believe most persons like to hike with their hands free. However, if you are devoted to your hiking staff, it gives you a sense of security and you enjoy carrying it, stay with it.

WHISTLE. Those persons who have participated in search-and-rescue operations for lost backpackers would probably place a whistle among the essential items of equipment. A lost hiker can soon shout himself hoarse. A shrill whistle can be heard much farther than a shout, and takes less effort. It is a good idea for parents who are taking children on a backpack trip to give them each a whistle, after instructing them when to use it.

In *bear country* a blast on the whistle when approaching thick cover is a good idea. Some backpackers carry a bell attached to their pack in bear country. I carry a whistle, and in bear country a good bell, costing about $.50 and $1 respectively.

SURVIVAL KIT. A survival kit may or may not be worthwhile to carry, depending on the length of trip, type of terrain, and your familiarity with the region. Or, you may want to carry only one or two items from the survival kit (see Appendix H), such as a smoke cartridge for signaling and some survival foods.

NONESSENTIAL EQUIPMENT

There are a few other items of equipment, which are frequently carried by backpackers, which can generally be considered nonessential equipment. Since it has been stressed that the knowledgeable backpacker takes primarily only essentials, plus some emergency gear, it might well be asked why nonessential gear is even mentioned. It is simply that there are a few additional items of equipment which will make your pack trip more enjoyable under certain circumstances, if you feel the added weight is justified.

CAMERA. A camera is not an essential item of equipment but on many trips it will be desirable. A 35mm camera and case weigh about 20 to 40 ounces. One way of saving weight on this item is for several or more hikers to go together, and the one with the camera can simply take duplicate or extra shots where desired. The others sharing in the camera shots take a corresponding weight of the "cameraman's" share of the common equipment.

BINOCULARS. Unless you are an ardent bird watcher, and you expect to be doing some serious birdwatching during your backpack trip, give concentrated thought to the matter before you add the weight of a pair of binoculars to your pack. A satisfactory pair of binoculars might weigh 8 ounces to a pound. A monocular may weigh only 4 or 5 ounces. They may prove interesting, and even useful, in scanning the countryside, watching animal life, etc. At any rate most backpackers manage to get along without these instruments. It's *your* decision.

FISHING EQUIPMENT. If you are going into an area where there are lakes or trout streams, you will probably want to take some fishing equipment. This will usually be either a fly rod, spin-cast rod, or spinning rod, and a reel to match, plus a small box of lures and some extra line. Don't go overboard on accessories. A landing net is nice, but it isn't essential. Neither is a creel. If you intend to wade streams you will want a pair of tennis shoes or lightweight waders. In addition to providing the pleasure of catching fish from wilderness streams or lakes, the weight of the fishing equipment will probably more than make up for itself by the lighter food load (meat) that will need to be carried. This will depend primarily upon your knowledge of the area and your experience as a fisherman.

POCKET THERMOMETER. Some persons carry a pocket thermometer. I have one which I occasionally carry. They weigh only about 1 ounce. It is interesting to wake up on a frosty morning and to guess how cold it is. Then look

at your thermometer and see what the temperature really is. Cost is about $4.

BACKPACKER'S TROWEL. A backpacker's trowel, made of high-impact plastic and weighing about 2 ounces, can be useful. It is particularly helpful in digging a small hole about 4 or 5 inches deep for the disposal of human waste. The cost is about $.40.

WIND METER. Wind meters weighing about 2 ounces are available from mountaineering equipment shops. You may find it interesting and helpful on a windswept mountain ridge to know just how strong the wind is. Few backpackers carry a wind meter, however. The cost is about $6 to $8.

ALTIMETER. Altimeters are available, in a weight range of 3 to 5 ounces, that will tell you your altitude. Conceivably they could be of some help in route finding. I have an altimeter and have carried it on a few backpack trips but

Backpacker's trowel made of high-impact plastic. Length 11", weight 2 oz.

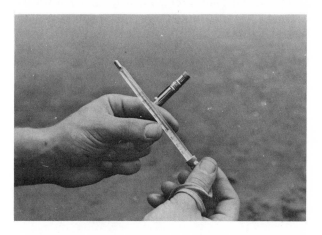

A pocket thermometer. When someone says "It's colder than blazes," you can give them a more scientific answer. (Cost about $3.50.) Photo by Lou Clemmons.

seldom used it. The type I have can be readily mounted, by a suction cup, on the dash of your recreational vehicle and mine most often is in my pickup truck, rather than in my backpack. Cost ranges from about $20 to over $100. Not recommended for the average backpacker.

PEDOMETER. Theoretically a pedometer should be a useful item of equipment in backpacking, since it measures distances. I have owned one for many years. Once it is calibrated to your stride, I find it reasonably accurate on level terrain. However, it is very inaccurate in the mountains, and that is where I do my backpacking. I never carry one on a backpack trip. The cost is about $8 to $10.

WEIGHING SCALE. A lightweight spring scale is useful in measuring out loads of common equipment, at the start of each day, for distributing to members of your backpack group. I have such a scale. Sometimes I carry it but more often I do not. Large parties would probably find it more useful then small groups. My scale weighs 7 ounces and cost $9.50.

MAP MEASURER. This is a small instrument with a tiny wheel that can be traced over an irregular path on a map to find the distance to be traveled. Some persons carry these on the trail, others use them only in planning of the route at home. They weigh about one ounce and cost about $3 to $5.

WATCH. In your escape from the "schedules of civilization" you may feel that a watch has no place on a backpack trip. Normally there is no need to set a rigid itinerary. However, a watch can still be helpful. You should know roughly how far you can travel over mountainous terrain in an hour, or a half hour. With this knowledge, and a watch, you will know where to look for certain checkpoints on your map. Thus, a watch is an aid to following your progress on your map and staying oriented. You will want to make camp, get supper cooked and dishes washed before dark. A watch will give you a good idea as to how many hours of daylight remain for these activities. If all persons are to meet back in

camp at a certain hour, after an afternoon of fishing, it will be pretty hard to do without a watch.

GUIDE BOOK. A guide book can be an aid in the planning of your route that takes place at home. If it is accurate and detailed enough (some are neither) it may be of help in staying on the trail in unfamiliar terrain.

NOTEBOOK AND PENCIL. A small notebook (or 3″ x 5″ note cards) and a pencil stub will be useful in keeping a log of the trip, noting changes in your check list for the next trip, leaving a note at a base camp for your companions, etc. A *wood pencil stub* (with a metal protector for the tip) about 4 inches long is recommended rather than a ball-point pen. A ball-point pen will not write well on a greasy or slightly soiled surface, which is apt to be the case with note cards or a notebook carried in your pocket and worked on when your hands are sweaty, or covered with sun protection cream or mosquito repellent.

PLAYING CARDS. Many persons will say that a deck of playing cards has no place on a backpack trip. However, if you have ever been tightly cooped up with two or three companions for a day or two, waiting out a severe rainstorm or snowstorm, you may change your mind. A deck of miniature playing cards weighs about 1½ ounces. If your companions are chess fans, you might consider a miniature chess set.

PAPERBACK BOOK. It may be desirable to take a paperback book for essentially the same reasons you would carry a deck of miniature cards. Or, maybe you simply like to read a bit in the evening. A paperback book will usually weigh about 5 to 7 ounces.

WALLET. Most backpackers leave their wallets in their vehicle at the trailhead. There are several items that may be in your wallet, however, that you may need in the back country. These are camping permit (if required), fishing license (if you are to be fishing), and fire permit (if required, and if you may want a fire). A good way to carry these items is in a plastic bag, with a small piece of cardboard for stiffener, and with a rubber band around the whole business.

SUMMARY OF RECOMMENDED EQUIPMENT

Now that we have discussed packs, sleeping gear, clothing, food, cooking equipment, other equipment, etc., let's see what it adds up to in an actual backpack trip. First we will consider only that equipment, food, clothing, etc., which

Spring scale, useful in measuring daily loads of food and common equipment for distribution to hikers.

is considered necessary to do the job, provide reasonable comfort, and assure your well-being. Recommended items, adequate for a backpack trip of up to one week, are used in making up the lists in Tables 10.1 and 10.2. Equipment and other items are considered in *two* categories. First, the *personal* items, which are those items for your personal use and benefit only. Each hiker must make his own decisions on what he wants to carry in this category. Secondly, the *common equipment*, consisting of those items shared by the group as a whole. You probably won't have all the items that are recommended in these lists. Where you have a different or substitute item, make the proper allowance for weight.

TABLE 10.1 RECOMMENDED PERSONAL EQUIPMENT

Item	Approximate Weight (Ounces)
Packframe and packbag	66
Sleeping Gear	
Sleeping bag	56
Foam pad (hip-length)	6
Ground cloth (coated nylon)	
(not needed if tent is used)	*11
Shelter	
Tent (one-man tent, as described in Appendix C, or	
similar design)	*36
Tent stakes	8
Two-man tent; one man sharing half the weight, assumed	
at 6 lb. for tent, fly, poles, stakes; or 48 oz. per man	
(Weight includes small whisk broom and sponge.)	48
Equipment	
Cord (30 feet of $\frac{1}{8}$ nylon parachute cord)	2
Flashlight (Mallory type) and spare bulb	3½
Iodine tablets	½
Knife (folding pocketknife)	3
Litterbag (cloth) about 9″ x 12″	1
Map and compass	3½
Matches (waterproof container), candle stub	2
Personal first aid kit	7½
Sunglasses	2
Washbasin (plastic bowl)	1½
Water bottle (1 qt., plastic, filled with water)	35
Eating utensils	
Plastic cup, spoon and bowl	6
Toilet articles	
Comb	¾
Insect repellent	1½
Small towel, washcloth	3½
Soap	2
Sun protective lotion	1¼
Toilet tissue	2
Toothbrush	½
	251 oz.
Other Items	
Watch (carried on person)	2

* One-man tent assumed in arriving at total weight

TABLE 10.2 RECOMMENDED COMMON EQUIPMENT

Item	Approximate Weight (Ounces)
Group First Aid Kit	10
Camera (35 mm)	30
Film, 3 rolls (1 oz. each)	3
Repair Kit	6
Cord (75 feet of ⅛″ nylon parachute cord)	6
Metal Mirror	2½
Cooking Gear:	
Backpack stove, wind screen, two pans, small frying pan, burner tip cleaner, eye dropper, funnel, match supply, and cloth carrying bag.	39
Hot-pan gripper, two tablespoons, G.I. can opener	3
Fuel for backpack stove (1 qt. in aluminum fuel bottle)	30
Dishwashing (small sponge, pot scratcher, biodegradable soap)	4
	133½

TABLE 10.3 OPTIONAL PERSONAL EQUIPMENT

Item	Approximate Weight (Ounces)
Sleeping Gear	
Pajamas	11
Shelter Gear	
Coated nylon sheet, for under floor of one-man tent	6
or	
Polyethylene sheet, for under floor of two-man tent (½ total weight of 20 oz.)	10
Equipment	
Bear bell	2
Binoculars	9
Camera	30
Fishing equipment (rod, reel, small box of lures)	19
Fishing license	0
Folding drinking cup	1
Hiking staff	20
Monoculars	4
Notebook, pencil stub	1
Paperback book	5
Pliers, small needle nose	4
Rubber bands (assorted sizes)	¼
Snakebite kit (suction type)	1½
Spare flashlight batteries; 2 batteries, 1 oz. each	2
Waders, lightweight plastic, for fishing	22
Whistle	½
Toilet Articles	
Feminine hygiene items	—
Foot powder	4
Hand lotion	1
Lip salve	½
Rubbing alcohol	3
Shaving gear:	
Safety razor and blades (shaving cream, mirror and washbasin can be shared as an item of common equipment)	1½

SUMMARY OF OPTIONAL EQUIPMENT

This is the point where many backpackers get carried away. They take too many things (often just gadgets) that they think they might need and then never use. Consider your optional items carefully. If you are not sure you are going to need an item (excepting first aid and emergency items) better leave it at home, especially for the first few trips. As with recommended equipment, the optional equipment items are divided into two categories, personal equipment and common equipment. Tables 10.3 and 10.4 list optional personal equipment and optional common equipment, respectively.

TOTAL PACK WEIGHT

In arriving at the total pack weight to be carried by each individual we will again assume a week-long trip for a group of three persons. The weight of the individual packs should be about as follows:

RECOMMENDED PERSONAL EQUIPMENT. As outlined in Table 10.1, the weight of the recommended personal equipment is 251 ounces, including packframe and fitted packbag.

RECOMMENDED COMMON EQUIPMENT. The recommended common equipment was outlined in Table 10.2 and amounted to 44½ ounces per person.

OPTIONAL PERSONAL EQUIPMENT. Some items of optional personal equipment that may be desired were outlined in Table 10.3. A total of 55 ounces of optional personal equipment is assumed.

OPTIONAL COMMON EQUIPMENT. (See Table 10.4.) A weight of 20 ounces per person of optional common equipment is assumed. This would provide 60 ounces of optional common equipment (3¾ pounds) in a group of three persons.

DUPLICATE AND EXTRA CLOTHING. As discussed in Part 5, Table 5.1, the only recom-

TABLE 10.4 OPTIONAL COMMON EQUIPMENT

Item	Approximate Weight (Ounces)
Altimeter	4
Bags, plastic (spare bags for lunches, trail snacks, equipment, etc.)	1 to 3
Carborundum stone	2
Cooking gear:	
Grill, with folding legs	28
Reflector oven	42
Frying pan, teflon	12
Food soaking jar, 1 pt.	2
Folding bucket, plastic coated cloth, about 2 gal.	6
Guide book	6 to 12
Miniature playing cards (for foul weather)	1½
Nail file	¼
Pliers (small needle nose)	4
Rope (50 to 75 feet of $^5/_{16}$" diameter nylon)	24 to 36
Shaving gear: shaving cream and plastic washbasin	9
Snake bite kit: antivenin & ethyl chloride	11
Survival kit	5 to 20
Tennis shoes, one large pair, for crossing streams	32
Tent, two-man size or larger. Two-man is assumed, weighing 6 lb for tent, fly, poles, and stakes. (Weight includes small whisk broom and sponge.)	96
Thermometer	1
Trowel	2
Weighing scale	7
Wind meter	2
Wood pile cover (plastic sheet, about 6' x 8')	6

TABLE 10.5 WEIGHT SUMMARY

Category	Approximate Weight (Ounces)
Recommended Personal Equipment	251
Recommended Common Equipment	44½
Optional Personal Equipment	55
Optional Common Equipment	20
Duplicate and Extra Clothing	39
Optional Clothing	30
Food	138
Total	577½ ounces (36 pounds, 1½ ounces)

mended duplicate clothing is socks, duplicates of the combination of socks that you use for hiking (about 5 ounces). For extra clothing (protection), a light down jacket will weigh about 18 ounces and a wind shell jacket about 4 ounces. These will provide protection down to about 20° F. A nylon poncho, large enough to go over both hiker and pack, is recommended and will weigh about 12 ounces. These items total 39 ounces.

OPTIONAL CLOTHING. Some persons may want to take pajamas, hiking shorts, or perhaps some other items. A total of 30 ounces of optional clothing is assumed.

FOOD. As discussed in Part 8, the total food weight was 414 ounces, or 138 ounces per hiker.

Thus, we have a total pack weight of about 36 pounds. For a group larger than three persons the weight would be slightly less because of additional sharing of common equipment. If you want to sacrifice some comfort and convenience, and eliminate all nonessentials, reduce optional equipment, etc., this weight can be reduced to 30 pounds or a bit under.

Some persons may want to take a tarp for rain protection, or to depend upon their poncho for both rain protection on the trail and emergency protection from rain at night. This depends largely upon the season and the experience of the backpackers. If you are doing all cooking over a wood fire the weight of the backpack stove and fuel is eliminated. A small party of male adult backpackers will normally want to make more sacrifices than a larger mixed group which includes women. If you have a group of "bottomless pit" teenagers, about 2 pounds of food per day, or more, may be required.

In a remote area you can leave a cache or two of food along the trail on the way in for a few meals on the way out, and this will reduce the weight. Also, as the food is eaten the food load per person is reduced by about 1½ pounds per day.

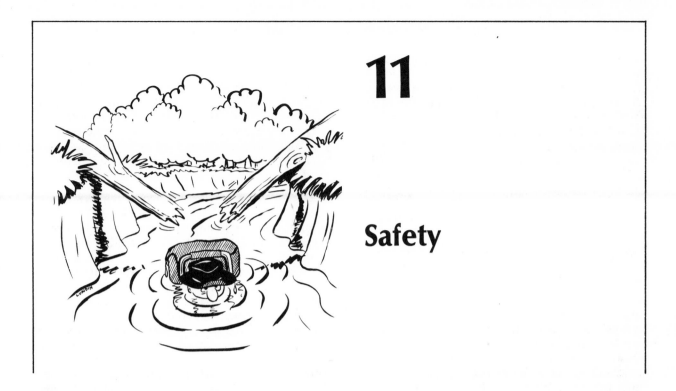

11

Safety

SAFETY VERSUS FIRST AID

You should by all means know your first aid well before you attempt a full-scale backpack trip. You should also carry a good first aid kit and possibly a snakebite kit (depending upon the region and the season). The subject of first aid is well covered in a number of readily available books. Therefore, there is no lengthy discussion of first aid in this book. One point should be emphasized. It is far better to *practice safety* on the trail, and in camp, than to have to use first aid.

CAUSES OF ACCIDENTS

It takes considerable know-how to plan a backpack trip and a daily routine that will take you safely from place to place in a wilderness or other remote area. The main contributing causes of accidents on a backpack trip are as follows:

(a) Lack of preparation
(b) Exposure
(c) Being in a hurry
(d) Getting too tired

LACK OF PREPARATION. There are many areas of preparation. There is the matter of food and equipment preparation. These may be relatively simple, depending upon how often you backpack and the state of readiness of your food and equipment. Other important aspects of preparation are to be mentally and physically

prepared. If you are just recovering from a deep emotional experience, going on a backpack trip may be unwise. You may think that a backpack trip will aid in your emotional recovery. If there is any doubt, you should seek the advice of your physician or another qualified counselor. The activity and mental stimulation of tasks at home may be better for your recovery than the exertion, fatigue, and routine of a backpack trip. Especially on a backpack trip where many miles are to be covered, an individual sometimes hungers for mental activity. On long, routine paths, or on steep switchbacks in the hot sun, the mind can become dull and bored. It is not uncommon to do a certain amount of day-dreaming in such instances and thinking about a recent bad emotional experience may not be healthy.

There is also the matter of *body conditioning.* If you have kept yourself in good physical condition throughout the year, then a minimum of special exercising and hiking may be sufficient. However, practically everyone needs some special physical conditioning before a backpack trip. Perhaps you have been so unfortunate as to acquire a cold, an aching tooth, or similar illness just recently and you are not fully recovered. You need to be honest with yourself as to your true physical condition and if you are not up to par you should probably cancel out. This requires a lot of courage, after preparing and looking forward to the trip for perhaps many weeks.

Other important preparations include a careful study and evaluation of the route, probable weather, stream crossings, etc. These may be fairly routine and simple or they may be quite complex. It varies with the qualifications and experience of one or more members of the party who are acquainted with the area and have backpacked in it at the time of year under consideration.

Still another phase of preparation is to become familiar with the experience, equipment, and physical condition of any newcomers to the group. This may present little or no problem, or it could develop into a very serious problem. If serious problems develop on the trail, because of a newcomer's lack of preparation or experience, it is then too late to do anything about it except to take emergency or makeshift measures.

EXPOSURE. Regardless of the anticipated weather you should always be prepared for the unexpected. This particularly applies to spring and fall backpacking, when *extreme* changes in weather may occur over a very short span of time, and to hiking in the high mountains at any time of year. Exposure in this discussion is intended to mean that type of exposure which may lead to *hypothermia.* Low temperature, wind, and wetness are the important contributing factors to hypothermia. Always have spare, warm, dry clothing with you, even though you don't anticipate the need for it. Take every precaution to keep the clothing that you are wearing dry, through control of exertion (and perspiration), removal, or addition of clothing as needed, and protection of yourself and your clothing from wind and rain. In other words, learn to keep yourself comfortable in the out-of-doors. Carry protective clothing for warmth and rain, even on short hikes.

BEING IN A HURRY. If your trip is properly planned, there should be no need for getting in a hurry. You should not plan to make more than ten to fourteen miles per day in mountainous areas where you can use reasonably good trails. If you are going to be rock hunting, fishing, or engaging in some other activity during the day besides hiking, this distance must be scaled way down. You should stay near the trail, or stick to suitable terrain with which someone in the party is familiar. Then you should avoid such mishaps as running out of water, coming up against blind cliffs or precipices and having to retrace your steps, or falling and breaking a leg by trying to hike through terrain that you should not have attempted.

Even with these precautions, you can still have an accident because you got in a hurry. Let's assume you have a stream to cross. You could take off your shoes and wade across at a certain point, but you don't want to take that much time. Instead you decide to use a tree which happens to bridge the stream near where you want to cross. It is not a very good bridge and it is dangerously high above the water, but you decide to risk it. On the way over one hiker's pack throws him off balance and he goes into the river, breaking a leg in the process. This accident was caused because you were in a hurry (and failed to use good judgment).

GETTING TOO TIRED. Don't see how many miles you can cover on a backpack trip. It should not be an endurance contest. It is always better to underestimate your ability to cover miles than to overestimate. It is extremely difficult to judge distances and traveling time in mountainous terrain from a map. Where you must do this, multiply scaled distances by a factor of two or three and you will probably be about right. However, there are still some unknown factors. Unless some member of the party has been on the trail before, you don't know for certain how good the trail is. Neither do you know how many times you may temporarily lose the trail and spend time to pick it up again.

Five or six hours of hiking (with a full pack) for the first day or two will be enough unless you are a seasoned hiker. Seldom should you plan to hike more than eight hours per day. When you get too tired you are a safety hazard to yourself and others. You will stumble and you may fall where ordinarily you would not. Your reactions are slower. You can easily hurt yourself doing simple camp jobs or other things that usually would not be dangerous at all. For example, I once witnessed a very tired hiker breaking wood by laying sticks on a log and stomping on them with his foot. One of the pieces flew up at an odd angle and caught him just above the eye, making a bad cut which bled profusely. Had this person not been "dog tired" he would probably have easily dodged the flying stick. If you push yourself to the point of exhaustion you are inviting trouble. Why not settle for fewer miles, a more leisurely pace, and enjoy yourself?

When you get too tired your judgment and thinking are also impaired. You may find yourself doing things—or planning to do things—that ordinarily you would not do. *Extreme fatigue* acts in much the same way as a *drug.*

ACCLIMATIZATION

If you live at a relatively low elevation and are going backpacking into the mountains, you should give some serious thought to the matter of acclimatization. There is less oxygen in the air at high altitudes and your blood has to make certain adjustments in order to supply enough oxygen to your body. However, even after acclimatization there is always less oxygen in the blood at high altitudes than at sea level. If you live at a low altitude and are to be backpacking at 7500 feet elevation or more, try to move into the area a day or more *before* you start to backpack. The time required for acclimatization will depend upon the specific altitude, the degree of exertion, and how rapidly you ascend to a higher altitude. If you go too high too fast you are apt to suffer from "mountain sickness" or "altitude sickness." The symptoms are queasy stomach, possible vomiting, diarrhea, drowsiness, headache, loss of appetite, irritability, lack of mental alertness, and chills.

It is always a good idea to drive to the trailhead the day before you intend to start hiking. A good night's sleep at the trailhead will do much to help your body acclimatize to the higher elevation. If you must start hiking the next day take it particularly easy for the first day or so. You should also avoid a route that takes you *rapidly* to a higher elevation.

If you find the symptons of altitude sickness coming on, slow down in your exertion, or lay over for a day. Avoid heavy eating, alcoholic beverages, and smoking. Limit your physical activity. Aspirin may be helpful in relieving the symptoms. If these measures are not effective you should descend to a lower elevation.

Major serious symptoms may occur at 9000 to 10,000 feet elevation and above. Some of the major symptoms are unusual fatigue (possibly complete collapse), shortness of breath, a racking cough, bubbling noises in the chest, and bloody sputum. *These symptoms are serious.* The victim should be moved to a much lower altitude *immediately* or he may die within hours. If oxygen is available it should be administered to the victim.

WEATHER CHANGES

A very important contributing factor to accidents and tragedies in the wilderness is weather. For example, after a few weeks of early balmy spring weather a party of hikers takes to the mountains. The days are bright, the weather is warm. Wild flowers have started to appear. Temperatures at night may be barely freezing. Off goes the party of backpackers, wearing normal mild weather hiking clothes, light jackets, etc., and carrying corresponding equipment. But . . . after they are on the trail a few hours, or perhaps a day or two, a storm front may move in suddenly. Within several hours' time temperatures may plunge to far below freezing. Heavy snowfall causes the party to lose its way. Panic sets in. The matches which the party has are quickly used up in trying to start a fire under adverse conditions. Within a matter of a few hours the party is hopelessly lost. One or more members may perish. In the spring of 1971 three such accidents occurred in the state of New Mexico within a few weeks' time.

This type of tragedy is fairly frequent in the spring of the year. It also happens to parties of hunters in the fall, with a fair degree of regularity. It sometimes happens to day hikers (often hiking solo), who take to the mountains on a nice, early spring day with the intention of taking a short hike of just a few hours and returning the same day. Never underestimate the fury of the wilderness and its harshness on the unprepared, under adverse weather conditions.

Unseasonably warm weather can cause snow runoff at a much more rapid rate than normal. Mountain streams which were easily waded at the same time the year before are now a foot or more higher. Don't take lightly the tremendous force of 10 or 12 added inches in depth of a fast-moving mountain stream. It can cost you your life.

So—*be prepared* for sudden changes in weather when you enter the mountains, particularly in the spring or fall of the year, when sudden deep snowfalls can make trails impassable and easily lost to hikers. At these seasons temperatures can change 50 degrees within a few hours' time. Have the necessary clothing and equipment for such an eventuality. Don't depend upon matches alone for starting a fire under such conditions. When you are in a semipanicked state of mind you are not going to want to whittle sticks of wood into shavings or "fuzz sticks" or take the necessary time to gather good fire-starting materials, as you would in a normal situation. Have a long-burning, hot-flame plumber's candle, fire-starting jelly, or a similar material in your fire-starting kit. Remember, it is one thing to sit in your easy chair at home and halfheartedly plan what you would do in such an emergency situation in the woods. It is quite another thing to be in the woods, trying to cope with that situation, unprepared, and with time running out.

For those who hike into the mountains, make it a routine that you carry a pack, even for a short duration hike. The pack should contain added clothing, fire-starting materials, first aid kit, drinking water, a few items of emergency food, knife, etc. Follow this practice whenever you go out, if only for a day, regardless of how brightly the sun may be shining or how warm the day when you start out. If you have come from some distance away for your hiking or backpacking adventure, make inquiry in advance of weather conditions in general and possible very recent changes in weather. Don't hesitate to cancel or alter your plans if weather conditions warrant. That dollar you saved by not making a last minute long distance phone call to inquire about the weather may look pretty small later on.

Backpackers who venture forth in the early spring or late fall, or who go into the very high mountains at any season, should study the table below and note the effect that wind has on the effective temperature. If you have ever ridden in the back end of a pickup truck at thirty miles an hour on a cold morning, you will realize how important it is to consider not only the temperature but the temperature-wind combination. As will be seen from the chart, if the outside air temperature is 30° F, and the truck is traveling twenty-five miles per hour, the effective air temperature is 0° F.

HYPOTHERMIA. Exposure to the elements, leading to hypothermia, is one of the most common tragedies in the out-of-doors. Hypothermia is *loss of body heat.* The victim does not need to be exposed to either extreme cold or high altitude in order to suffer fatal hypothermia. The exposure temperature is often above freezing, frequently between 40° and 50° F. The altitude may be relatively low, even near sea level. He may be wearing normal and adequate clothing for protection on a 40° day. However, there are other factors present. Perhaps the victim has been hurrying to reach a certain objective and has perspired extensively. He probably failed to remove unneeded clothing when he started to perspire and his clothing is now wet with perspiration. Wetness of clothing may also have been caused by rain or snow, and failure to put on rain gear in time. Another factor that is commonly present is wind. Wind actually *refrigerates* wet clothes by evaporating moisture from the surface.

If you are hurrying toward an objective and any member experiences the conditions de-

TABLE 11.1 WIND CHILL FACTOR

When the temperature/wind speed factor falls in the area shaded below, frostbite, especially of the face, is a serious hazard.

When Thermometer Reads	When the wind blows at the m.p.h. below, it reduces Temperature to								
	Calm	5	10	15	20	25	30	35	40
+50	50	48	40	36	32	30	28	27	26
+40	40	37	28	22	18	16	13	11	11
+30	30	27	16	9	4	0	-2	-4	-6
+20	20	16	4	-5	-10	-15	-18	-20	-21
+10	10	6	-9	-18	-25	-29	-33	-35	-37
0	0	-5	-21	-36	-39	-44	-48	-49	-53
-10	-10	-15	-33	-45	-53	-59	-63	-67	-69
-20	-20	-26	-46	-58	-67	-74	-79	-82	-85
-30	-30	-36	-58	-72	-82	-88	-94	-98	-100
-40	-40	-47	-70	-88	-96	-104	-109	-113	-116
-50	-50	-57	-85	-99	-110	-118	-125	-129	-132
-60	-60	-68	-95	-112	-124	-133	-140	-145	-148

To measure speed of wind without instruments: When CALM (smoke rises vertically); 1-12 m.p.h. (just feel wind on face, leaves in motion); 13-24 (raises dust or loose paper, snow drifts, branches move); 25-30 (large branches move, wires whistle); 30-40 (whole trees in motion, hard to walk against).

For the properly clothed, there is little danger down to -20° but caution should be used with regard to all exposed flesh. At below -20°, take no unnecessary chances.

(Courtesy of Sport House, Concord, Massachusetts.)

scribed above, give up on your particular objective for today, or for this trip. Don't plunge on until you are exhausted! BIVOUAC! Select the best spot that is immediately available and get out of the wind or rain. Try to get on the lee side of a ridge, or behind rocks, trees, or other natural barriers from the wind. Use a tent, tarp, ponchos, natural shelter, or whatever is necessary and available. Build a fire and concentrate on making your camp or bivouac as comfortable as possible. Conserve your energy. *Move slowly and deliberately.* If your clothing is wet, change at once into dry clothing (if available) or climb into a dry sleeping bag after removing clothes. Dry the wet clothes by the fire. Eat some food and preferably drink some hot liquid. Don't go to sleep as long as there are any symptoms of hypothermia. The symptoms are these:

(a) incoherent, slurred speech
(b) violent fits of shivering
(c) fumbling hands, stumbling gait
(d) drowsiness
(e) exhaustion
(f) shallow breathing

When the above symptoms are present hypothermia has already set in. The temperature of the inner core of the body is no longer a normal 98°. It is lower than this; how much lower depends on how long hypothermia has been present. It could be as low as 85°. If it drops to 80° the victim will be unconscious and if it falls several degrees lower death will occur.

When the signs of hypothermia *first* appear treatment should start *without delay*. Make the best shelter that surroundings and your equipment will provide but start to work on the victim immediately. Don't place the victim in a cold sleeping bag. Have one of the well members of the party, wearing only underclothes, pre-warm a dry sleeping bag (under which as much insulation as possible as been placed). The victim should then be placed in the sleeping bag with the well person, so as to warm the victim by skin-to-skin contact.

Warm stones or canteens filled with hot water, properly wrapped, can be placed in the sleeping bag. If the patient is able to drink, give him hot soup, hot coffee, or other hot drinks. This can be followed by small amounts of high energy food, depending upon the patient's reaction. Try to keep the victim awake. *Do not leave the victim alone*, even for short periods.

Continue the treatment until the patient shows definite improvement and the symptoms have disappeared. The patient can then move around a bit, properly clothed, to determine his reaction to mild exertion. The next step is to try to evacuate the patient to "civilization" but only if he is well rested and ready for it.

RAINSTORMS

A little wetting on a warm day won't hurt you, but don't try to continue hiking in a bad storm. Seek the best shelter you can find, make yourself comfortable and wait it out. If there is a hard rain, put up a plastic sheet or a tarp on a ridge line, and keep yourself and your equipment dry. If your pack is not waterproof or you are not sure whether it is, by all means take extra precautions to keep it and its contents dry. If your pack gets thoroughly soaked it will be so heavy you can hardly lift it, let alone carry it. Besides, if everything in it is wet or damp you will have a mess. If you are wearing a poncho or other good rain gear, and there are trees in the area, you can huddle under a tree. It is surprising how much protection is afforded by a good size tree, with thick branches and foliage.

LIGHTNING

In many mountainous regions sudden electrical storms are very common at certain seasons of the year. Your chances of being struck by lightning are small, but it does pay to have some basic knowledge of how to protect yourself. In an electrical storm you should observe the following precautions:

MOUNTAIN PEAKS. Stay off mountain peaks, especially those which are relatively sharp and prominent. At a good distance downhill from the peak, say several hundred yards, you should be quite safe. A mountain with a broad ridge or rounded top is less dangerous than those with sharp, prominent peaks. In any case, in event of an electrical storm, get off the top of the mountain as fast as possible.

CLIFFS, CAVES. The overhang of a cliff should be avoided. It is a very risky place to be in an electrical storm. If you are under the overhang, a bolt of lightning coming down the cliff is likely to jump across the edge of the overhang and pass through your body. Likewise, do not seek shelter in a small, shallow cave. It is better to get wet (and stay alive). Only fairly large caves are safe. If you do seek shelter in a cave, or under a very large overhang, do not stand but sit. Stay back from the cave entrance and avoid the walls of the cave. A *sitting* position near the *center* is best.

CREVICES. Avoid a crack or crevice that leads up the slope of a hill or mountain. These may be good attractors of lightning, especially if filled with damp earth or if there is a trickle of water flowing.

PROMINENT OBJECTS. Lightning may be attracted to a prominent object on the landscape, such as isolated or very tall trees, buildings, large boulders, etc. If you yourself are the most prominent object on the landscape, you should sit or lie down. You can also move into the general area of some other more prominent object, but keep a distance away from it equal to about twice its height. Don't get directly under it.

SIT OR LIE. Wherever you seek shelter, it is best to sit or lie on the ground during an electrical storm. Pick out a dry spot if possible and insulate yourself from the ground with clothing, packframe, loose rocks, etc. A fully inflated air mattress is a good insulator.

SOLO TRAVEL

Backpacking by yourself in remote areas is not recommended. If you should break a leg, or get sick, you have a serious situation which could cost you your life. Having a companion will provide a very significant added margin of safety. If one person gets sick or injured the other person can take care of him or go for help. A *minimum* of *three persons* is actually recommended. One person can then stay with the sick or injured hiker while the other goes for help. Another good reason for having a companion or two is that pack loads will be lighter because of the sharing of cooking utensils, general camp equipment, and other common gear. Additionally, for most of us (even though we may shun large hiking groups) a companion or two to share our "adventures" makes a backpack trip more enjoyable. Regardless of the size of the party, it is important to let someone know when and where you are going and your itinerary, just

in case you do not return when you are supposed to. A ranch or farm near the roadhead or a Forest Service office in the nearest town are good places to leave such information. Further, a relative or close friend back home should by all means have this information. They should also have the license number and general description of the vehicle in which you will be traveling to the takeoff point. If an emergency back home requires that someone get in touch with you while you are traveling on the highway, this information will be of utmost importance to state police or others who are attempting to find you.

Forest Service personnel and other professional outdoorsmen sometimes go into remote areas alone. It is part of their job. However, not only are they usually expert woodsmen, but their headquarters knows where they are and will soon be looking for them if they do not show up or check in according to a prearranged plan. Further, such persons usually travel by horseback and having a well-trained horse provides an added margin of safety.

On some of the well-known, regularly maintained and frequently traveled trail systems, such as some sections of the Appalachian Trail, a few hikers will be found traveling alone. If it is a section of the trail that is known to be frequently traveled the risk in traveling alone is certainly not as great as in solo travel in some of the wilderness areas or other remote regions. However, it should be recognized that there is risk involved in *any* solo travel away from "civilization." Important factors to consider are your experience, your knowledge of the area and trails, and the time of year and probable weather. Each year many hundreds of dollars are

The Sportsman smoke signal, made by the Superior Signal Co. of Spotswood, N.J., provides a dense cloud of smoke instantaneously. It may be a worthwhile item to some backpackers. It is often very difficult to quickly produce a dense cloud of smoke for signalling purposes from materials at hand.

spent in locating lost or injured hikers, and the searchers are subjected to additional risk and possible accident in doing so.

CROSSING STREAMS

A considerable number of accidents occur in crossing unbridged streams. It takes time to remove shoes, socks, and possibly trousers, in preparation for wading a stream. It takes additional time to put these items back on after the stream is crossed. Therefore, most hikers look for a quicker way to cross the stream. Before crossing a stream by any means other than a bridge, you should unbuckle the waist strap of your belt, and preferably loosen the shoulder straps. Then you can slip out of your pack quickly if a mishap occurs.

Sometimes, with some reconnoitering up- and downstream, rocks will be found which will serve as suitable stepping stones for crossing the stream. If they are properly placed and reasonably large and stable—fine. You have your "bridge." However, beware of making long hops from one rock to another with a fully loaded pack. You are not nearly as nimble with a large pack on your back as without and it can easily throw you off balance. Also beware, in early morning or cool weather, of stepping on ice-covered rocks. Your lug soles won't help a bit.

Another possibility is a log or tree trunk which bridges the stream. A log which is so close to the water that it gets wet from spray can be extremely slippery. It may be better to pass it up.

If you can find a stick or pole of sufficient length, it can be of some help in crossing a stream on a log. It is generally best to place the pole in the water on the downstream side of the log and "lean into it" a bit as you cross. Then, if you should fall into the river you will not be swept into the log and maybe trapped against or under it by the fast-moving water.

If it is a tree trunk that bridges the crossing, and there are projecting branches or "stubs" on it, the branches may be of some assistance in steadying yourself as you cross. But beware. Such projecting branches may be readily caught on a corner of your pack and throw you off balance.

Before you cross any stream on a log or tree trunk you should carefully consider the character of the stream below. How far down will you fall if you should slip? Will you fall onto jagged rocks or boulders? Study all such crossings deliberately and critically before you start across. Even though it takes longer, wading the stream may be best.

Generally a mountain stream will be swiftest at its narrowest point. It will often be deeper there also. Therefore you should usually select the widest part of a river for wading. Swift streams should be crossed at a quartering angle downstream.

Streams that originate in glaciers can be especially tricky to wade. The gray-colored, silted water often makes it impossible to see the bottom in water only 6 inches deep. Using a stick or pole as a probe in such water and as a "third leg" will aid in crossing.

The experience and physical ability of the hiker must always be considered when a hazardous stream crossing is to be attempted. Don't goad a novice, or anyone else, into attempting a dangerous stream crossing that he feels is beyond his capability. The stronger, most experienced members of the party should try the crossing first, if the decision is made to attempt it. It may be a good idea for those persons to carry across the packs of the less experienced. Also, a rope tied around the waist (bowline knot) of each member during his crossing and held by persons on the bank is a good safety precaution. If there are hikers on both shores some members may feel more secure with two ropes around their waist, one going to the far shore, the other being held by persons on the near shore.

If there are stream crossings to be waded which are knee-deep or more, a pair of hiking shorts will prove useful. Depending upon the company you are in, your undershorts may also be satisfactory.

When crossing a stream each step should be made carefully and deliberately. Be sure your forward foot is firmly positioned before taking the next step. Hurrying across may lead to a broken limb or other disaster. If you are crossing

Author crossing stream in British Columbia. "My pack was heavy and I was not sure of my footing, so I chose the safe way." Photo by William A. Lee.

on a log and it is wet, or if you are fatigued, play it safe. Sit down astraddle of the log and ease yourself across by bumping along on the seat of your trousers, using hands for leverage.

Wading streams in bare feet is *not* recommended. Your footing will be unsure and there is always the risk of cutting or bruising your foot on a sharp rock or other material in the stream bed. Where there are streams along your route that will require wading it is recommended that tennis shoes be carried for the purpose. One large pair may suffice for all members of the party and they can be retrieved, with a hand line, after each person has crossed the stream. Where there are many crossings along the route, each person may prefer to carry his own tennis shoes. Where crossings are close together the tennis shoes can then be left on for walking between crossings. Tennis shoes dry out quickly and can be worn around camp as a welcome change from hiking boots. If there are only a few "mild" stream crossings, a pair of rubber-soled shower slippers may give adequate protection to the feet. Some persons, in wading a stream, remove their hiking boots and socks, put the hiking boots (minus socks) back on, and wade across in their boots. The water can then be dumped from the boots and the dry socks and wet boots put on again. This practice is not recommended, however.

Stream crossings that lie along your route should be considered, insofar as possible, *before* you leave home. Get all the information you can on depth and nature of crossings, possible recent floods, etc. When you are out on the trail you may find some crossings are more hazardous than anticipated. A fast-moving mountain stream a foot deep requires careful evaluation. A depth of 16 or 18 inches may dictate that the party must turn back. If the risk is great, give up the particular objective for this trip.

ABANDONED BUILDINGS

As you hike through the wilderness or other remote areas you may come across an abandoned building. In foul weather it may appear desirable to seek shelter in such buildings, if there is enough of the building left to offer some shelter. However, there may be some problems if you should decide to move in. Vermin and rodents such as bedbugs, fleas, mice, etc., may be unusually plentiful in such a place. If you move in you may decide to move out again and into a tarp shelter or whatever other shelter you are carrying. When walking about such a building, inside or outside, be very careful of boards with nails lying about. They may penetrate your boot, cause a puncture wound, and give serious trouble.

COOKING IN TENTS

During foul weather it may appear desirable to do your cooking inside your tent. This practice can present several severe safety hazards, however.

First, you are liable to set your tent on fire. The hazard is especially great when your cook stove is first started, before the fire is under control and regulated. With the flame out of control and some possible spilled gasoline, you have a perfect setup for burning down your tent, the occupants, and any equipment in the tent. If you feel you must cook in your tent, light your stove *outside* the tent and get it well under control before moving it inside the tent. Have your escape route planned—in case you need to get out of the tent in a hurry. (For example, have a sharp knife ready to cut through the back side of the tent, if the back of the tent is your position during the meal.)

Second, in a good tent, all zippered up because of the weather, there can be danger from lack of oxygen.

Third, consider the possibility of doing your cooking under a separate fly, away from your tent, if cooking under a shelter is necessary. This will be much safer than cooking in a closed tent. Also, some tents have a vestibule where cooking can be done with less danger than bringing the stove into the main tent. In *bear country* cooking in or near a tent may result in food odors that will attract bears to the site.

Also, seriously consider a cold meal, if these alternatives do not seem satisfactory. Better to eat a cold meal than to cook a hot meal and not be alive to eat it after it is cooked.

HATCHETS, SHEATH KNIVES

A hatchet is a useful and important item of camp equipment. So is an axe. You should know how to use them safely, pack them properly, and keep them sharp. They are *not* required items of equipment on most backpack trips, however. Wood can usually be had by simply picking it up off the ground when a wood fire is desired and permitted. A jack saw will usually do the few really necessary jobs that a hatchet would ordinarily be used for on a backpack trip. A satisfactory jack saw weighs as little as 4 ounces and an average hatchet about 28 ounces; that is a pretty good reason in itself for leaving the hatchet at home. A sheath knife may be taken, but a good pocketknife will do the essential jobs that a sheath knife would be used for. Also, in reference to sheath knives, it is usually a good idea to keep your belt free of equipment on a backpack trip. Most of the better packframes employ a waist strap, and a waist strap cannot be properly used when there is equipment on your trouser belt. Hatchets and sheath knives are a common source of accidents in camping. They represent a hazard when used by persons who have not had good instruction and experience in their use. Firearms are in the same category.

INSECTS

Except in unusual circumstances, insects are simply a nuisance, rather than a threat to safety. At certain times of the year, in some areas, insects such as mosquitoes or flies may be so thick as to require the use of a head net that fits over a broad-brimmed hat and ties around the neck. Long-sleeved shirts and trousers are also important. Use reasonable precautions and you will probably avoid being bitten by spiders, scorpions, and the few other insects which do represent some degree of hazard. Before you put your shoes on in the morning, shake them hard to get rid of any insects that might have crawled inside during the night. Or, you can carry a very lightweight plastic bag and put your shoes in this at night. Do not pick up loose rocks on the ground without first turning them over with your foot. There may be a scorpion underneath, and you could get a bite on the hand. Don't thrust your hands into thick vegetation, cracks in rocks, holes in stumps, or other places where you cannot see well. In other words, use reasonable precautions and insects should present no problem to your safety.

Ticks are found in many sections of the United States, frequently in mountain valleys and forests. They cling to the underside of leaves and brush, or to grass, usually along trails used by animals. When an animal or person comes along the trail the ticks fasten on to the unsuspecting traveler as he brushes by. They then dig in and suck blood. Their prevalence in a given area often varies from year to year. An area having few ticks one year may have many the next time you visit there. Ticks vary in size from about ¼ to ½ inch in length. They are usually dark brown in color and always have eight legs. They attach themselves to the skin and bite by probing their entire heads into the flesh. If they have not started to probe they can be brushed off easily (but carefully). Once they have fastened themselves, special measures are necessary. Light a match, blow it out, and apply the hot end to the exposed part of the tick. He will back out. Or, cover the entire tick with grease or oil. When in tick country hikers should frequently *inspect one another* during the day for possible ticks that may be on outer clothing or on exposed skin areas, such as head, neck, chest, and back of legs, where another person can see the area better than yourself. In tick country take time to shake clothing out frequently. Inspect underclothing occasionally. Look carefully for ticks around your waist, on the skin under your belt. Certain serious diseases are spread by ticks, in addition to the painful bite that they may inflict. Only a very small percentage of ticks carry such diseases, however.

POISONOUS PLANTS

Poison ivy, as well as poison oak and poison sumac, is a widespread plant that everyone should learn to recognize. If you have recognized a poisonous plant and know that you have touched it, immediately wash the affected part with water and soap. Chances are that a rash or blisters will not develop. If you are particularly allergic to poisonous plants, you should carry a lotion, such as calamine lotion, which you have found to be effective in treatment.

On a well-planned backpack trip it should not be necessary to eat wild plants to supplement the food which you carry. About ⅓ ounce of prepared dehydrated salad provides a generous serving for one person and there are some tasty dehydrated salads available. The energy spent in carrying several ounces of dehydrated salad in your pack will probably be far less than the energy required to search for, find, and clean some wild-growing salad substitute at meal time. There is always the possibility of *wrong* identification of wild plants, unless you are an expert, and this can lead to severe illness—or worse. Water hemlock grows along many mountain

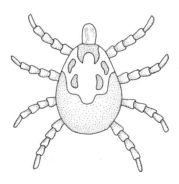

TICK (enlarged). Many varieties of ticks are found in the United States. All have the same general shape and eight legs. A well-fed female tick will be about one-half inch long, others much smaller. Examine your skin and clothing frequently when in a tick area.

streams and is very poisonous. Other common poisonous plants are wild cherry, oak, elderberry, and black locust.

SNAKES

Some persons have a very morbid fear of snakes. To avoid going into the mountains or desert because of that fear is very foolish, but not to have some knowledge of snakes and take a few *reasonable* precautions is equally foolish. Rattlesnakes are the most widely distributed of all our poisonous snakes. You may hike hundreds of miles without seeing a rattlesnake. Then, probably when you least expect it, there is one in your path. Rattlesnakes are found over most of the United States. They do not travel much in the daytime as they do their hunting for food mostly at night. In hot weather they will never be very far from shade. Unless you step on a rattlesnake or get very close to it, it will move out of your way if you give it a chance. Following are a few precautions you should take when traveling in country where there may be rattlesnakes.

Wear long-sleeved shirts and trousers. A rattlesnake may penetrate these when it strikes, but they offer significant additional protection, compared to bare skin.

When bushes are in or near your path, walk several feet out around them, rather than brushing up against them. Then, if there is a rattlesnake coiled there, it won't matter. Otherwise it may strike. Stay out of dense grass, brush, and foliage, insofar as possible.

In climbing either up or down hillsides, do not put your hands or feet down in places where you cannot fully see whether they are clear. Putting your hand over the edge of a blind cliff is asking for trouble.

If a stone or log is in your path, just assume that there is a rattlesnake coiled on the blind side and act accordingly. If you cannot see over the object, step up on it, then down, or go around.

Carry a snakebite suction kit in rattlesnake country. Also carry a sharp single-edge razor blade, to shave the hair from the surface of the skin so that you can get good suction. In using a suction type kit, wet the rim of the rubber suction cup with your tongue, to further aid in proper suction. A tube of ethyl chloride (a compound used for spot freezing of the skin surface) provides additional treatment *if you have had expert instruction in its use*. The same applies to an antivenin kit. If you carry ethyl chloride be sure to get the metal tube type of container with the small valve at the top rather than the glass bottle type of container. Make no

mistake about it, antivenin kits and ethyl chloride are dangerous materials to fool with.

If the trail goes along cliffs, walk several feet out from the face of the cliff. Then if a rattlesnake is coiled on a ledge of the cliff, you will probably avoid being bitten. A bite on the face, or on the trunk of the body, is much more serious than on an arm or leg.

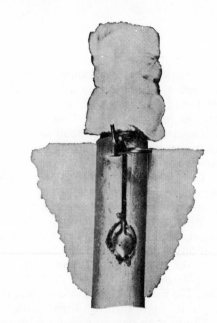

COYOTE GUN. This is the "business end" of a coyote gun, with a "wad" of scented bait projecting a few inches above ground. (The remainder of the gun is buried.) A coyote, tugging on the bait, discharges the gun and gets a shot of cyanide (and certain death). If you come across such a device leave it alone. Courtesy of Humane Coyote Getter, Inc.

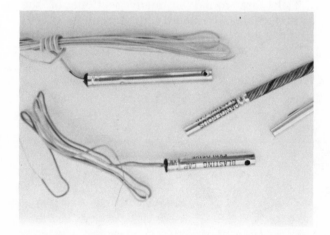

BLASTING CAPS. Two types of caps are shown. Those with wires are electric caps. Such caps are often found in an area where there has been construction work or mining. They are very dangerous. If found, leave them alone and report their location to the nearest authorities.

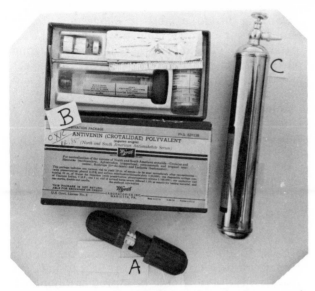

ANTIVENIN KIT (B), ETHYL CHLORIDE (C), AND CUTTER SUCTION KIT (A). These are good items to have when traveling in a remote area where rattlesnakes are prevalent. The same antivenin is also effective for water moccasin and copperhead snakebite.

It may be of some comfort to know that most persons in good health (except very young or very old) would recover from the average rattlesnake bite even if it were not treated, but don't count on it. Know the first aid treatment for snakebite and use it if the occasion arises, which it probably never will. If you are interested in statistics, in the United States about 3400 persons are bitten each year by poisonous snakes. Of this number about sixty persons die. It is believed that intense fear on the part of the victim is an important factor in most of these deaths.

ANIMALS

Normally there are no animals in our wilderness areas that will cause you any harm if you leave them alone and do not get too close to them. They will usually go out of their way to avoid you. *Never* try to corner or capture a wild animal. This applies to everything from a chipmunk to a deer or bear. Particularly avoid getting close to young deer fawns or bear cubs. The mother will usually be close by and may give you a hard time.

Most persons are aware of the potential dangers involved in getting close to *large* animals. On the other hand many persons are careless when it comes to *small* animals and rodents. Skunks are frequent visitors to backwoods camps. Like most other animals they are looking for tidbits or scraps of food that may be lying about, usually around the cooking area. They usually appear tame, sometimes visiting camp in daylight. However, consider this: if you should get close enough and should agitate a skunk into spraying you, your clothes, or your equipment, you have a real mess. It requires special measures and plenty of time to clean up yourself and your equipment when you are close to home. In the backwoods it is next to impossible. Also consider the fact that the skunk may be *rabid*. This very real possibility also exists with chipmunks, ground squirrels, and other playful little animals. It is not too unusual that a small animal in the wilds which is overly friendly is also rabid. Now, suppose you should get bitten by getting too close to such animals or possibly in trying to feed them. It may only be a scratch but you are now faced with a real dilemma. You can either consider the wound as just another small scratch, or, you may consider the possibility of the animal being rabid. In the latter case you can pack up your gear and head back for "civilization" and . . . the uncomfortable consequences of a series of *rabies shots*. Stay away from all wild animals, large or small! You should also consider that bubonic plague may be contracted by handling of small animals and rodents. This serious, but not common disease is transmitted by the bite of an infected flea. Observe all wild animals from a respectful distance and do nothing more than observe. If you want a close-up photograph use a telescopic lens.

When in camp keep food stored out of reach of animals, preferably in bags suspended by ropes from trees or on a very high rope line. Keep food out of tents and away from where you sleep. Most animals have a keen sense of smell, and they will sometimes enter a camp area in search of food. Food stored in your tent may encourage the animals to come in. On rare occasions a bear or other animal may enter a tent during the night, even though there are persons sleeping there, if you have food stored in the tent with you. A candy bar in your pocket is food, and the smell is readily picked up by some wild animals.

BEARS. The most dangerous wild animals are *not* the completely wild ones, but rather those that are partially tame. Normally wild animals are more afraid of you than you are of them. The bears in some of our National Parks are examples of partly tame wild animals. In some areas of the Parks, the bears become so accustomed to people that they are no longer afraid of them. In fact, they may become quite aggressive about coming into camp, stealing food or begging for it, and getting into mischief. As long as you leave these animals completely alone, and keep food and other attractions out of their reach, there is normally nothing to fear from them. When you start feeding them by hand, teasing them, and so forth, it is a different story. You may end up without a hand, or worse!

As you hike along a mountain trail, if you see many good-sized rocks that have been freshly turned over, a bear has probably been along that trail recently. A bear will often do this in looking for beetles, grubs, ants, and other insect "tidbits." He will also tear apart stumps and rotten logs. The presence of fresh bear dung may also indicate that a bear is in the area. Most bears have a keen sense of smell but poor eyesight. You may see a bear coming toward you before he sees you. If you do, "ease away" and go around. Don't run unless you are sure the bear is chasing you. He may be coming toward you only in order to get a closer look and identify his "intruder." If you run, a bear is more likely to chase after you, whether or not that was his original intention.

A particular danger when traveling in bear country is to come upon a bear unexpectedly, at close range. Their reaction when surprised is generally unpredictable. If you are traveling where thick vegetation, brush, or terrain may lead to a surprise encounter with a bear, carry a whistle or bell. (If you don't have these, loud conversation or other noise will help.) Blow on the whistle frequently when you are in or near thick brush. The bell can be fastened to your pack where it will provide a continuous sound as you hike. Bears hearing the noise will take off in the opposite direction.

I have backpacked in the Canadian Rockies and some of the areas had a good population of bears, both grizzly and black bears. Certain precautions must always be taken in bear country. Wardens and other knowledgeable personnel in such areas generally advise selecting your sleeping area not closer than 300 feet to the area where you have been cooking, or where food is stored. Not only food, but the odors of such items as insect repellent, sunburn lotion, shaving cream, toothpaste, cosmetics, etc., may attract bears. When you leave the area during the day or go to bed at night put all such items in a bag with your food. Suspend the bag at least 15 feet off the ground. The best suspension system is to string a rope between two trees and tie your food bag at about the center of the rope. An alternate method, somewhat less desirable, is to suspend the bag from a lone branch of a single tree; the tree should be of small diameter (8" to 10") and relatively free of good-sized branches near the ground.

Cooking *inside a tent* is dangerous at any time. In bear country such practice may be an invitation to disaster. There will then be strong food odors in and about the tent—a perfect invitation for a bear. The tent, your clothes, and other articles will all have the food odor.

Female personnel should not camp out in known bear country during their menstruation period. The odor associated with menstruation may attract a bear.

Before going to bed, wash off from your body any insect repellent, sunburn lotion, etc., since it will have some odor that may be attractive to bears.

Do not leave unwashed utensils and dishes near your sleeping area during the night. All garbage, food scraps, food wrappers, etc., should be meticulously burned in a fire if you have an open fire. If not, it should be stored and handled *as food*, away from animals, until you come to an area during your trip where it can be burned. *Do not bury garbage.* You may bury it where is is a safe distance from your sleeping area, but the next backpacker who comes along may unknowingly make his camp near where you have buried garbage, a serious situation.

Bears like to follow streams, or the shore of a lake. Keep your camp back a good distance from

Bear bell on pack, commonly seen and used in bear country.

such places. Bears also follow trails, the same trails that you follow during the daytime. Again, *keep your campsite away from the trail.*

Bears very seldom attack sleeping campers but it has happened. If it happens to you, play dead. You can't fight a bear and win. Campers who have played dead have proven that with this technique you are likely to get by with the fewest possible injuries. If you are on the trail and are charged by a bear in an area where there are no climbable trees, throw off your pack and, again, play dead. Lie on your stomach and clasp your hands over the back of your neck. It is entirely possible that the bear may be satisfied to simply rummage through and tear up your pack. Regardless, the still, prostrate form of a human is least subject to attack, as proven by many persons who have encountered bears.

These are the rules for bear country. If you are not willing to take these precautions you had best do your backpacking in a region which is free from bears.

HUNTERS

In many areas of the country the fall of the year is one of the ideal times to go backpacking. The daytime temperatures are invigorating, the woods are colorful, and there is usually less "competition" from other backpackers. Many persons, because of work schedules, have no choice but to go in the summertime.

There is one aspect that should be carefully considered in planning a fall backpack trip, however. That is the *hunting seasons.* In some areas there are too many hunters in the woods during the hunting season, particularly during *deer* and *elk* seasons. Most backpackers would prefer to plan their trips around these hunting seasons so as not to be in the woods at the same time as the hunters. This can be easily done by consulting the State Fish and Game Department and obtaining a copy of the hunting regulations and seasons. The season varies from state to state and often varies from area to area within the state, so specific information on hunting seasons is necessary.

The risk during hunting seasons other than for deer and elk is something to be evaluated on an individual basis and a knowledge of practices in the particular area. A "city hunter" sitting on a tree platform near the carcass of a dead horse, waiting for a bear to visit the carcass so he can collect a "trophy," isn't much of a risk. Most bird hunting is usually done in open areas, away from the woods, with short-range shot guns and, again, would not usually be considered a risk to the backpacker in the woods. But heaven help

and protect the backpacker who goes into an area that is saturated with hunters (from experts to raw novices) armed with high-powered rifles and hunting for deer or elk.

PREDATOR TRAPS

A possible source of danger, particularly to backwoods travelers in the Western States, is predator traps. These take a variety of forms, which normally are of no consequence if you are reasonably alert, but they are not to be fooled with. The U.S. Fish and Wildlife Service is one branch of the government that engages in predator control. An example of one predator device is the cyanide gun. A cyanide gun takes a special cartridge and discharges a load of cyanide. It is sometimes used in controlling coyotes in an overpopulated area. The gun mechanism is usually buried *below* the surface of the ground except for one *small* projecting part. This is the "business end" which is baited with food or a scent attractive to coyotes. When a coyote finds the bait and tugs at it he gets a shot of cyanide in the mouth, which results in quick death. Poison meat and poison grain are sometimes used in predator control also, but a hiker should have no occasion to expose himself to these hazards.

Still other devices used in animal control are game traps. These generally take the form of a cage, which is baited so as to cause the door of the cage to close when the animal tugs at the bait. Bears are frequently live-trapped by such devices in order to transfer them to another locality.

There are rather strict procedures pertaining to the use of devices such as those mentioned. One of the procedures is to place conspicuous signs at all places where these controls are employed, warning persons that such a device is close by and not to tamper with it. Obviously, such warnings should be rigidly observed. As you travel in remote areas, if you should come across any piece of mechanical equipment or other man-made item, leave it strictly along. Blasting caps are an example of such equipment, frequently found in remote areas. They have turned more than one hiking and camping trip into a tragedy. If you should discover a blasting cap, *don't touch it!* Note its location carefully, and report it to the nearest Forest Service Office or similar agency.

WATER SUPPLY

It is very important to keep in mind when planning your day-to-day route the location of all sources of water. If potable water sources are more than four or five hours apart, you should seriously consider another route or make very certain that you have ample water for every member of the party, plus some to spare. In determining whether a spring or other water source is safe for drinking, observe the plants and aquatic life in and about the spring. The water may be crystal clear but, if it is completely free of small aquatic insects and other life, it is highly suspect. The water in many high mountain streams and from most springs in the mountains will be safe to drink without treatment of any kind, but not always. If there is any doubt, boil it or treat it with iodine or other water purification tablets. When you wash dishes throw the dirty dish water on the ground *away* from the campsite, *not into* the stream. Unless publicly approved, swimming and bathing in mountain lakes and streams should only be done in very remote areas, never in generally frequented areas. In many of the high mountain lakes swimming can be quite dangerous.

WATCH YOUR STEP

When hiking on a wilderness trail, don't walk along with your head in the clouds. Watch your step! Few wilderness trails are level like city sidewalks. There will be holes, loose stones, tree roots, and other things in the trail over which you may stumble and fall. When you stumble, it is much more difficult to recover your balance with a full pack (or if you are tired) than it is without a pack. Stepping at an odd angle on a loose stone may give you a wrenched ankle, which will be very unpleasant to say the least. It can even mean the end of the trip.

Keep your eye on the trail. This doesn't mean you can't glance up once in a while as you hike along, but govern the length of your glances according to the difficulty of the trail. If it is really rugged, you had best watch where you "pick 'em up and set 'em down." If you like to admire the scenery under such circumstances (and who doesn't?) stop frequently on your feet for a few seconds in order to do so.

Remember when hiking through rugged country or through brush that your pack projects beyond your body outline and that places where your body may squeeze through, or just slip by, may not allow your pack to do so. When you are going along at a good clip and your pack suddenly catches a tree limb or other projection, it can be a rude awakening, and it can mean a spill. If you are crossing a "bridge" provided by a fallen tree and your pack catches on a limb, it can tumble you off the tree and into the creek or whatever else is below.

In going up a short steep slope that has loose rock on it, go up one hiker at a time. Those standing below should be out of the way where they will not be struck by rocks dislodged by the person making his way up.

CAVES, MINE SHAFTS

Unless the trip is specifically planned to include the exploration of caves (under expert guidance), they should be avoided. Special equipment and clothing is required in the science of cave exploration (speleology). Abandoned mine shafts will be found in some remote areas. Avoid them like you would avoid the plague.

YOUR GENERAL WELL-BEING

Although not exactly in the category of accident prevention, there are certain things you can do on a backpack trip that will benefit your general well-being and thus help you to get more enjoyment out of the trip. Here are a few of them:

DRINK WATER FREELY. You will frequently be so engrossed in what you are doing that you will actually forget or neglect to drink enough water. You will probably be perspiring considerably, and your body will lose water as well as salt. Make a point of taking a drink of water at least once each hour. If you are perspiring freely or have been exerting strenuously, it is a good idea to take a bit of salt with it, or take a salt tablet one to three times a day. The extra salt is very important.

AVOID OVERFATIGUE. Don't push yourself to exhaustion. Especially go slow for the first day or two until you see how much you can take. Get at least eight hours of sleep each night, and preferably nine or ten.

In addition to inadequate sleep, fatigue can also be caused by concern and worry. If you have never carried a 35-pound pack for twelve miles through the mountains on a hot day, you will have some apprehension the first time you try it. While you are on the trail, this apprehension is going to increase the fatigue that you would normally experience from such physical effort. After the hike is accomplished, this apprehension is going to give way to a sense of elation because of your accomplishment, and some of your fatigue will disappear. It is not unusual for beginning backpackers to become so fatigued during the last few miles of hiking into a remote area that they can "hardly take another step." Upon reaching camp they are so elated that they then want to go for another hike around the area. The cure for fatigue due to apprehension is *practice*. When you are confident of your ability and you keep your efforts within the bounds of that ability, this kind of mental fatigue is no problem.

If you have been so unfortunate as to acquire a blister or sprained ankle, concentrating on the pain will cause fatigue in a hurry. If you have properly treated the blister or other problem, take your mind off it. Think about a recent pleasant activity or a contemplated one, but don't allow yourself the luxury of concentrating on the pain or other negative thoughts. Your mind and your attitude have a real and important bearing on how well you feel and how fatigued you become. Carry on a conversation, hum a tune, or joke with one another to avoid monotony. The miles and the hours will pass much faster and at the same time be more enjoyable.

KEEP REGULAR. Your daily routine will be changed quite a bit from your normal habits when you go on a backpack trip. Individuals who have very regular bowel habits at home may find themselves having difficulty on a backpack trip. Two to four milk of magnesia tablets, taken daily, will provide a mild and harmless laxative and keep you "regular." Some are mint-flavored. Regardless, they are easy to take. More stubborn cases may require the use of glycerin suppositories, and a few of these may prove useful. They too are harmless.

A SUNTAN. No matter how great the temptation, do not try to acquire a suntan on a backpacking trip. Most of the hikers who do so end up wishing they hadn't. You will get plenty of sun without purposely exposing yourself. Even though they wear a hat, long-sleeved shirt, etc., most persons need the help of a protective cream or lotion on their hands and face to keep the skin from getting too dry and uncomfortable. The back of the neck is particularly susceptible to sunburn. Your pack may offer some protection, depending upon how high it is and the angle of the sun. A broad-brimmed hat will help. A bandana worn as a neckerchief is good. Don't overlook the backs of your hands when applying sun protective cream. It's a susceptible spot. If your nose gets dry and "crusty" inside, put a bit of cream on a paper tissue, and coat the inside of your nose with it.

YOUR FEET. Take care of your feet. They must get you where you are going and bring you back again. Carry some moleskin patches in your pocket. *At the first sign* (don't wait for a rest stop, meal stop, or until camp at night) of a tender spot on your foot or toe, stop and put a moleskin patch over it. In this way you will probably avoid a blister. If you do not have moleskin, put plain adhesive tape over the tender spot (not a Band-Aid) and leave it there. When you have a chance during the day, wash your feet. Use clean socks and change them daily even if they do not appear very dirty. If your feet sweat considerably, you will want to change your socks more often. In this case, have a pair of extra socks handy and change them as necessary. Hang the sweat-soaked socks on the outside of your pack, so that they will dry as you hike along. The use of a good foot powder may also be desirable.

EATING. Try to eat regularly (but not too much at one time) even though you don't feel the need for it. Have some trail snacks in your pack and do some "nibbling" between meals. Never eat heavily or even normally just before you are about to undertake a hard climb or other strenuous physical activity. Before starting a really hard climb, eat very lightly, if at all. For example, eat some candy. At intermediate points during the climb eat some dried fruit or candy if you feel the need for it. When the climb is finished then eat a bit more—to hold you until time for the next regular meal. Some persons eat less on a backpack trip than they do at home. Others eat more. Regardless, being on a backpack trip should not be reason for stuffing yourself with food. You will feel better and enjoy the trip more if you keep this in mind. *Never* eat large quantities of food in an attempt to combat fatigue. For true physical fatigue you need *rest* and a *moderate* quantity of food, if any, preferably eaten after the rest.

DISHWASHING. One of the most common illnesses in backpacking is *dysentery*. This is usually picked up from unclean dishes or from soap left on dishes during the dishwashing operation. Prevention is not difficult. You may rough-clean your dirty dishes and they may look satisfactory. Regardless of how clean they may appear, however, this should always be followed by washing all dishes and cooking utensils thoroughly in *hot soapy water*, followed by *a good rinsing in very hot water that has been boiled for a few minutes.* An important camp rule is that each person drinks only from his own canteen and that eating utensils are never shared.

KEEP CLEAN. Don't be too fussy about your clothes. They are going to get dirty, but good. However, good body cleanliness can still be maintained. In warm weather plan to bathe fully every day. With a few changes of water, plus some skill and dexterity, you can take a

Careless backpackers built a fire here against the large log, which was almost completely burned through. An afternoon shower probably put out the fire after it was abandoned. There was other burnable material in the immediate vicinity and a forest fire could have resulted. There were also designated campsites in the general area for use by backpackers and this was not one of them. Photographed by the author in the back country of one of our large National Parks.

full-fledged bath using a small plastic bowl. Or, you may prefer to carry a plastic washbasin for the purpose. Water for bathing can be heated in cooking utensils over the campfire, and the shadows of the night will provide the necessary privacy. Getting back to clothes again, don't be too fussy about their appearance, but a few reasonable precautions will help a bit. Don't wipe your hands on your trousers after cleaning the fish. Don't sit in the dirt when you can find a clean rock or log to sit on. When your hands get black from the cooking pans, wash them instead of wiping them on your clothes.

Remember that the temperature of the body is greatly affected by the temperature of the extremities (head, arms, legs). Therefore, bathing your face, hands, and arms frequently on a hot day will help you to keep cool and feel better, as well as to keep clean. That piece of thin toweling in your hip pocket will come in handy when you want to sponge off. In the dry climate of some of our western states, you may prefer to remain wet and let the air do the drying. If you have an opportunity during the day, wash off your feet and legs also.

FIRST AID

You may make trip after trip into the

wilderness and never need to use any first aid beyond putting a Band-Aid on a cut finger. The nature of first aid, however, requires that the supplies and techniques be available for use at a moment's notice. There are a number of good books on first aid and this book therefore does not go into the techniques of first aid. It is desired, however, to stress two things: (1) practice safety, so that you will avoid the need for first aid, and (2) know your first aid well and have the essential first aid supplies and knowledge at your fingertips, ready for action if and when an emergency occurs. How long has it been since you thoroughly reviewed a first aid book? Are you sure you know the difference between sunstroke and heat exhaustion? The symptoms and treatment are very different. Heat exhaustion, in varying degrees, is quite common. Do you know your first aid well enough that you will not panic when the need occurs to really put it to good test? Giving an injured or sick person the wrong first aid treatment is frequently worse than if you gave them no treatment at all. Look over the contents of your first aid kit and review the techniques!

Aftermath of a forest fire. This photo was taken soon after a fire had ravished many acres of good forest land, not far from the author's home. Within one to three years' time insects will move in and will "finish off" the charred trees that remain standing. Please put out your fires!

12

On The Trail

HOISTING PACK

There are several ways of getting a loaded pack onto your back. If there is a rock ledge or fallen tree nearby, about waist high, you have a ready-made loading platform. Balance your pack in an upright position on the platform, facing the shoulder straps. Slip one arm through its shoulder strap (usually the left arm first), then the other arm and the pack is on your back.

When there is no convenient "loading platform" nearby—the usual case—a different approach must be used. The usual approach is to lift the pack by its shoulder straps, momentarily balance the pack on your bent left knee while putting your left arm through the left shoulder strap, bend the body forward at the same time rolling the pack onto your back and slipping the right arm through its shoulder strap. If it comes easier, balance the pack on bent right knee first, and slip the right arm through its shoulder strap. Regardless, the whole process should be done in essentially *one continuous motion.*

With a good rock or tree trunk to lean your pack against you can also get it on while you are in a *sitting position* on the ground. Back up to your pack, in a sitting position, and slip your arms through the shoulder straps. In getting up from the sitting position with a full pack, first turn your body so that you are in a *kneeling position* on the ground. Then push up from the ground with your arms and your legs, into an upright position.

Still another method of getting your pack on is to simply have someone else hold it in position while you slip into it. However, most backpackers prefer to get into their packs without help. A possible exception is a husband-wife team where the husband helps the wife into and out of her pack, and also young children.

After the pack is on your back lift it by the bottom ends of the two vertical frame members and adjust its position on your back. Then tighten your waist belt. The waist belt must be *very tight* if it is to serve its purpose of transferring a major part of the pack load to the hips. The shoulder straps should be quite snug. The pack should ride high and the shoulder straps should serve primarily to hold the pack in place, rather than support the load. The pack should not "hang" from your shoulders when you are carrying it.

Getting out of the pack is essentially the reverse of getting into it. In removing your pack from a standing position, lower it to the ground in one continuous motion, but *be careful not to drop the pack* so that it hits the ground hard. You can very easily damage a packframe by "dumping" a heavy load onto the ground. If you are tired and your pack is heavy, the "safest" way to get out of it is to kneel on the ground and then "turn over" into a sitting position (the reverse of getting the pack on while in a sitting position).

Shoulder straps here are holding load in place but the load is not "hanging" by the straps. The waist belt is properly supporting most of the load.

Shoulder straps too low. The shoulder straps as shown here are riding too low and are supporting much of the pack load. Waist belt should be carrying more of the load.

The top end of the shoulder straps should be positioned so that they pass close to the neck, never far out on the shoulders. This is an adjustment that should be made at home.

When you are planning to make a short "breather" stop along the trail, look for a log or smooth rock on which your pack can rest while still on your back. It is much more tiring to stand still with a full pack on your back, for more than a few minutes, than to walk with it. If a trail stop is going to be more than three or four minutes long it is best to remove your pack.

SETTING THE PACE

Most backpack trips are made for pleasure and most backpackers are not too much concerned with how many miles they cover in a day. However, a day on the trail is usually started with some "goal" in mind, even though it may not be far in distance. Also, depending on the terrain there are certain fundamentals in hiking to be adhered to if the miles that are covered are to be in relative comfort and with the least expenditure of energy.

In hot weather try to get an early start on the trail. You can hike more miles on a cool morning, with less expenditure of energy, than

in a hot afternoon when the sun is bearing down. Usually the larger the group the more difficult it is to get an early start in the morning. It may be good to sacrifice a hot breakfast for a cold one just to get an early start. Even if you call a halt by midafternoon, the early morning start will usually pay off if there is a specific distance to be covered.

The natural inclination of many hikers is to start off in a burst of energy, while they are fresh and then taper off or perhaps give out relatively soon. This is the wrong approach. A steady, even pace can be maintained for more hours and more miles will be covered in greater comfort than with a fast pace which will require more prolonged rest stops and may even result in collapse and illness.

During the first hour some halts may be required for adjusting pack loads, relacing boots, and similar adjustments. After that the frequency of stops will usually depend on the nature of the terrain and whether the hiking is on essentially level ground, uphill, or downhill. Set rules of taking a break of so many minutes out of each hour will seldom be beneficial in the ever-changing terrain of mountain travel.

On level ground walk with a determined pace, never hurried, but as though you were going some place. Never run, trot, or even walk extremely fast with a pack on your back. Keep hands out of pockets and don't carry gear in your hands. Normally if there is gear left over that you have to carry in your hands, you are not properly packed. Although your pack will interfere somewhat, swing your arms a bit rather than letting them hang like dead weights. *Don't saunter or stroll.* Too slow a pace is just as tiring as too fast. Anyone who has ever led a slow-moving, stubborn, one-speed pack animal along a wilderness trail knows how tiring an unnaturally slow pace can be. If possible settle into a *rhythmic* stride, which is not hard to do on a good smooth trail. However, on an uneven trail and rough terrain it is very difficult, if not impossible, to maintain rhythm.

If you are climbing an uphill slope use a slow but steady pace and stop on your feet for a few seconds as necessary, rather than pushing yourself to the point of giving out and then stopping for a much longer period. The steeper the grade the shorter your stride will be. On very steep grades the *rest step* should be used. The rest step allows a short period of rest between *each* step: (1) one foot advances to a new position; (2) the knee of the rear leg is locked and that leg momentarily supports the entire body weight. The unweighted advance leg rests. (3) The rear foot advances to rest. An alternative to this method is: (1) transfer all weight to forward leg and lock knee; (2) let trailing leg go limp; (3) advance trailing leg to forward position. Since the grade is steep the steps will be short. If you are at high altitude (8000 feet or more) make a conscious effort to *breathe deeply* with *each* step. Deep breathing will help to make up for lesser oxygen at high altitudes and is helpful in preventing altitude sickness. Take every precaution to avoid unnecessary sweating, particularly if the weather is cool.

As you travel uphill you will from time to time be able to see the top of the ridge and as the top draws near, the spirit soars. However, when you finally reach the ridge top you find that there is another ridge beyond that (and the spirit falls). This process will probably be repeated many times during the day. Just when you think you have it made another long, steep grade comes into view. This can be very damaging to the enthusiasm. The "cure" is to forget about the ridges ahead, maintain a slow but steady pace and let your mind drift to more pleasant thoughts rather than concentrating on the miles ahead.

Traveling downhill is not as difficult as uphill hiking but it is not as easy as it appears it should be. Your feet and knees can take a real beating in downhill travel. Before starting downhill it

may be desirable to add a pair of socks to reduce the motion of the foot within the boot. Boots should also be laced up snugly. Your stride will be increased, but resist the temptation to walk fast. With each downward step there will be a certain jar or shock. This should be *cushioned* by bending the knees slightly. Downhill travel is tiring and rest stops are just as important as in uphill travel.

Traveling *cross-country*, off the trail, can be very difficult. In wooded and mountainous areas it can be essentially impossible. Your trip should normally be planned so that trails are followed. Thick brush, boulder fields, and blind canyons can quickly take the fun out of cross-country travel in rough terrain. Traveling with a heavy pack in such areas can also be dangerous. It is easy to loose your balance and take a tumble.

If you should feel a bit light-headed while hiking, stop and prop one foot up on a rock or log (with your arm resting on your thigh). Then lean over (keeping your pack on) so that your head is at about the level of your hips. If this doesn't help, call a rest stop and take off your pack. Then lie down on your back and *prop your feet higher than your head*. In a few minutes you should feel fine again. Before continuing on your way, take a drink of water with a little salt in it and eat some candy or other trail snack. Never neglect your water intake. Take a good drink at least once an hour but not huge amounts at any one time. Never ration yourself to see how long you can go without water. When the weather is hot, and even on a cool day when exerting heavily, you need to replace the salt that is lost through perspiration. Don't take too much salt at one time, however, and *always* take it with plenty of water.

Do not cut across switchbacks. They are there for a reason. The switchback represents the easiest, most energy-conserving route up (or down) the slope. Further, cutting across switchbacks leads to erosion.

Take every precaution to avoid sweating when the weather is cool. On a cool morning you may start hiking while wearing an extra shirt, sweater, or other heavy clothing. In your desire to keep moving down the trail, you may forget or neglect to stop and remove unneeded outer layers of clothing when you warm up. This is a serious mistake. Heavy exertion can take the place of a lot of clothing insofar as keeping you warm is concerned. It is far better to be a bit cool when you are exerting than to be perspiring. On a cool day, if you allow your shirt to become wet with perspiration your body is going to cool down rapidly as soon as you stop or slow down in your exertion. Wet clothing quickly loses its insulating value. Also, the evaporation of the water from your perspiration-soaked shirt or jacket will cool your body too suddenly. This is why *several layers* of clothing are better in cool weather than a single heavy layer. You have a better range of adjustment to suit the outside temperature.

When on the trail, hikers should walk in single file and should not follow one another too closely. It is very annoying to have a hiker follow so closely that each time you stop or change pace a bit he has to do likewise to keep from running over you. On the other hand, hikers should keep together as a group, unless they specifically plan to break up into more than one group. The leader should not need to make frequent checks to determine where certain members are. Stragglers should be eliminated at home before the trip starts, not on the trail.

A factor that will sometimes govern the distance between hikers is *dust*. If there is much dirt in the trail it will often become ground to a powderlike consistency. This is particularly true on trails that are heavily traveled and those frequented by animal packtrains. Each hiker will stir up his own little dust cloud in hiking along such a trail. Walking in one another's dust is not only unpleasant but it is actually harmful to your lungs and to your health in general. Therefore it is recommended that on dusty trails the distance between hikers be such that walking in dust clouds is not necessary.

For groups of more than several persons, depending upon the experience of the members, the leader should appoint an "assistant" to bring up the rear. If it is a large group assistants should be placed at intervals along the line of hikers. By their experience they will know when the pace should be slowed or speeded up and when to take "breathers." By visual contact hikers will in turn know when to change their pace. In most of the short stops that hikers will make during the day, of a few seconds to one or two minutes in duration, they will be stopping in their individual places, not as a group. If too many stops are made as a group, an "accordion effect" results. When the leader stops it takes from a few seconds to a few minutes for the nearest and farthest away hiker, in turn, to catch up. By the time those farthest away have caught up (or before) the leader is ready to move on again. This can be pretty exasperating, particularly to those farthest from the leader. One of the reasons you came on this trip was to "get away from it all," including crowds of people (remember?). Your backpack trip will give you more of a feeling of a wilderness adventure as an individual if your trail pace and stops are patterned along the lines described.

Animal packtrains may be encountered on some of the main trails of our national Forests and Parks. These animals and their handlers have the *right of way* over foot travelers. When you see such a packtrain approaching, step well off the trail (on the outside edge) and stand quietly while they pass. Any sudden movements you may make can readily cause some animals to shy and give their handlers real trouble. Practice courtesy.

TRAIL STOPS

Give a little planning to your rest stops. Try and select an area with a nice view, interesting foliage, or some other attraction. If it is a hot day try to stop in the shade. On a cold day stop in the sun. However, if you need a rest stop before you reach such a place take it where you are, rather than pushing yourself to exhaustion.

When you make stops along the trail during which you remove your pack (whether they are rest stops, lunch stops, or whatever else), *keep your equipment together*. Don't set your pack in one place, lean your fishing rod against a tree in another place, and put your camera or canteen on a rock in still another place. It is recommended, in such temporary stops, that you set your pack on the ground and that camera, binoculars, canteen, or anything else that is not in the pack be set on the ground beside it. In this way you will probably avoid such problems as getting two or three miles down the trail and suddenly remembering that you left your camera hanging from a convenient limb on a nearby tree at the last rest stop. In stopping for lunch, set your pack and gear back far enough from the work area (where you are getting lunch) that other hikers do not have to stumble over it and possibly step on some piece of gear in the process. Such stepped-on (and possibly broken) gear is usually considered to be the responsibility of the hiker who left it there, *not* the person who stepped on it. It is best to lean your pack against a tree trunk, bush, or rock, away from the work area, and put any other items of equipment right beside it. Fishing rods not fastened to the pack should be propped against the pack or something else so that they are off the ground. More than one backpack trip has been seriously affected and bruised feelings have resulted from leaving fishing rods lying on the ground and having them stepped on. The same general idea applies in camp also. Stow your gear in one place, insofar as possible, and keep it away from the general work area where others are working and walking about.

STAY ORIENTED

To be oriented means to know where you are. Unless you have been over a trail before and know it well, you probably cannot stay oriented without a map and compass. Before starting out on a new trail, especially one in a remote area, make every reasonable effort to find and talk to some person who is familiar with that trail. Ask them about *check points* and *prominent landmarks* that will help you to stay on the trail. Inquire about those places where you are likely to miss a turn and lose the trail.

From the time you leave the roadhead, follow your progress on the map. A stream crossing, a swamp, a spring, and a mountain peak in the distance (that will provide a compass bearing) are all good check points that will appear on a topographic map and help you to stay oriented. A fallen tree across the trail, an abandoned cabin, a prominent rock formation, and so forth, are possible check points that you should ask others about because they won't appear on a map.

Keep in mind where the trail is going. The purpose of a trail is to get from one point to another. It will usually be the shortest route, consistent with the terrain. Many trails in the West, as well as some other regions, are laid out to accommodate horses and pack animals. If you find yourself scrambling among boulders, confronted by very many logs in the trail, going through thick brush, or using your hands to negotiate a steep slope, then you are probably on a deer trail and *off* your chosen trail. Trails having very many of the obstacles mentioned would not normally be used for horse travel.

You may be following one of the trail systems that has its own distinctive markings. In a National Forest it may be a blazed trail, laid out by the Forest Service. In some of the National Parks the trail markers will be orange colored, rectangular pieces of metal, about 3‴ x 5″, nailed to a tree at a height of about 6 to 8 feet above the ground.

Depending on the wilderness, national forest, or other area you may be in, and the frequency of usage of the trail, its general condition may be very good, fair, or "pretty rough." A main trail will usually have small, neat signs at the takeoff from the roadhead showing the trail name or number and the distance to the major objectives. Along the trail, at points of intersection with other trails, there will frequently be additional signs showing where those trails go and the distance, as well as the remaining distance of your trail to its objective. Where the trail cuts into the mountainside, the outside edge will frequently be reinforced with logs or stones to prevent erosion. On steep slopes, more stones or log formations will often be laid across the trail for the same purpose. Such trails are usually very easy to follow. Except for reading the signs along the trail and an occasional reference to your map, no significant effort is required to stay on the right trail.

If you believe that all trails in our national park or wilderness system are as described above, prepare yourself for a rude awakening. It isn't so. On most government trails there will still be the sign at the roadhead, but that may be the last one you will see for a good while if you are in a remote area. Availability of manpower for maintaining the trail and infrequency of usage simply make it impractical to accomplish any more maintenance than perhaps the occasional removal of a large tree that falls across the trail and makes it impassable for horses. The blazes may be very old and faint or obscured from sight by growing limbs.

Deer paths that intersect with your desired trail may be more used than the trail itself and can easily lead hikers to follow them and get off the main trail. The trail that appears as a good solid line on the map you are holding in your hand may be faint indeed, in actuality, and overgrown with weeds and brush. I well remember one trail turnoff that has been marked for many years by a rusted horseshoe and a more rusted condensed milk can, hanging by a rope from a low bush (no other marking).

Is all of this bad? Not by a long shot. Few of us that have frequented such areas would want it any other way. We do not particularly look forward to "progress" and improvements dictated by advancement of "civilization" into such areas. This will call for replacement of such markings by small neat signs and "brushing up" the trail, and the area will then be frequented by more people.

This is simply mentioned so that you won't take too much for granted in your pretrip planning when you study that nice, pretty map, with its very distinct lines marking the trails. What may appear as a very easy problem in path finding when the map is spread out on your living room table at home may be much more of a problem when you are out there in the mountains with the sun boiling down, perhaps a bit fatigued, and trying to figure out "where the heck the trail went to."

As you progress along the trail, keep a mental or written record of important check points that you pass and the time of day that you pass them. Fix in your mind the approximate time that you should arrive at the next check point. When you arrive at a check point, make sure that it is the particular check point that you think it is. (There may be lots of stream crossings, more than one spring, and more than one fallen tree in the area where you are looking for such a check point.)

Keep a mental note of your general direction of travel. The trail will continue in a given general direction as shown on the map except where it is necessary to temporarily deviate to avoid difficult or impassable terrain. These deviations may not be apparent on a map and at times they may amount to complete change in general direction. In some unusual situations it is possible to get so turned around that you may start back down the trail in the direction you just came from. In foggy or stormy weather, where there is no sun to aid you in determining general directions, it is a good idea to take a look at your compass occasionally.

Your trail may top out on a windswept, rocky ridge where there are no trees to be blazed. You may assume that it goes on down the other side of the ridge, but when you look there you don't find it. The heat of the noonday sun, fatigue, and your anxiety to keep going ahead may impair your judgment. You finally pick up a trail on the other side of the ridge and follow it. However, you may have picked up a deer trail and after a while you decide it's the wrong one. *Backtrack!* Don't go cross-country, even for a short distance, in the hope of picking up the right trail. Chances are that going cross-country will require more time and energy than back-tracking. There is a good chance that you may cross your desired trail at a place where it is a bit obscure, not recognize it, and keep right on going. You may soon become thoroughly lost.

Your trail may lead down into a dry arroyo. You assume that it crosses the arroyo and continues on up the other side. However, when you look for the trail on the other side it is not there. In all probability the trail has gone right up the middle of the arroyo (or down) in order to pick up a better section of terrain for climbing out. There may not be any trees lining the arroyo which are suitable for blazing, hence the trail is not marked there (and right when you most needed the marking). Water rushing down the arroyo after an occasional rain has obliterated any sign of the path on the ground. These little problems add to the difficulty (and pleasure) of backpacking. They are most apt to occur in remote areas, off the beaten path. That ten dollars per day and food that the ranch boy wanted for guiding your party may start to look rather insignificant about this time. *Before* you go into remote areas be sure that your technique, your knowledge of the area, and your general preparedness are a match for the job at hand.

MAP AND COMPASS

The maps most commonly used by backpackers are the topographic (or topo) maps, available from the U.S. Geological Survey and some equipment supply firms. They show the topography or surface configuration of the land. Contour lines, brown in color, show elevation above sea level. All points on a given contour line are at the same elevation. Comparison of adjacent contour lines shows *differences* in elevation. Where contour lines are close together the lay of the land is steep. The farther apart the lines are the more level is the land. Natural features shown on a topo map include lakes, streams, springs, swamps, and forested areas. Trails, roads, and buildings are also shown.

The 7½ and 15 minute quadrangle maps are most commonly used by backpackers. On the 7½ minute series one inch on the map represents about 2000 feet on the ground. In the 15 minute series, one inch on the map represents approximately one mile on the ground.

When a topo map is held in reading position (right side up), true north is toward the top of the map. This will be verified by a small diagram at the bottom of the map, which shows not only the direction of true north, but also the *declination* (or variation) and the direction of magnetic north, and the difference in degrees between the two.

To *orient* a map means to place it in such position in front of you that north on the map is

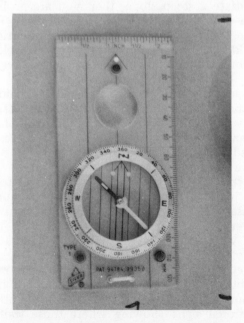

A good compass, with attached base plate, direction-of-travel arrow, and straight edge. This type is most useful for orienting a map, taking a field bearing, and following that bearing.

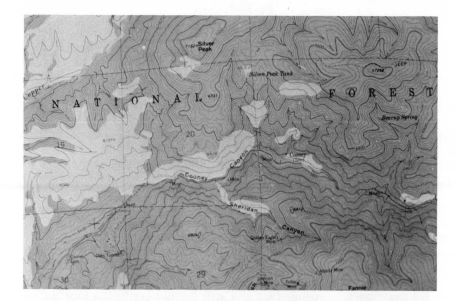

This is a section of a U.S. Geological Survey map. This is the type of map most frequently carried by backpackers.

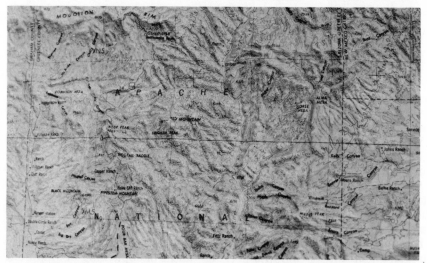

This is a plastic relief map. These maps are not suitable for carrying in the field. They are very useful in getting a "bird's eye view" of the area you are packing into and studying it over before the trip. These maps are available from Hubbard, P.O. Box 105, Northbrook, Ill. 60062 or from the Army Map Service, Fort Sam Houston, Texas, 78234.

This is a close-up view of a small section of the map shown above. A framed map of this type, of your favorite backpacking area, makes a nice wall decoration for your den or study.

the same as north on the ground. This can frequently be done by lining up known features in the terrain, such as mountain peaks, lakes, streams, etc., with the same features on the map. To do this you must know the position on the map where you are located and be able to recognize prominent features in the surrounding area.

Because of the magnetic declination it is possible to make errors in going from map to a compass bearing and vice versa. When the declination is east of true north and you are going from a compass bearing to a map, the reading is *increased* by the amount of declination. When going from map to compass the declination is *subtracted* from the bearing. (For a westerly declination the procedure is reversed.) It is easier to work with a map, and avoid the possibility of errors in going from map to a compass bearing and vice versa, by drawing a *series* of *magnetic* north lines across the face of the map. If the declination is 15 degrees east of north, draw a series of parallel lines across the map, one inch apart, which are parallel to the magnetic north index arrow at the bottom of the map. Thus, all of these superimposed lines will be 15 degrees east of the true north-south meridian lines on the map.

With the magnetic north lines drawn in on the face of your map, it is much easier to use. Place your compass on the map with the direction-of-travel arrow pointing toward your desired direction on the map. (One edge of compass base plate should touch both starting point and destination.) Then, hold the base plate of the compass firmly onto the map in that position with one hand. With your other hand turn the compass housing until the orienting arrow on the bottom of the housing is parallel to the nearest magnetic north line which you have drawn on the map. (You should disregard the compass needle.) The compass is now set for the correct bearing and you are ready to travel.

In some situations a hiker will know that he is on a certain trail as shown on a map, or along the bank of a stream, but not know just where along the trail or stream he is located. To determine his position he will need to look around and locate at least one identifiable landmark on the terrain that is also shown on the map. Perhaps in the area he just came from he can identify a mountain peak that is also on his map. He then takes a *back-reading* on the peak. This is done by sighting with the compass with the direction-of-travel arrow pointed *toward* you instead of away from you. The bearing is transferred to the map, compensating for magnetic declination is doing so. The bearing line passes through the landmark, on the map,

and will intersect the trail that you are on. The point of intersection is your approximate location on the trail.

Maybe you will know the *general* area you are in but do not know your *particular* location in the area. Solving this problem is similar to the above example except that *two* mountain peaks or other landmarks will need to be known. It is preferable that the landmarks be located so that your line of sight to each will intersect at approximately a 90-degree angle, or as near to 90 degrees as possible. Take back-readings to each landmark, and transfer the reading to your map. Draw the bearing lines through each landmark and project them until they intersect. The point of intersection is your approximate location. If you can get a similar bearing on a third landmark which you recognize, that bearing line should intersect at the same point as the other two and will further verify the location of your position.

Perhaps you do not recognize any landmarks in the area, either from where you have come or ahead. You are now *lost*. It is time to *backtrack* if you can. If you do not know your way back it is time to bivouac and initiate survival procedures.

You should practice using your map and compass, and orienting procedures, when you are in familiar country. Such practice can also be done close to home during a day hike. Then you will have more confidence in your efforts when you are in relatively unfamiliar country and trying to get your bearings. In your training and practice, use a good reference book such as *Be Expert with Map and Compass* by Bjorn Kjellstrom. This book is available from many mountaineering and backpacking equipment supply firms.

MAPS AND TRAIL INFORMATION

On most backpack trips you should provide yourself with some maps of the area, as well as sketches and notes that you make yourself. Depending upon the area that you choose for your backpacking adventure, the following are sources of maps that will usually be found helpful.

U.S. FOREST SERVICE. The U.S. Forest Service has maps of the National Forests and Wilderness Areas, which are available to the public free of charge. These may be obtained by writing to the Supervisor of the National Forest for the forest or wilderness that you are interested in. A list of the national forest and wilderness areas is given in Appendix E. The Forest Service maps generally show trails, streams, springs, prominent mountains, fences, and buildings (if any). They do not have contour lines. These maps are very useful to have and to use in conjunction with the U.S. Geological Survey maps. I use them regularly.

If you have some questions concerning the area you plan to pack into, write to the nearest Forest Service office. I have always found members of the Forest Service to be very helpful in furnishing information on forest and stream conditions, trails, and in supplying similar data important to the planning of a backpack trip.

U.S. GEOLOGICAL SURVEY. The maps published by the U.S. Geological Survey will be found very helpful in most backpacking. These maps show all of the important natural features, as well as trails, roads, and isolated buildings. Elevations are shown by contour lines and this is an important feature when traveling in rugged terrain. These are called quadrangle maps. An index (free), as well as the maps themselves, is available from the U.S. Geological Survey. (See Appendix F for address.)

TRAIL ORGANIZATIONS. Detailed maps and information on the Pacific Crest Trail are available from the Sierra Club. Information on the Appalachian Trail is available from the Appalachian Trail Conference. Helpful information on the Long Trail, which winds along the Green Mountains in Vermont, can be obtained from the Green Mountain Club. (See Appendix F for addresses.)

OTHER SOURCES. The Chamber of Commerce of a city in the general vicinity of the area of interest will frequently be able to furnish some maps and information which will be of value. Large cities often have local hiking clubs, and the City Chamber of Commerce can furnish names and addresses of these clubs, if you are interested. Some states have a State Chamber of Commerce, usually located in the capital city. Practically all states have a state fish and game department, or its equivalent, which can furnish information that will frequently be helpful in your planning. Some of the suppliers listed in Appendix A have maps and books available giving detailed information on areas of particular interest to mountaineers and backpackers.

CARE OF MAPS

To protect your maps from moisture, dirt, and wear, it is recommended that you use transparent plastic which is available for this purpose in sheet form. You can get this from some of the suppliers listed in Appendix A and frequently at local stationery stores. When the paper backing is removed from one side of the transparent plastic, an adhesive surface is exposed onto which your map or map section is placed to accomplish a bond.

On many backpack trips you will only be concerned with a small area of the map. Instead of carrying the complete map, you can use a razor blade to cut out the area of the map you are interested in and reinsert it after the trip, using transparent tape. In cutting out the area you are interested in, include some adjacent area for orienting purposes.

Large maps can be folded with an accordion style fold, which is easy to do. With the map face up, draw an imaginary horizontal line from west to east, dividing the map into two equal halves. Now fold the map along this horizontal line, back surface to back surface, with the printed side of the map on the outside. Next, starting at the northwest corner of the map, fold it *accordion* style, into sections about 4 inches wide. When the folding is completed the northeast corner of the map will be on the outside. With this type of fold, you can read your map in the field without unfolding the entire map.

Transparent map cases, with grid lines marked on the case surface, are available from most of the suppliers listed in Appendix A and from many office supply stores. These are convenient for use in wind and rain and will keep your map clean.

LEAVING THE TRAIL

There will be some occasions during backpack trips when you will want to temporarily leave the trail you are following. This may be for the purpose of exploring a particular area, rock hunting, fishing, or some similar objective. If it is just a short trip you may not need to mark your path in order to find your way back to the main trail again. For a longer distance, possibly an overnight hike to a particular point of

A map case will protect your map in wind and rain, and also keep it clean. Photo by Lou Clemmons.

interest, it may be desirable to take some special precautions.

You should *not* blaze trees, bend over bushes, or pile rocks in order to mark your trail. When you leave a main trail and want to mark your path, there are several ways of doing so that will require relatively little energy and will not mar the landscape. First there is the matter of simply making mental notes of your position, prominent features in the terrain, and following your progress on a map or sketch of the area. Stop and look backward occasionally. It is surprising how different the same area can look when viewed from various angles. If you come to a particular spot where you think you may have trouble staying on the trail on the way out, make a note of it on a 3″ x 5″ card or in a small notebook, take a compass reading on the back trail and prominent objects, and record them.

If you want to mark the trail in some stretches, you can use a grease pencil to make a small marking on rocks. It will deteriorate in a few weeks and you will have not marred the landscape. You can also use 8- or 10-inch lengths of crepe paper and tie them to tree limbs and bushes with a single overhand knot. They too will deteriorate in a few weeks, and in much less time if there is rain. A somewhat more permanent marking, but one which will also deteriorate in several months, is 10-inch lengths (about 1 inch wide) of lightweight cloth, such as parachute cloth. Put a number on each strip of cloth with a felt tip marker before leaving home. When you mark the trail with it, enter a description of the back trail in your notebook, identifying the note with the number on the cloth strip. The purpose of marking a trail, as suggested, is to find your way back along the same route.

You can therefore pick up the cloth or paper markers on the way out. You may miss a few, but they will deteriorate.

Occasionally during a backpack trip it may be desirable for trip members to be temporarily separated. This may occur during a period of fishing, wildlife observation, and so forth. It is recommended in such a case that all persons travel with one or more companions rather than alone. Sometimes it happens that you don't know whether a group or certain individuals are ahead on the trail or behind. This can cause some anxiety, as well as wasted effort in locating them. For example, some persons by prearrangement may be traveling parallel to the trail but 100 yards or more to one side. This sometimes happens when fishermen are fishing a section of mountain stream that parallels a trail. Engrossed in what they are doing, they fail to notice whether certain companions have moved on ahead. They finally make their way back to the trail, but they don't know whether to hurry and catch up or sit down and wait.

This problem can be solved in several ways. If it is a small group, persons traveling along the trail can use a stick and make a distinctive mark (such as an "X," "—," or "O") where there is soft dirt in the trail, doing so each several hundred yards or more. Other companions coming along the trail will see that mark and will know that the person or group assigned that particular mark is somewhere ahead on the trail. Distinctive colors of crepe paper, tied on tree limbs or bushes, or small cards bearing initials or a name (and hour) and impaled or tied to twigs, can be used in the same manner. The last person(s) coming down the trail can pick up the pieces of paper or cards and burn them at the next camp site.

13

In Camp

GIVE YOURSELF TIME

As you hike along your trail, you will probably see many "picture book" campsites. Quite frequently, however, you may not find such a campsite when you need it most (when it's time to make camp). Once you have agreed on a time to make camp, you should usually take the first acceptable campsite that you reach within a half hour after that time, unless you are familiar with the area and know absolutely that a better campsite is only a short distance away. If you do this, you will probably avoid such problems as being caught in the darkness on the trail, still faced with finding a campsite, making camp, cooking your supper, and washing dishes. It takes the fun out of these activities if you have to do them after dark. It is also hard on flashlight batteries and dispositions. If you are traveling in the vicinity of a stream in late afternoon, don't leave that stream and go chugging off up the mountainside unless you know that there will be a water supply when it's time to camp. Better to camp early and have some leisure time than to be caught in an unfamiliar area, away from any water supply, and having to make a dry camp. *Give yourself time* to properly prepare your chosen campsite for the night, and to cook your evening meal. This usually means making camp a minimum of two hours before darkness.

CHOOSING A CAMPSITE

Many of the conditions pertaining to selection of a camp in general camping also apply to campsites for backpacking. However, some deserve special emphasis. One of the prime requirements of a good campsite in backpacking is *water*. If wood fires are permitted and you do your cooking over a wood fire, you will also want to select an area that has a good wood supply. (If you are cooking over a portable stove, then wood is no problem.)

In planning your trip, the length of travel each day should be gauged so that you will have a stream, spring, or lake available as a water supply when it comes time to make camp. It is far better to underestimate how far you will travel in a day than to overestimate. It is possible to make a "dry camp" away from any water supply, but this should be avoided if possible.

You do not need to cook and eat in the immediate area of your campsite, however. For example, the general area chosen for camp may be along a stream that offers no nearby level places for beds. However, there may be a good level knoll several hundred yards above (higher than) the stream. You can lay out the sleeping bags and other gear on the knoll and take a five-minute hike down to the stream at mealtime, if that is a better place for your cooking.

Avoid making camp near bogs, marshes, or any other areas that contain stagnant water. These are natural breeding places for mosquitoes. Meadows with poor drainage are also likely areas for mosquitoes. During insect season a campsite on relatively high ground, which will be exposed to any breeze, should be chosen. In the western mountains, depending upon the elevation, mosquitoes are usually quite prevalent during June and July. Gathering some advance information on the mosquito aspect, prior to your trip, will be time well spent.

In cool weather you will want to pick your campsite so as to be protected from the wind. If you are in a canyon you can depend upon the wind blowing up the canyon during the day and down the canyon at night. A campsite on the lee side of boulders or a grove of trees is a good choice if you want to avoid the wind.

In cool weather you may also want your campsite to be exposed to the sun as early as possible in the morning. You can use your compass to determine where the sunny spots will be in the morning (or to be in the shade, if that is preferred).

Anticipate the course of temporary streams or flash floods if it should rain. Don't have your bedsite in such an area. Pick out a spot that looks like it would drain well in the event of rain. *Do not ditch* your bedsite. Ditching mars the ground and leads to erosion.

Near the bottom of a rock slide is a poor place to camp. The rocks may slide some more. Directly under a high cliff or near the bottom of a steep slope is a dangerous place to camp. Animals moving about, or changes in weather, may dislodge stones or boulders and send them down into your camp area.

The natural inclination of a group when entering a clearing that they have chosen for a campsite is to select the biggest tree in the area and drop their duffle there. Soon after they will be laying out their beds in the same spot and otherwise preparing the camp for the night. The dead wood that you find lying on a forest floor comes largely from live trees, and it has to come off the tree sometime. It might come loose during the night while you are under it. Avoid picking out the biggest tree in the area and making your bed under it. (It may also attract lightning.) If you are camping where there are trees, pick out medium-size trees and look them over carefully for dead limbs before you decide to make your bed there.

Hikers have been known to make their beds right in the middle of ant colonies. Look the ground over, as well as looking for nearby dead trees or dead limbs.

When you first enter a prospective camp area, don't set up camp immediately. Spend a few minutes walking around and looking it over. Hikers are frequently in too much of a hurry to set up camp. Then when it is about set up they discover one or more features that make them wish they had chosen another spot. The first thing to do in looking over a likely campsite is to *take off your pack.* Walking around with your pack on is more likely to make you want to hurry and get the job over with.

You should try and select an area that is generally level, and in particular has enough fairly level places of "sleeping bag size" or appropriate tent size to accommodate the number of persons in the party. However, no area will be absolutely level. A few inches in elevation where you choose to sleep may mean the difference between whether you stay dry in the event of rain or whether water runs into your sleeping bag area. Observe which way water is likely to *flow* over the ground in case of a hard rain. The *nature* of the *ground surface* is also an important consideration. Rain will not soak into hard packed, bare ground as it will into a forest floor or ground that has a covering of pine needles, grass, etc. Bare ground also means more difficulty in keeping your bedding and other gear clean. Spread out the individual sleeping sites, rather than clustering them too close together. Again, one reason you probably had for making this trip was to get away from crowds. Most people like some privacy. This applies on a backpack trip as well as at home.

A good view from your campsite is nice but it should normally be one of the lesser considerations. Unless it is a base camp or layover camp, most of the time you are there you will be asleep.

On some backpack trips you will be packing into a *base camp* and then working out from there each day, returning to the same camp at night. In setting up such a base camp, give some consideration to locating it near prominent features in the terrain that will help you find it when returning at the end of a day's activities. For example, in a dense forest where the view is limited and many areas look pretty much alike, finding your way back to camp can turn out to be quite a chore. On returning to camp in a dense woods you may pass within a hundred yards of it, never see it, and go right on by. (You now have a problem.) Try to set up such a base camp near a prominent tree, an unusual rock formation, the fork of a river or some other irregular feature in the terrain that will be of assistance in locating it.

SETTING UP CAMP

One of the first things to do in setting up camp is to decide where the *cooking area* will be. If you are cooking with a backpack stove this may be a rather minor problem. However, it is usually desirable to have boulders, trees, or some other type of windbreak when using a stove, even though it has a wind screen. A suitable place near the cooking area, in the form of a rock slab, clean grass or pine needles, etc., on which to spread out food and cooking and eating utensils, is also desirable.

If you are using a wood fire for cooking, and the campsite has been previously used, you can probably find a fire ring or place where an open fire was built by previous backpackers. This is the place you should usually build your fire, so as not to make new scars on the ground. The only exceptions 'would normally be where the original fireplace was improperly selected. It might possibly have been built under low overhanging tree branches, near other burnable materials that cannot be moved, against a large log, etc.

Having selected the site for cooking and eating, the hikers can now choose their individual sleeping sites. The reason for selecting the cooking site first is that in bear country the sleeping area should be well away from the area where food is to be cooked, eaten, or stored. If you are not in bear country then this is not a major

consideration, although you will probably prefer not to have skunks, raccoons, and other small scavenger animals in your sleeping area either. If you are in bear country don't take the matter lightly. It is suggested that you refer to the section on animals and bears in Chapter 11.

In unpacking their packs hikers should bring their share of the food, cooking gear, and any items of common equipment which they have been carrying, over to the cooking site. Food should normally be hung in bags off the ground, even for very short periods and even though hikers are in the area. With everyone engrossed in setting up their sleeping sites it is quite possible that small animals may get into the food supply, in daytime, without being noticed. After the evening meal, more elaborate measures for protecting the food for the night should be taken, usually by hanging a bear bag high off the ground, again . . . if you are in bear country. Remember that leaving food within the reach of animals is inviting them to a treat, and *they may accept the invitation.*

If your packbag is waterproof, or if you have a waterproof cover for it, there is no need to put it inside a tent or to have it at your bed site. It is recommended that it be suspended off the

Hoisting the "bear bag."

Suspending pack for the night, out of the reach of animals. Either a rope line between two trees or a high limb on an "unclimbable" tree is recommended. Photo by Lou Clemmons.

Sleeping bag, hung up to dry. Photo by Lou Clemmons.

A pair of moccasins provides a welcome change from hiking boots, after a hard day on the trail.

ground from a tree limb or a high rope stretched between two trees, away from your bedsite. Don't leave packs on or near the ground. Some "irresponsible" porcupine or deer may feast on pack straps or other sweat-soaked equipment for the salt that is in them. Also, food odors on packs may bring a bear into camp during the night.

Parachute cord or other stout cord should be used to put up short clotheslines. Towels and damp articles of clothing, or freshly washed socks and other items, can be hung on the clothesline. Try to hang clotheslines away from the main area of camp and out of the way of hikers who will be moving about the camp area. Leave a white rag or article of clothing on the line at all times so that it can be clearly seen and hikers will not walk into it and possibly hurt themselves.

You can stow your clothes in your pack or under your sleeping bag to keep them dry. Dry clothes under your sleeping bag will provide additional insulation from the cold ground. Don't stow your clothes in these places, however, unless they are absolutely dry. A more desirable way of stowing clothes is to make a

clothes hanger from a stick of wood, about 1 inch in diameter and 16 inches long, and put your clothing on this. Using a stout cord about two feet long, tie a small loop at the center of the cord, then tie the ends of the cord to the ends of the stick. With another piece of cord, tied to the loop at the center of the first cord, suspend this "hanger" from a tree limb. Drape your shirt and trousers on the hanger and pin socks and other small items of clothing to it. If you suspect rain, better place a plastic bag over the whole business, bottom side up. Punch a small hole in the bag through which to thread the rope that suspends the hanger from the tree limb. Reinforce the edges of this hole with tape. Do not close the bag at the bottom. If you have a tent, articles of clothing which are a bit damp can be hung from a ridge line inside the tent.

YOUR BED

If the spot you select for your bed is not absolutely level (the usual case) you will be most comfortable if you put the head end of your sleeping bag at the higher end. Go over the ground carefully (on your hands and knees), and remove pine cones, rocks, and sharp twigs before putting down your ground sheet. Spend a good five minutes in doing this—more if the spot is not fairly smooth—and it will pay off. When your sleeping bag is on the ground and not in use keep it rolled up, at least loosely, with the head end in the middle of the roll. This will keep ants and other insects out of the bag.

If you are using a tent it is recommended that you go over the tent site on your hands and knees, and remove sharp objects, just as you would before putting down a ground sheet for your sleeping bag. The floor of a backpacking tent is not rugged. It can readily be punctured or torn by irregular objects on the ground. Also, if you are using a tent it is recommended that you remove your hiking boots before you enter the tent, or, crawl around on your hands and knees inside the tent. Otherwise you will track unnecessary dirt into the tent. Also, heavy lug soles are hard on tent floors.

If a poncho or rain fly of some kind is pitched over your sleeping bag, make sure that the outer edges of any ground cloth you may be using are well *within* the area covered by the rain fly. Otherwise, any rain running off the fly will fall on the exposed edge of the ground cloth, be unable to soak into the ground, and will run under your sleeping bag. You will become much wetter than if you used no ground cloth at all. If you use a ground cloth, mark one side of it (using a felt tip marker) with the word "UP" in large letters before leaving home. When you use the ground cloth, lay it on the ground so that the side marked "UP" is always the top side and the opposite side is next to the ground. The ground side will collect dirt over a period of usage, and there is no point in having this dirt next to your good sleeping bag. In using a clear plastic ground cloth, in particular, it is not always obvious which side was next to the ground the last time it was used.

If you use a tarp it will hopefully have grommets along the edges. A plastic tarp may not have grommets. In that case you can use round, smooth rocks for anchoring the sides. A 1-foot length of $1/8$ inch diameter shock cord, inserted in the ridge line, will provide "give" and help avoid tearing the plastic. Use plenty of rocks, very roughly the size of an indoor baseball, and anchor the sides securely so that they will not flap during the night. A little breeze can make a loose tarp flap loudly, and it sounds even louder when you are trying to sleep. You can also tie down corners or edges of plastic tarp with heavy cord and small, smooth stones about an inch in diameter. Push the stone into the plastic and tie your cord around the bulge in the plastic on the opposite side.

Remember that it is the confined air in your sleeping bag that keeps you warm. Fluff it up well before going to bed. A feature of a down sleeping bag is that it has good resiliency. It will compress into a small bundle when pressure is applied and will spring back into a large volume when the pressure is released. It will therefore compress *under your body* while you sleep.

If you wake up cold at night, reach your arms outside of your sleeping bag and fluff up the sides and top with your hands. Now roll over, moving the sleeping bag with your body, so that the fluffed-up side is next to the ground and the compressed side is skyward. You are now lying on your stomach and you will need to roll over on your back carefully, without turning the sleeping bag with you. Do this and then fluff up the sides and top again with your hands and you are in business. By this time the sleeping bag hood is probably not where you want it so you may need to do a little more twisting and organizing. However, the sleeping bag has now been fluffed up on all sides, and you should sleep warmer for awhile. If you have a liner in your sleeping bag there is not much point in trying this trick unless the liner is made of very smooth material and also firmly anchored to the inside of the sleeping bag at several points with tie tapes because it will get hopelessly twisted. If you are brave enough you can of course step out into the night air and fluff up your sleeping bag the "easy" way.

Walk around the area before dark and note the location of any large stones or logs that you may walk into or trip over after dark. Dead limbs at eye level are dangerous. Break them off or hang white rags, a towel, or paper on them, to avoid injury after dark. This precaution applies to the area around your sleeping site as well as the camp in general.

BEFORE YOU GO TO SLEEP

Before you retire for the night, make sure you have certain items within reach of your sleeping bag. You may want your flashlight during the night. Once you have it you should be able to find other items within reach without too much groping around. After a hard day of hiking, regardless of how much water you drank during the day or in the early evening, it is not uncommon to wake up thirsty during the night. Have your canteen handy (within reach), with water in it. Just before going to sleep it may be a good idea to take one or two aspirins. You may not have a headache, but you will probably have a few muscles that are a bit tired and achy. A couple of aspirins will help you relax, ease those aches, and get a good night's sleep. If you are not under an insect screen, then have your insect lotion within reach in case you have to "do battle" during the night. Do you have the habit of thinking about the next day's activities just before falling asleep? Several 3″ x 5″ note cards and a pencil stub within reach will be useful for jotting down certain reminders for the next day.

If the weather is at freezing or below, it is best to put your flashlight (and canteen) *inside* your sleeping bag. It shortens the life of batteries if they are exposed to freezing temperatures.

THE FIREPLACE

Where it is safe and permissible to build a fire in the camp area, the fireplace will usually be the center of camp activity. Hikers will frequently be found at the fireplace, whether to cook, to eat, to talk, or just to sit and stare at the fire. Because of the heavy traffic at the fireplace, the soil around it will frequently become ground to a fine dust from the passage of many feet. It is therefore recommended that you plan your camp layout so that the place for the cooking and campfire is at one end or one corner of the camp rather than near the geometric center. This will cut down on unnecessary "by-traffic" of persons who are simply going from one point in the camp to another.

Open containers of food, butter, etc., may have dirt kicked into them if they are set on the ground or on low stones around the cooking fire. Bags of food may be stepped on and split open. It is therefore recommended that your "work table" for meal preparation be removed from the immediate vicinity of the cooking fire. Choose a spot about 15 or 20 feet away from the cooking fire; it should be grassy, covered with pine needles, or provide a flat rock or an otherwise nondusty area. This is the place to lay out eating utensils, silverware, food, and condiments for that particular meal. It will usually be a cleaner and better spot to wash the dishes also, rather than in the immediate area of the fireplace.

The cook needs still another work space. He needs a small clean area, away from foot traffic, where he can sort through food bags and equipment after the meal is over, while others are washing dishes. Find a small, clean spot about 20 to 30 feet in some other direction. Here the cook will have the room and the necessary solitude to concentrate on what he is doing as he sorts through food bags, finding the right bags for the particular meal, getting the individual bags back into the larger carrying bags, and so forth. Here he will make up equitable loads for each hiker to carry, or following the supper meal will put the food into suitable bags for hoisting off the ground.

When fire-starting conditions are difficult (just after a hard rain for instance) take more than the usual amount of time to gather a good supply of dry wood before you try to start a fire. Damp hikers are frequently somewhat impatient to get a fire started, and this impatience may lead to more delay in the long run. An inadequate supply of dry twigs, etc., will be quickly used up, perhaps before larger pieces of wood start burning. Then you must take time and go look for more fire-starting material, and the time spent in gathering the supply for the first attempt has been wasted. Possible sources of good fire-starting materials on a rainy day are the underside of downed timber which is partially propped off the ground by limbs, the overhang of a cliff, the underside of a pile of driftwood near a stream, hollow tree trunks, and on the ground under trees having dense foliage. Don't overlook used paper tissue, candy wrappers, etc., which you may have in your pocket. Pine needles are excellent fire starters, and where they form a thick carpet on the forest floor some dry needles can usually be found, even after a good rain.

When you go to bed at night the fire should be *thoroughly extinguished* by dousing it with water. Be just as careful to ensure that it is completely out as you would if you were leaving the area. There should be no need for having a fire going at night. However, if for some reason you do keep a fire going at night you should take turns watching it. An unattended fire is potentially very dangerous. It is unsafe if you are asleep, even though you are only a few feet away.

LOSING GEAR

It is easy to mislay eating utensils, knives, and other small items of camp gear and leave them behind when you leave camp. There are several things which can be done which will minimize the possibility of losing such items. First, do not set such items down in out-of-the-way places. Immediately after using such items as knives and matches, put them in an assigned place. Very small items, like a can opener, can be tied to a larger piece of equipment. Second, small items such as silverware can have the handles or other surfaces coated with a bright colored, nonlead paint, which is nonpoisonous and will make it easy to locate. A small piece of bright colored rag can also be tied to the item. Third, spend the last five minutes before leaving camp in walking around the area and making a last check to see that some item of equipment has not been left behind. Specific individuals should be in charge of specific items of all common equipment. Those individuals should have a check list and should use it to check off all items for which they are responsible before the group leaves each lunch site and campsite and moves on down the trail.

SANITATION

It is very important in choosing a toilet area that it be in a spot that is not likely to be chosen by some future party as a campsite. Few things are more disgusting than to find a good potential campsite and then to discover exposed human feces nearby, complete with toilet paper littering the ground or impaled on the branches of bushes and fluttering in the breeze.

Toilet areas should be well off the trail and away from potential campsites. A thicket or brushy slope in uneven terrain is usually a good location. It is important to be well away from streams, brooks, or potential stream beds, such as a gully. Whether the soil is loose enough to permit the digging of a shallow hole, or whether loose rock, bark, or other debris is available for covering all "evidence" should also be considered.

"Cat sanitation" methods should normally be used and a hole 4 to 6 inches deep dug with a rock, stick, or the heel of your boot. After use cover the hole with dirt, rocks, etc. Be considerate of those who will come after you. It is a good idea to carry matches to the toilet area and to burn used toilet tissue. However, if you are in a thicket, or there is much burnable material lying about this may be unsafe. In such case toilet tissue also should be thoroughly covered and never left above ground to blow about. It is a good idea to have a washbasin, soap, and water available back at camp, for use upon your return.

Large backpacking groups should carry a small shovel for the digging of a latrine. They should also carry lime, or a similar substance, that can be used to aid decomposition, control odor, and keep flies away. Obviously all such holes should be filled in carefully before leaving the campsite.

Urination does not require such "cover up" effort, but the same rules and precautions should be taken to select an area away from any campsite and away from watercourses.

Fish heads and entrails lying about, and swarming with flies, where somone has cleaned fish, are not a pretty sight. They should be burned in a hot fire, along with other garbage. If a fire is not available they should be carried in a plastic-lined *litterbag* to the next site where a fire is available.

CAMP SPIRIT

A proper camp spirit has a lot to do with making the trip an enjoyable experience for everyone concerned. When you take to the woods on a backpack trip it is seldom that everything works out exactly as it was planned at home.

There are always some unknowns. If you knew precisely what experiences and problems you were going to have, what the weather would be, and so forth, it would no longer be an adventure. Each individual should be *mentally* and *physically prepared* to make the most of the situations that are encountered, whether they are good or bad. You will probably plan your next backpack trip by "including out" those hikers that display "camp spirit" along the following lines:

1. They did not check out their hiking boots; nor did they take the time to make a few conditioning hikes before the trip. After a few hours on the trail they start to complain of sore feet, an uncomfortable pack, and so forth.

2. They did not check out their equipment before leaving home. They have trouble with some of their gear and frequently ask to borrow some items (not common equipment) from other hikers.

3. They "surprise" the other hikers by hauling out a transistor radio the first night in camp, and play it long and loud, even though it was specifically agreed that such equipment would be left at home.

4. They always manage to stay in their sleeping bag until someone else gets up in the morning and has the fire going. When breakfast is about half-cooked they straggle out and finish dressing.

5. They take needless risks that are a threat to their individual safety and to the trip in general.

6. When meals are being prepared, they always seem to have some item of personal equipment that needs attention at that particular time, or they may simply wander off and go fishing or exploring.

7. They frequently hold up the group from starting their next activity, as planned and agreed to by the majority.

8. They are chronic complainers about the weather, the trail, the food, the fishing, or a dozen other things.

9. They brag about their equipment. If some hiker is getting along with blankets from his bed at home it isn't necessary to call his attention to the luxury of a goose down sleeping bag. A single glance on his part at a good sleeping bag will do the job very nicely. If he wants details he will probably ask for them.

10. They raid the food supply. They may also take more than their share of a certain food without first asking others if they have had all they want. (The cook is in charge of the food supply, and he is responsible for seeing that everyone gets enough to eat. Getting into the food supply without the cook's permission is strictly against the rules.)

11. They fail to keep litter picked up around

their tent site and do not assist in keeping the general camp area clean. "Leave no trace" means nothing to them.

12. When others are ready to "sack out" for the night they can be depended upon to remain up long afterwards, filling the night air with loud talk, tramping around camp, rummaging through gear, and so forth.

On a backpack trip you will be with your companions for twelve to fourteen hours each day. This is more hours per day than you usually spend with members of your immediate family. All personalities have certain idiosyncrasies (except you and me). Sooner or later one of your companions is going to say something or do something that you do not like. To avoid spoiling a good trip, hold your temper. Take a walk, bite your fingernails, or go kick a big boulder, but don't "spout off." Make an extra effort to get along with other members of the group and to be considerate. Give someone else the first cup of coffee, the first plate of food, the first drink at the spring, the first cast at a trout pool, and show other kindnesses. It will pay big dividends in the long run and assure maximum enjoyment from the trip for the time and effort you have invested. The rule "Do a good turn daily" is a good plan to follow.

When the trail is long and hard, the weather foul, and the food burned (how bad can things get?), dispositions have a way of getting "on edge." *Thorough planning* and *preparation* at home and setting *reasonable schedules* on the trail will do much to counteract this. Be kind to one another. Punctuality, helpfulness, and cheerfulness all have an important place in backpacking. If you are to meet with individuals or a group at a certain place on the trail at a specified time, be a few minutes early rather than a few minutes late. When the time for meals is established, all members should report promptly to the scene of action. Everyone should help with the operation from the time cooking is started until the last dish is washed and packed. Be considerate of the group's welfare. That piece of cheese that someone decides to snitch from the food supply for a private snack may be just what the cook was planning on to flavor a pot of macaroni at the next meal. The old sleeping bag feels mighty snug on a frosty morning, but someone has to get up, start the fire, and put the coffee on. Why not you this morning?

DON'T LITTER

The wilderness and national forest areas are yours. Take care of them as you would any other prized possession. Be thoughtful of those who will come after you. Don't leave a trail of debris as you travel through the backwoods. Police your campsites carefully before you leave them.

All refuse which is not completely burned should be packed out. There should be *no exceptions*. This includes all cans, bottles, and metal foil. If you were able to carry them in full you can carry them out empty. It is a good idea to make your own *stout cloth* litter bag, from new muslin or percale cloth material, with a drawstring at the top. *Plastic* bags, even fairly heavy plastic, are usually unsatisfactory. Litter in the bag will frequently rub a hole through the plastic and cause some of the contents of your pack bag to become blackened or soiled.

When on the trail, hikers should not throw candy and gum wrappers, bits of string, plastic, tape, and other litter on the ground. Such material should be put in the pocket and burned at the next camp—or, *packed out*. Although single, uncrumpled layers of foil will often appear to burn if thrown in a hot fire, most frequently there will be very small flakes of the "burned" foil left in the fireplace, after the fire is out. Therefore, all foil should be packed out.

Take an interest in wilderness legislation and in other legislation that seeks to preserve a part of the natural beauty of this country for the generations to come. Don't take too much for granted. If you are in doubt as to how to proceed, Appendix G is a partial list of some well-known organizations that are fighting the battle to ensure that your children and mine will have clean air to breathe, clean rivers, and wilderness and forest areas for wholesome recreation. These organizations need your support. Please give it to them! As a starter, why not write to your congressman and ask him to take action toward preventing mining in wilderness areas. (It is now permitted.)

14

Backpacking with Children

Some parents may want to try a family backpacking trip. I have taken many backpack trips with my family, some when the children were quite young, and most of them were thoroughly enjoyable. Family relationships can grow stronger in doing things together and backpacking is no exception. As for fishing and other outdoor recreation, if the first family backpack trip is enjoyed by the wife and children they will probably have enthusiasm for future trips. If too many problems occur on the first trip, it is quite likely that father will have to seek other companions for his subsequent backpacking adventures.

Of major importance to the success of a family backpack trip is the *experience* of the parents. They should not attempt taking the children on a backpack trip until they, particularly the father, have had extensive experience themselves. Parents can tolerate such misfortunes as losing the trail, overextending themselves (with resultant aching feet and bodies). getting gear wet, spending sleepless nights, etc. Such events take on different proportions from a child's viewpoint and may be sufficient to thoroughly discourage them from wanting to undertake any more backwoods adventures.

EQUIPMENT

Good quality backpack equipment is fairly expensive and when you are attempting to outfit an entire family with packs, sleeping bags, hiking boots, etc., the price tag may be beyond your budget. In many areas it is possible to *rent* all kinds of equipment used in backpacking, and this may be the solution. Especially for the first few trips, until the parents can see how the children are going to take to this new family sport, it would be wise to rent or possibly borrow much of the special equipment needed. Also, plan your first trips for *warm* weather, when a minimum of equipment and relatively inexpensive equipment is required (compared to cold weather backpacking).

PRECONDITIONING

Thorough preparation is of the utmost importance. The family should take a number of day hikes, three to five miles in length, in preparation for the backpack trip. Try to choose a wooded area or other terrain for these preconditioning hikes that will be interesting to the *children.* If these hikes are too monotonous it may so discourage the children that they won't want to take any backpack trip. Hiking boots should be carefully checked out. If the trails for your chosen backpack trip are good (and they should be) some children may be able to get by with canvas or tennis shoes. Almost any rubber-soled boot, above-the-ankle type, will serve adequately for the first few short backpack trips (provided they fit properly). During the preconditioning hikes, *check the children's feet periodically.* They frequently will not inform you of sore feet until a blister has already formed and they are in real trouble.

For the preconditioning hikes, have the children carry the packs that they will carry on the backpack trips, if any. Add a light load to the pack, such as rain gear, jackets, food items, drinking water, etc. Check to see that the packs fit properly. If the children complain of sore shoulders or other discomfort with a light load, the pack may be too large, too small, or there may be some other problems. Better to remedy the difficulty now than to wait until the group is on a backwoods trail.

Make some effort to keep the children interested as they hike. Point out animals and birds, unusual rock formations, clouds, etc., to them. Try and get a "feel" for their best pace, and things along the way that keep them amused and in good spirits. To get anywhere on a backpack trip you must set a reasonable pace and stick to it. Children often want to start out in a burst of energy and then quickly slow down. Before they get too tired, call a brief rest stop. Have a fruit drink and some candy.

Guide books to flowers and trees, birds, and/or animal tracks will probably increase the children's enjoyment in hiking. With some help and encouragement from mom and dad they may become quite knowledgeable and interested in these aspects of nature, depending upon their age.

There are hazards in the woods and the children should become acquainted with some of them. Point out poison ivy and poison oak to them, if there is any. Teach them to exercise caution in stream crossings so that they do not slip on a wet log or hurt themselves in wading a stream. If there may be poisonous snakes in the area, tell the children to avoid thick terrain, to watch where they step, and not to put either hands or feet into places where they cannot see well. It takes some tact and diplomacy to point out such hazards without alarming a child unnecessarily. Don't dwell on hazards too much. Spend at least an equal amount of time in showing them the beauty of the outdoors, and stressing that with reasonable precautions they are completely safe.

PREPARATION

Thorough advance preparation is especially important in planning trips with children. *Never* take young children on a trail that you have not been on yourself and know every step of the way. A simple *overnight* trip should usually be their first backpacking experience. In subsequent trips you can increase the duration and distance. Try to pick a scenic area, within three to five miles of the trailhead, for a camp. Children love *water*. A camp near a river or lake, that provides shallow areas where the children can play and wade, may be ideal. Avoid areas with a high population of poisonous snakes and thick brushy terrain. A parklike area is much better. Avoid making a trip at the height of the mosquito or black fly season, if these may be a problem. If the weather is hot try to get an early morning start by camping at the trailhead (if necessary) the evening before, even though only three or four hours of hiking may be required. If rain is a possibility, take every precaution to see that you have adequate shelter, and suitable rain gear for hiking. A wet camp, wet gear, and wet clothes will *not* increase the children's enthusiasm for backpacking.

Depending upon the age and sex of the children, a tent or tents of their own can increase their enjoyment of the outing. It might be one of the plastic tube tents that are commercially available. Or, you can make a simple "pup tent" from a sheet of plastic, suspended with a rope ridge line and weighted along the ground edge with rocks.

If you have a family dog, and dogs are permitted in the area you are packing into, it may be a good idea to take the dog along. Although dogs are not generally recommended on a full-scale backpack trip, on a short trip with children it may heighten their enjoyment considerably to have their favorite pet along.

Include plenty of candy in your food list. Also keep in mind some foods that your children particularly enjoy, when you are making up the food list. Even if you intend to cook on a portable stove, get a fire permit (if required) if wood fires are allowed in the area. Children always enjoy a fire, even if it is only a small one. They may be able to toast marshmallows or

Tents are recommended when backpacking with children. Photo by Owen Thero.

roast hot dogs over the fire. Possibly you can make them some popcorn. Try having the children drink various brands of dehydrated milk at home to see which they like best, before taking it on a backpack trip. Also, children who refuse dehydrated milk may relish it if chocolate flavor is added, or they may prefer drinking it as hot chocolate.

Babies who cannot yet walk would seem to be a problem on a backpack trip. Yet they are often less of a problem then toddlers who have just started to walk. The latter can often keep a couple of adults busy just looking after them. Waiting until the toddler is subject to some degree of verbal guidance may be best.

Most children eight to ten years old can carry small packs, containing sleeping bags, articles of clothing, and other lightweight items. Obviously dad and mother will end up with packs which are a little overweight, but the distance to camp should not be long. If you have a special area that you like to pack into that is perhaps 6 to 8 miles from the trailhead, you may be able to get a rancher or outfitter to pack your gear (especially the heavy items) into your camp while you walk in carrying light backpacks. This would especially apply to a trip of several days or more, where the food load would be a considerable portion of the total load. After the food is eaten, you could probably carry out the remaining load without difficulty, if you packed carefully to start with. Also, in going into many of the attractive areas you will find that the way in is predominately uphill from the trailhead. Coming out of the area is considerably easier since it is mostly downhill travel.

In planning the trip, discuss some of the plans with the children, so that they feel they have a

Good equipment helps to maintain the interest of older children. Photo by Fred Mulholland.

real part in it. During actual preparation, let them perform some minor tasks in getting food and equipment ready. Sunburn and dehydration are potential problems with children, just as they are for adults. Long-sleeved shirts and long trousers, as well as a hat are recommended for all members.

Checklists are just as important in backpacking with children as they are in a group of adults. In addition, it will give older children an added sense of responsibility if they are made accountable for certain items on the checklist. Certainly they can be responsible for their own clothing and equipment. (This will also save time and work for the parents.) Let them assist in planning the checklist and impress upon them the necessity of assuring that all items on the checklist are accounted for, before leaving home and after the group is on the trail. Depending upon the age of the children, let them also be responsible for certain items of common equipment, that are for the benefit of the entire group.

ON THE TRAIL

Small children will usually stop and rest when they are tired but older children may not. The older children may set goals for themselves that are beyond their capabiltiy and may experience bodily harm from overexertion. Some restraint may need to be placed on them, particularly if there is rivalry with other children in the group.

A harness with a leash can be an aid and comfort to mothers in controlling very young children. This is especially true for precipitous

Backpacking family on the trail. Photo by Owen Thero.

trails and those that wind along swift streams, as compared to parklike areas.

Generally the *slowest* member of the group should be in the lead, or between the leader and another adult who brings up the rear. In order to keep the group together you will have to gear your pace to that of the slowest member. Sometimes slowness of the children's pace will be directly in proportion to the monotony they are experiencing. Talking, singing, pointing out items of interest will help relieve the monotony. Depending on the age and physical stature of the child, don't be too hasty to relieve him of part of his load when he starts to complain of a heavy pack. Promise a rest stop and a snack within the next ten minutes at an interesting place. The child who complains of being too tired may "explode" in a burst of energy once you reach camp.

Watch carefully for *sunburn* and *dehydration* in children. They cannot be expected to take the preventive measures against sunburn that an adult would take. A good case of sunburn can spoil their trip and be a burden to the adults. Encourage the children to drink water and other liquids frequently. They are apt to neglect this unless reminded. Have plenty of fruit flavoring, cocoa, malted milk, etc., along as an assist in getting the children to keep their liquid intake at a high level.

Side trips off the main trail to points of interest will increase the children's interest, if the side trips are not too long and do not take away too much energy needed for the main trip. A *whistle* on a cord around each child's neck will help in locating them if they get out of sight, and also give them a sense of security. It is a good precaution.

Children are prone to throw gum and candy wrappers, Kleenex, etc., along the trail. Teach them from the beginning the importance of using a litterbag and burning all burnables when (and if) a fire is available. Impress upon them that nature is sensitive and cannot fight back against man. The motto "Take nothing but photographs, leave nothing but footprints" should be stressed to children from the beginning of their first backpack trip.

Teach children to keep a respectful distance away from all wild animals, even very small ones. First, the animals should not be disturbed in their natural environment. Also, if they are regularly fed by people they may get so accustomed to this that they will die when no one is around to feed them and they must scrounge their own food. There is always the possibility of animals being *rabid*, particularly the overly friendly ones. If your child should get bitten by an animal this poses a real problem, and the vacation may end right there.

IN CAMP

Don't be too anxious to set up camp when you first reach your destination. Let the children "goof off" a bit. Depending upon their age and experience, let them have a part in choosing the area where they are going to sleep and pitch "their" tent. Instruct them in proper storage of their bedrolls and other camp articles during the daytime. Explain how and why many articles of gear and clothing should be kept off the ground and how they should be stored. It is a good idea to set boundaries as to how far the children can go from camp without an adult being along.

It is never too early to teach children backwoods manners and wilderness preservation. Designate a toilet area and instruct the children in digging a "cat" hole and covering all "evidence," including toilet paper. When it is time to wash up or do dishes, impress upon them that these tasks are accomplished well back from any water supply, and explain the reason.

If there is some fishing to be had, let the children have a try. Don't expect them to stay at it very long, however, if the fish are not biting. If dad goes off fishing by himself for too long a period of time, neither mother nor the children are going to appreciate the lack of attention. Be prepared to exercise a lot of patience and restraint. Remember the trip was planned for the children. Try and view it from their standpoint. If your child catches a fish, makes a "discovery" on his own, comes up with a good suggestion, etc., applaud or commend him properly.

A difference of several years in age can mean a big change in the amount of gear a child can carry, the kind of terrain he or she can cover,

Children enjoy helping with the cooking. Photo by Fred Mulholland.

length of trip, etc. Don't be misled, however, that more energy and enthusiasm automatically qualifies youngsters to carry adult loads. Be reasonable. There will also be a change in the type of activity which they will enjoy. They may develop into "serious" trout fishermen, or, if their indoctrination to fishing has not been up to par, they may want nothing to do with it. Perhaps rock hunting, bird watching, or photography will spark their interest. At a fairly early age there will be times when they will want to take a friend along on their backwoods trips. Encourage them! The time will come all too soon when your children will be taking trips "on their own," and probably into areas and terrain that mom and dad wouldn't even want to attempt. Enjoy your family while you can!

BREAKING CAMP

Breaking camp each day and moving to a new area can be a chore with a group of adult backpackers. With children it can be even more so. If you find a camp spot that the children enjoy, stay there for a couple of days, or even for the entire trip. You can make daily hikes out from a base camp, and see new areas, without moving the camp. This particularly applies to families with small children who are not yet capable of carrying their share of the gear.

ENJOY YOUR VACATION—BACKPACK

Every year thousands of families take to the highways for their vacation, in all types of recreational vehicles. Many of them spend much of their time in crowded camp grounds, often with much less privacy and feeling for the outdoors than they would have in their backyard at home. They "visit" the National Parks (more crowds), spend time in the souvenir shops and main points of interest, then speed to the next National Park (to repeat the process). If a family has the proper equipment, and some backpack experience they can vary this routine, get away from the crowds, and make the vacation one which all members will thoroughly enjoy. The next time you plan to visit a National Park or similar scenic area, take along *backpack* equipment and supplies. Get information in advance on the hiking trails and backpack campsites in the park by writing to the superintendent of the particular park. Order topographic maps of areas that have trails which are of possible interest. When you arrive at the park get more information on the particular trail you have in mind, type of terrain, campsites available, fire permits required, etc., then select the trail that is commensurate with the *experience* and *age* of all members of the family. Take off for a few days into the backwoods and really enjoy a wilderness vacation. Admittedly, some of the trails in the National Parks, and the backwoods campsites, will be fairly crowded, but nothing like the recreational vehicle campgrounds and points of interest that you can drive to in an automobile. *If* your experience is up to it avoid the popular trails and areas of the Park in favor of a more remote and little-used area. It can be a truly enjoyable vacation, one which all members of the family will enjoy and fondly remember for years to come.

15

Preparing for a Backpack Trip

SETTING A DATE

One of the first things that needs to be done in planning for a backpack trip is to set a date for the trip. This may seem like a simple thing, but it does require some thought. For a full-scale backpack trip, the date should be set at least a month in advance, and preferably somewhat longer. In using dehydrated foods, some of them may be ordered through the mail and about three weeks should be allowed for delivery from the time you send in your order. It is desirable to package the food at least a week in advance because there are usually some unexpected matters that come up during the last week before a trip, and you will want to get as much of the routine preparation out of the way as possible.

Trying to get three or more persons to agree on a date for a trip can be quite a job in itself. At the same time you should reach agreement on an *alternative* date, in the event that you have unexpected bad weather move in just prior to the takeoff date, someone gets sick, or there is some other emergency. With the planning and preparation that is required for such a trip, when someone backs out for reasons of "personal convenience" just a few days before takeoff, this is usually reason for "exclusion from the club" as far as future trips are concerned. At the minimum, it means repackaging of practically every food item, which is no small job. If only three persons were going, and someone backs

out, it possibly means cancellation of the trip. In remote areas a group of three is considered a minimum from a safety standpoint.

When you set a date, every member of the group should work conscientiously toward that date. At the same time you need to condition your thinking to the fact that if a real emergency occurs or definite bad weather moves in you will delay the trip to the alternative date. There are types of persons who, after setting a date and telling their friends, neighbors, and others about the proposed trip, feel that it almost amounts to a bad mark on their reputation if they do not take off as planned, regardless of what comes up in the meantime. That is why agreement on such matters and on an alternative date is important.

Do as much of your trip preparation as far in advance of the trip date as possible. Nothing is more frustrating than working right up to the time of takeoff in repairing or locating equipment or doing numerous other jobs that could have been done weeks in advance. You will enjoy the trip much more if you can spend the week or two prior to takeoff in making daily conditioning hikes and so forth without being bothered by a lot of last minute details.

BE PREPARED

If possible, store the equipment that you use in backpacking in a special place. Since it all goes in or on your pack, it doesn't take up much room. A few medium-size cardboard boxes will usually hold all of it. The time to make repairs or changes in your equipment is as soon as possible after a trip. Don't wait until just before another trip to get it in order. If something needs repair, repair it; if it needs sharpening, sharpen it. If you plan to try out a new piece of equipment or a new food, do so well in advance of another trip. In other words, "Be prepared." Many of these preparations need to be done right after each trip, and most of them can be done weeks before the next trip. Following are recommendations on a few jobs in this category.

1. Immediately after each trip thoroughly air and sun your sleeping gear and any items of clothing which are not washed. Store sleeping bags in a fluffed condition, rather than rolling them tight. The ideal way is to suspend them vertically from a hanger and not roll them at all. Never store a sleeping bag in its stuff bag.

2. Immediately after the trip you should make some notes on how menus and food quantities worked out. Did you have too much or too little of some foods? Make some notes for reference in planning for your next trip. Were some foods unsatisfactory? Make a record now!

3. Make some notes as to what you intend to do differently on your next backpack trip. Admit your mistakes, and plan how you are going to correct them.

4. Go over your checklist after every trip. You will probably want to make a few changes. Keep your checklist and notes from trip to trip.

5. Soon after each trip wash pan bags, silverware bags, any cloth food bags, etc. Replace any worn drawstrings or tie strings on such bags. Thoroughly wash all cooking and eating equipment. Replace soap, pot scratchers, sponges, and so forth. Replace wire bails on cooking pots with new wire. Store this gear in large plastic bags to keep it clean.

6. Repair or replace any equipment or clothing that is torn or broken. Lubricate zippers on packs and clothing. A soft lead pencil or a candle will work well, or there are special zipper lubricants available.

7. Clean hiking boots and the lugs on the boots. Use a waterproofing material, after cleaning, if the need is indicated. Did you have any trouble with your boots on the last backpack trip? Do they need repairs? New insoles? This is the time to check them over, have any necessary repairs made, and then try them out on some practice hikes.

8. Did all items of clothing perform their intended function on your last trip? Do you want to try out a different item of clothing for one that did not perform satisfactorily? Now is the time to do it.

9. Do any items of rain gear or equipment need a new coat of waterproofing compound? Do it now and then check them out under a shower or garden hose.

10. Did your backpack stove perform satisfactorily? Do you need to mail order any new stove parts? Regardless, it is a good idea to get out your stove and check it over, just to be sure it is in good operating condition.

11. Sharpen knives, fishhooks, and so forth.

12. Try out a new trail food. The place to first try it out is at home.

13. Review your first aid technique. Check over the contents of your first aid kit. Replace aspirin, moleskin, etc. Check the rubber suction cups on snakebite kits. After several years the rubber frequently becomes hard and brittle, and the suction cup may be worthless for the purpose intended, even though it has never been used.

14. Check over fishing equipment, rock hunting equipment, cameras, and other special gear.

15. Replace "old" matches in match containers. Matches that are more than six to nine months old do not work as well as "fresh" matches. Only wood stick or "kitchen" matches are recommended.

SELECTING NEW EQUIPMENT

One advantage in belonging to a hiking or backpacking club is that you can talk to others about their backpacking gear and see the equipment in use. You can get firsthand information on the virtues and deficiencies of various items of equipment that you cannot get from reading retail catalogues. Even though you may still do most of your backpacking with a small group, belonging to a club can provide these and other benefits that you could not obtain otherwise.

From time to time some of your equipment will need to be replaced. With most gear there must always be some compromise between weight and ruggedness. A cast iron skillet will last a lifetime, but that doesn't make it a good piece of backpacking gear. You will enjoy carrying a lightweight teflon or aluminum skillet much more, and it will serve the purpose, even though it needs to be replaced periodically. You may buy a pair of hiking boots that will last five years or more, and with each step you take you may have to pay for that durability by lifting an extra pound of weight. A lighter boot may need to be replaced every one or two seasons but that is of no consequence if you have enjoyed many miles of extra comfort in hiking as a result of less durability. If you are buying a fishing rod for backpacking, buy one with a detachable handle and with sections nearly equal in length.

Avoid heavy, overdesigned equipment and clothing. This particularly applies to war surplus items.

When you order equipment from catalogues, be sure to note the difference between weight of the item and its shipping weight. If in doubt, write to the supplier and ask for a clarification of weight before placing a positive order. When ordering hiking boots, ask what the *weight* of the boot is in *your size*. The catalogue weight given for some of the hiking boots can be quite misleading.

ORGANIZING

Would you like to participate in a backpack trip that is a comedy of confusion, frustration, wasted effort, and hurt feelings? It's very simple. Just take any group of reasonably well-qualified hikers and backpackers, and assume that because of their experience you don't need to do any significant amount of planning or have any definite organization in preparing for the trip you have in mind. You will end up with too much of certain equipment (unnecessary duplication), not enough of other items, a conglomeration of food and menus, an itinerary that was supposedly satisfactory to everyone but which actually doesn't please anyone, and there will be other problems. Certainly in a small group of experienced backpackers the role of the leader is not as distinct or as involved as in a large group with varied and less experience, but someone still needs to "spearhead" the preparations. In a large group, intermittent preparation and coordination over a period of six weeks prior to takeoff is not unusual. You should have a few meetings of the group concerned, to plan your trip and to determine who is going to do what in getting ready for it. Following are some of the things that will need to be decided:

CHOOSING A LEADER. A leader for the group should be chosen to have general responsibility for planning and organizing the trip. He should also have overall responsibility for the welfare of the group and the conduct of the trip after it gets underway.

FOOD, COOKING GEAR. One person, hopefully someone skilled in cooking on the trail, should be in charge of menu planning, buying and packaging food, getting together cooking gear, etc., and distributing equal loads to each person in time to pack it with the rest of their equipment. In a small group the leader may also be the cook, but not necessarily. Someone in the group may be allergic to certain common foods or may have a strong dislike for some foods. It is best to find this out when the menus are being made up at home, rather than when the group is cooking in camp.

CHOOSING A ROUTE. Try to choose an area and a route into the area that some member of the party is familiar with. One or two persons should be responsible for getting together maps, literature, outlining an itinerary, and providing all possible information on the route.

OTHER COMMON EQUIPMENT. Someone will need to assemble other items of common equipment, and distribute an equal load to each hiker, such as: repair kit, group first aid kit, rope, and so forth. If it is agreed that one person carry a camera (or other item) for the benefit of all, then that person should be compensated accordingly in the weight of other common equipment that he is given to carry.

TRANSPORTATION. You will need transportation to the takeoff point. One approach is that hikers furnishing vehicles get their gas and oil paid for by the others. An alternative is for riders to jointly pay the driver at the end of the trip for car or truck expenses, based on mileage driven (say 10 cents per mile for passenger cars). Those furnishing vehicles should take special precautions to ensure that the vehicles are in good operating condition and not likely to break down on the way to the takeoff point. If a vehicle breaks down en route and the group has to wait at some remote crossroads while a fan belt or ignition coil is being brought out from the nearest town, it gets the trip off to a bad start. Preventive maintenance costs money, and a *generous* mileage allowance to the vehicle owner is essential.

Do the proper persons (drivers) have the full name and address of all hikers they are to pick up? (There are a lot of Johns in the phone book.) Searching out street names and house numbers with a flashlight at four o'clock in the morning can be quite a chore, and phoning persons at that hour to ask them how to get to their home can lead to a certain amount of difficulty.

FUNDS. You will need to purchase foods and certain common supplies well in advance of the trip. If you are hiring a guide or arranging for special transportation at the roadhead, a deposit is usually made toward this service. Each member should make an advance deposit toward these costs. There also needs to be a clear understanding as to whether any of this advance payment is to be returned to a trip member who later cancels out. Generally such advance payments are not refunded, either in whole or in part. When supplies are purchased for the trip or deposits made for a necessary service, the planning is already too far along to permit any refunds.

GENERAL PLANNING

There should be a *trip plan*, and every participant should understand it thoroughly. It is amazing how even very fundamental aspects, such as the length of a trip, can be misunderstood by some. It is not unusual to be far into the woods and then have an argument arise between some trip members as to whether the group was to return to the roadhead on a Saturday or on a Sunday. The date and the exact hour of the takeoff from home and the date and approximate hour of return to the roadhead are very important. There should also be a return date and hour, left with a responsible person back home, which will be a "cutoff" time. If you have not returned home by that time, it is to be understood that you have encountered a serious emergency or accident and that the responsible person at home is to take action accordingly. This is a very important and serious matter and should be treated as such.

AN ITINERARY. There should be an itinerary for the trip, starting with the hour that the group leaves the trailhead, outlining the expected travel for each day and camping place for that day. After the group is on the trail, the itinerary can be as flexible or as rigid as you want to make it, but there should be a plan. On a well-conducted backpack trip a group does not go into a remote area and simply wander aimlessly about for a week. Be careful, however, not to try and crowd too many miles or too many activities into one day. Be particularly careful in your planning that you will have a suitable campsite, especially with respect to water, when it comes late afternoon and it is time to camp.

A GUIDE. Are you going to hire a guide? If you are going into a remote area, away from marked trails, and no one in the group is familiar with the area, a guide can save a lot of headaches. He need not be a professional guide. A local ranch boy of high school age may be an entirely satisfactory guide. If he knows where the trail is and can stay on it, he will be of more service to you than a Ph.D. who can speak seven languages (and doesn't know where the trail is).

ROAD TO TRAILHEAD. Is there an automobile road all the way to the trailhead, or will special transportation need to be arranged for the last few miles of travel? If there is a road all the way to the trailhead, is it good in *all seasons*? Is a four-wheel drive vehicle required? If the road is dirt and an unexpected heavy rain makes it impassable, what alternate transportation is available? There has been more than one backpack trip that never got off the ground

because the planners failed to recognize the possible need for special transportation for the last few miles of travel to the trailhead.

PHOTOGRAPHY. As you discuss and think through the proposed trip, you will find that there are many questions to be answered and some "rules" to be made. Some snapshots or color slides are an important feature of most backpack trips. However, if some trip member insists on a "commercial quality" shot every time he takes a photograph, it is going to mean some delays. There are types who like to have the entire "safari" trip by a certain spot two or three times so they can get just the right shot. Unless the trip is planned for this type of photography, most members will not want to go along with it. It is best to talk these things out beforehand. For example, you can make a rule that photographs can be taken freely as long as the photographer doesn't hold up the group. Those persons who need tripods and too much other paraphernalia every time they click the shutter may find that the rest of the group is a quarter mile down the trail by the time they get set up.

WEATHER. Have you carefully investigated the weather and minimum temperature that can be expected for the area (and altitude) that you will be in? Is rain expected at that time of year? At high altitudes don't overlook the possibility of snow and severe winds. These factors are important in planning your sleeping gear, clothing, and possibly the itinerary. A long distance phone call to a Weather Bureau, Chamber of Commerce, Forest Service Office, or rancher in the area, just prior to leaving for the trip, is a good idea. This will serve to determine whether there has been a sudden change in weather, floods, forest fires, or similar conditions that may call for postponement or a change in trip plans. State police in some states maintain radio contact with units in other parts of the state and will be glad to furnish information on local road conditions.

INSECTS. Try and get some reliable information on the prevalence of flies, mosquitoes, ticks, and other insects in the area where you are planning your trip. At certain seasons insects can be such a nuisance as to call for unusual protective measures or perhaps postponement of the trip. A few weeks earlier (or later) there may be no problem at all. Get advice on locally used insect repellents and protective measures, such as head nets, gloves, bug dopes, sulphur, and kerosene.

WATER SUPPLY. Some trip member may be acquainted with the area where the group will be backpacking and may know the trails. He may recall where certain streams and springs are located and think that there is adequate water along the trail. Remember in such planning, however, that the flow of streams and springs may vary with the season of the year and that a spring that was flowing one year may be dried up the following year. If you write to the Forest Service or another knowledgeable organization for maps, this is a good time to inquire about the flow of certain streams and springs and other possible water supply along the trail. Never underestimate the seriousness of running out of water on a backpack trip. In some areas there may be no problem whatever. In other areas, and at certain seasons, some careful planning may be required.

STREAM CROSSINGS. One item of preparation is to determine what stream crossings are to be encountered on the trails you will be hiking. This in turn will dictate whether you should take one large pair of tennis shoes as an item of common equipment or whether each hiker should take his own, as an item of personal gear. If there are only a few scattered stream crossings, mild in nature, one pair of large tennis shoes to be shared by the group will probably do. However, if a given stretch of trail has, for example, four or more stream crossings in a mile of travel then it may be desirable for each person to have his own tennis shoes. For such stretches of trail the hikers will probably want to put the tennis shoes on and keep them on, even for the hiking between crossings. Then, when crossings are less frequent or the trail leaves the stream, each person will want to change back to regular hiking boots. Hiking for very long in wet socks or wet shoes invites blisters and sore feet. Wading streams in your hiking boots is *not* recommended.

TAKEOFF TIME. If the takeoff point is more than several hours' drive from your home, it may be desirable to drive there the evening before and camp at the roadhead. In this way you won't need to start hiking right after being fatigued by a long drive, and you can get an early start on the trail. When this is done, your breakfast the next morning at the roadhead should be planned with foods, utensils, and cooking gear which are carried separately for the purpose. The only items you should need to unpack from your trip gear are your sleeping bag and mattress. *Keep the breakfast simple.* Otherwise it will take too long and you will probably start up the trail on too full a stomach, which is not good.

Another reason for early arrival at the trailhead may be to allow time for acclimatization to the altitude. If some members live at much lower altitude than that in which they will be hiking, even an overnight stay at the takeoff point will be beneficial. In some cases a longer time may be required.

DOGS. The matter of taking dogs on a backpack trip is frequently a controversial subject. Even though dogs may not be forbidden in the area you are planning to pack into, having a dog along may be objectionable to other members of the party. That is why the matter should be discussed early in the trip planning. When a member shows up ready for the trip with his favorite dog in tow it is then too late.

In Canada the National Park Game Regulations state that all dogs in the National Parks must be kept on a leash. Further, taking dogs into the back country is strongly discouraged. The National Park Service in the United States has a similar policy. Also, in the United States the superintendent of the National Park has the authority to bar dogs and other pets from all or portions of the Park under his control.

Very often a dog owner will start out with his dog on a leash but once he is in the backwoods the leash comes off. Free-roving dogs harass wildlife and often kill small animals such as ground squirrels, deer fawns, and elk calves. The presence of dogs sometimes leads to encounters between campers and bears that would *not* have occurred if the dogs had been left at home.

TAKING FISH HOME. Some persons object to taking home (or attempting to take home) fish that have been caught in wilderness lakes and streams, and this includes the author. I am an avid trout fisherman but I have never kept more fish, while fishing in the wilderness, than I needed for the next meal. Further, I don't ever intend to. There are several reasons for this.

First, it is very difficult to stock most wilderness lakes and streams and the majority of them are *not* stocked. Trout or other fish are part of the wilderness environment. It is a source of great pleasure to many backpackers to catch trout in unstocked waters, and then release them, keeping only enough to eat for the next meal. Those persons who attempt to carry fish out of the wilderness are depleting the supply and eradicating a source of enjoyment for future backpackers.

Further, trout and most other fish taste really good only when they are freshly caught. Often those who attempt to carry fish out of a wilderness area will end up by throwing them away later. Where icing facilities are available, fish can be preserved for a time, if you want to do it, but this does not apply to wilderness backpacking.

It is therefore strongly recommended that if you fish on a backpack trip you keep *only* enough fish for the *next meal*. All others should be carefully released. As for other aspects of the wilderness environment, give some consideration to those who will come after you. Many persons would not want to be a member of a party that carried fish out from a wilderness lake or stream. That is why it is recommended that the matter be discussed in the planning that takes place at home.

STOPS EN ROUTE. Are you going to allow any stops on the way to the trailhead, except for food and gas? Most hikers who have gotten up at three o'clock in the morning to meet an early takeoff hour will not appreciate sitting in a hot vehicle while some member trips gaily from store to store, shopping for camera film, suntan lotion, fishing license, or some other item that he should have obtained weeks before. Are you going to allow shopping or sight-seeing stops on the return trip home? Once they are back at the roadhead, most hikers are anxious to return home. It's up to you, but it's best to have these things well understood beforehand.

OTHER ITEMS. Should hikers take their own bag lunch for the first meal on the trail? Are floods a possibility? If you are hiking along one of the big trail systems that "touches base" with civilization every few days, are certain supplies to be replenished along the trail? Are you going to allow smoking along the trail? Are you going to permit firearms to be carried? Are typhoid or tetanus shots recommended for trip members?

After you have discussed all of these factors and made your decisions, it is a good idea to have the basic trip plan typed, and a copy made for each member. Then there can be no misunderstandings. This particularly applies to large groups of six persons or more. The trip plan should outline the itinerary. It should also list common equipment which will be taken for the benefit of all members. It should list the basic "rules" that you have agreed to for the conduct of your trip.

THE LEADER'S JOB

The leader does not have an easy job. Except in very large and formally organized groups, the leader will be paying his way, along with other trip members , and the time that he has spent in planning and organizing the trip will be donated. Trip members should thus keep in mind that the leader is entitled to his share of fun from the trip and full participation in the various activities.

One of the most important tasks of the leader is to determine the hiking and backpacking capability of each member of the group, early in the trip planning that takes place at home. Probably most and perhaps all of the members will be well known to the leader and this may be no problem at all, but don't take too much for granted. A single newcomer to the group or an individual whose capabilities are not well known to other members can ruin a trip for the entire group. The newcomer to the group may overestimate his ability in the discussions and planning that take place in the living room at home. After a couple of hours on the trail he may throw off his pack, spread-eagle on the ground, and not want or not be able to go on. Mr. Leader, you now have a problem—and a very serious one. The other members will see many weeks of their own planning and careful preparation going "down the drain," and they probably wll not take kindly to you as a leader from now on.

Early in the planning at home, if there is any reasonable doubt about a trip members capability, particularly his hiking ability and general stamina, you had best take some very specific steps to find out for yourself. If there are some mountain trails near your home, you can designate a particular trail and ask this individual to make a few hikes over it with a full pack. Or, you can spend an afternoon hiking with him over some rugged terrain. A few hours of reasonably strenuous hiking, with a full pack, should be sufficient to tell the story, and it will be a good investment for everyone concerned.

It will probably be a good precaution for the leader to specify a maximum weight of pack to be carried, especially for newcomers to the group. I once backpacked into a wilderness area with an individual who represented himself as an experienced backpacker. During the first hour on the trail he consistently lagged behind the group and was not keeping a reasonable pace. I then had a talk with him and during the discussion I lifted his pack. It was immediately apparent that he was way overloaded. We discussed some of the equipment in his pack and it was obvious that he had many unnecessary and heavy items. We spent the next half hour hiding various items of equipment and clothing behind rocks, etc., to be picked up on the way out. From then on he did better in maintaining the pace of the group but it was very evident that he was not the experienced hiker he had considered himself to be. I climbed one long hill twice, once to carry my pack up and the second time to carry this person's pack. One experience like this and you soon learn not to take too much for granted in evaluating newcomers.

Someone has to make the decisions, and once the group is on the trail it is the job of the leader to decide on a course of action. There will frequently be differences of opinion. After the matter has been duly discussed, accept the leader's decision. If you are not willing to do this you should have stayed home. If the group is "honored" with a daredevil type of individual, it is a good idea to remind that person early in the planning phase that you (the leader) reserve the right to restrict his activities on the trail insofar as they may affect the welfare and safety of himself and the group.

If the group has found a leader who has had a lot of backpacking experience, as well as good leadership and management capabilities, take good care of him. There aren't too many of these types around.

PHYSICAL CONDITIONING

If you normally do considerable hiking and walking, you may be able to start a backpack trip with no special preconditioning and make out all right. For most persons, however, some special preconditioning is desirable to harden your muscles, toughen your feet, and check out your pack and pack load. Books or magazines, wrapped in towels or blankets, are good for simulating a loaded pack. Do not use rocks. Rocks are not a good simulation because the weight is concentrated in a small area, and carrying a load of rocks is hard on your pack sack.

PRETRIP HIKES. There is a lot of difference between hiking over level terrain and hiking through mountains, where normally there will be a lot of uphill and downhill travel. Try to arrange your preconditioning hikes in hilly country if there are no mountains nearby. Wear the same boots and combination of socks that you will be wearing for your backpack trip, and the same clothes, insofar as possible. This preliminary hiking should take place at least a month before your backpack trip and preferably longer. The situation is somewhat like studying for an exam in school. If you don't know the lesson thoroughly a week before, then you aren't going to be able to prepare yourself in a day or two. In preconditioning you should occasionally push yourself to where you are *thoroughly fatigued*, to increase your endurance and to find out just what your limitations are. This will also give you confidence when on a real backpack trip and you are faced with a possible situation that calls for unusual exertion. For about a week before takeoff, however, take only moderate (but regular) daily hikes and exercise, never pushing yourself to the point of fatigue. Never prepare yourself for a backpack trip by taking another backpack trip just before the "big one." After any such trip you need a week of limited activity before you will be back to normal. For a week or more prior to a trip get plenty of sleep. Avoid late hours, as well as the exertion and concern that comes from waiting too long before getting your gear, clothing, and food ready and packed. Take extra precautions to avoid contact with persons having colds or other communicable diseases. In other words, give more than usual attention to good personal hygiene.

OTHER EXERCISE. Backpackers who live in large cities may find it difficult to make regular hikes, in preparation for a backpack trip. Some persons condition themselves by carrying a loaded pack up and down the stairs in an apartment building. Jogging is a good way to get in condition for backpacking. It builds up endurance and also toughens the feet. Alternating jogging with walking trips, where a pack is carried, is good. When walking for pretrip exercise always wear the boots and combination of socks that you will be wearing on your backpack trip. It is recommended that the walking and jogging exercises be done at least five days a week interspersed with a couple of rest days.

If you resort to calisthenics to get into shape, skipping rope and running in place are good exercises. Also, doing partial knee bends (not deep knee bends) in a standing position is good. Fatigue in the knees is a very common discomfort in backpacking.

If possible try to acquire some suntan in the few weeks prior to a backpack trip. This is not for the purpose of hiking unprotected from the sun while backpacking. A hat, long-sleeved shirt, and long trousers are still recommended. In the high altitude sunlight of the mountains you will simply be less prone to severe burn if you have some suntan prior to the trip. If you plan to backpack part of the time in shorts, rather than long trousers, it is very important that the legs be included in this preliminary tanning process.

PHYSICAL EXAMINATION. If you have not recently had a physical examination it may be desirable to have one, well in advance of taking a backpack trip. The necessity of such an examination will depend somewhat on your age, how often you backpack, your general physical condition, and similar factors. If you have recently had an illness and have not fully recovered, don't start a backpack trip with the thought that it will cure your illness. Backpacking is a very strenuous activity and you need to be in good physical shape when you start.

Quite a few backwoods trails are frequented by livestock. If this is true of the trails you plan to travel it may be advisable to have a tetanus shot. Consult your physician on this.

ALTITUDE CONDITIONING. If you are going on a backpack trip in the high mountains and you are not accustomed to exerting at high altitudes, it is very desirable that you take a number of short hikes in mountainous country prior to tackling a full-scale backpack trip. No person functions as well at high altitudes, but some are much more seriously affected than others. Don't wait until you are on a backpack trip to find this out. (See Part 11, and comments on acclimatization.)

FEET. It makes a sorry situation when a hiker develops blisters on his feet, usually in the first few hours of a backpack trip (if it develops at all). Besides taking preconditioning hikes, soaking the feet in tannic acid about fifteen minutes daily (for seven to ten days) just before a backpack trip will toughen them up significantly. Use 1 ounce of tannic acid (available from drug stores) to 2 quarts of water. You can use the same mixture over and over for any one trip. It will turn very dark but that doesn't matter. Wipe your feet on *paper* towels after soaking. Tannic acid will permanently stain a cloth towel, and this could conceivably cause certain members of the household to take a dim view of your backpacking activities.

Hours of walking over rugged trails can bring about sore spots and problems with your feet that will never show up in normal daily activity. A particularly vulnerable area is the toes. Trim your toenails straight across. If you round the outer corners the nails will dig into the skin, causing irritation and possibly infection.

For persons who experience foot problems, it may be desirable to carry a small bottle of rubbing alcohol. Apply this to your feet each morning and at night while on the trip. Foot powder may also be a help.

From previous experience you will know which areas of your feet develop tender spots or blisters. Perhaps you have a bunion problem. Protect all such areas with moleskin before leaving home and leave the moleskin in place for the entire trip. A small polyfoam pad, placed between the large toe and the next toe, will usually be an aid to those who have a bunion problem.

EATING. Serious and experienced backpackers will train and condition themselves for backpacking, just as an athlete trains. They will keep themselves in condition throughout the year by regular physical exercise. Just prior to a backpack trip they will exercise regularly but not excessively. If they are of normal weight for their body build, they may want to add 2 or 3 pounds to that normal weight over a period of a few weeks prior to the trip. On a strenuous backpack trip it is better to *eat for energy* rather than try to maintain your precise body weight.

When undertaking heavy exercise which is not a part of your daily pattern of living, you will probably have more energy and feel better if you eat a bit less than necessary to maintain normal body weight. Strenuous, prolonged activity means fatigue. The prime remedy for physical fatigue is rest, or a change of pace, and a good night's sleep. Eating large quantities of food is *not* the cure for physical fatigue. When you are fatigued your body does not readily digest food.

You have to burn up about 3500 calories to lose a pound of body weight. If you eat regular, reasonably well-balanced meals with generous amounts of high energy foods on a backpack trip, your energy will stay at a high level, even though you may burn up somewhat more calories than you take in. If you start a ten-day trip at 2 pounds overweight and finish 2 pounds underweight you have done yourself no harm if you were in good physical condition to start with. When you get back to the daily routine at home your weight will soon return to normal.

This approach results in a higher energy level for many experienced backpackers. It also means that weight of food in your pack can be several pounds lighter per person than if you started at normal weight and finished at normal weight. On a reasonably strenuous backpack trip you may use up to 4000 calories per day or more. You do not have to replace that many calories each day during the trip, however, in order to feel well. This type of planning is not generally applicable to large groups, to mixed groups, or to teen-agers. It is primarily limited to small groups of adult sportsmen, who are accustomed to backpacking together and confident of their own ability and thoroughly familiar with the capabilities of the other members of the group.

Don't go "overboard" on your sugar intake during a backpack trip. Some backpacking literature advises that you not only eat more sugar at mealtime than you normally do, but that you eat a lot of candy between meals. This is wrong. Your body does not need that much sugar, and it may be harmful. Some increase in sugar over the quantity normally eaten at home is recommended, but certainly not the huge amounts that some literature indicates. It is recommended that you significantly increase your intake of fat and protein foods while backpacking. Fats are the main source of sustained energy and the energy is more slowly and continuously released than with sugar, which provides quick but not long-lasting energy. *Fats* should be consumed *regularly* but not too much at one time, since they do not digest readily, particularly at high altitudes. This will sustain your energy at a good level. Be reasonable on the sugar intake. There is some evidence that sugar increases cholesterol and some of the heart troubles associated therewith.

PRACTICE. You may have read all the books on lightweight camping and mountaineering that are available. You may know them by heart. But when you climb your first mountain with a 35-pound pack on your back and the sun is blazing down, there will be an element of doubt in your mind. You will be wondering whether you will make it or not or whether you will hold up your companions who may be in better shape than you are. On the first time up, that element of doubt will probably bother you just as much as the hot sun overhead. You won't have to say a word about it, it will still be there. After you have done it once, you won't be so worried. After you have done it a dozen times, you won't give it a second thought.

As with many other endeavors, advancement in backpacking techniques and added enjoyment comes largely from experience and persistent effort to improve. You should not attempt a week-long backpack trip until you have made a few trips that were several days in length. You should not attempt a trip of three or four days until you have made some overnight trips. Short trips are desirable in order to check yourself out and see how you do, as well as to check out your gear and to get thoroughly familiar with it.

WEATHER PROTECTION

A major decision in the planning of any backpack trip is to decide what is needed in the way of clothing and shelter for protection against the elements. This will largely depend upon the season, the particular area, and the altitude. Don't take this matter too lightly. To a lesser degree the planning will depend upon the individuals making up the party. For a mixed group, or a group of young persons, more protection would probably be planned under the same anticipated weather conditions than for a group of experienced male backpackers. The latter would normally be willing to take certain calculated risks that might not be advisable for some other group.

The difference of a few weeks in the time of the trip may dictate a difference in protective clothing and shelter. For example, the mountains of New Mexico are normally very dry in the spring of the year, through the month of June. Starting in early July, however, and extending through August, daily heavy rains can be expected in the afternoon. Therefore, a backpack trip in this area from April through June requires minimum rain protection. The same trip, taken in July or August, requires good personal rain gear and a good rain shelter at night.

Obtaining *advance information* on probable weather conditions, for the area you plan to pack into, is a very important factor in the planning of a backpack trip. Don't underestimate it!

USE A CHECKLIST

How many automobile trips have you been on where someone asked soon after the trip got underway, "Well, I wonder what we have forgotten?" When you are traveling by automobile, forgetting needed equipment may not be too serious. You can stop in some town and buy the forgotten item, if it is important enough. When you are in a wilderness or other remote area and find that you have forgotten something, it is a different story. Your money won't help there. If you think it isn't serious, try getting along without matches, toilet paper, soap, shortening, or some other essential item on a week-long backpack trip. It will make you a firm believer in checklists. Presumably, practically every item that you take on a backpack trip is essential, otherwise you would have left it at home.

Prior to doing any packing, make out a list of equipment, clothing, and other gear that you plan to take. If planning and packing the food and cooking equipment is assigned to another member of the party, you won't have to worry about that, but you will need to leave room in your pack for your share of this and other common equipment. As you make out the list of items that you intend to take, put down the weight of each one. Review the list a number of times, and be sure that you are not taking too many items of nonessential equipment or that there isn't some substitute item available that will do the job just as well and weigh less.

Checklists serve another important function in addition to serving as a means of reviewing every item of equipment that is to go in your pack and its weight. Hikers have left home on pack trips forgetting cameras, canteens, fishing gear, food in the refrigerator, and other items that they planned to take. When you finally pack your gear for the last time, check off every item of equipment against your checklist, as it goes in or on your pack. Then you will know absolutely that you have everything you planned for. If some items are to be carried separately (in the car) from your pack until you get to the takeoff point, make a special note of this and fasten the note to the outside of your pack, where you won't overlook it.

After you arrive at the takeoff point you should very carefully go over the items (if any) on your checklist that were not put in your pack or fastened to it when you left home. (Few

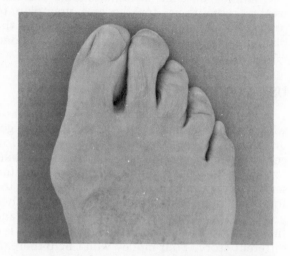

This picture shows the big toe of a hiker's foot folding under the second toe (a mild case). This is quite a common condition, often hereditary.

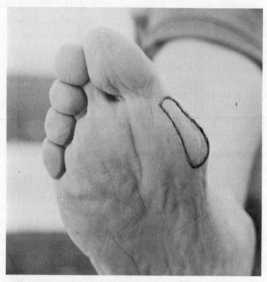

Although the "folding under" of the big toe as shown above is not severe enough to cause trouble in normal, limited walking, when on a hike a large painful bunion will usually form in the area outlined in this photo.

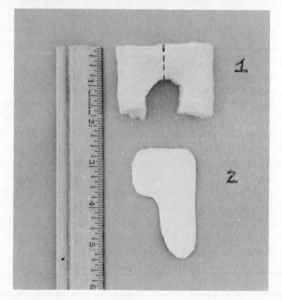

These items will alleviate the bunion and soreness caused by the above foot condition on a long hike. Item 1 is polyurethane foam, cut to about ½-inch thickness at center (half-moon) and tapered to about ¼-inch thickness at the outer edges. It is folded along the dotted line and wedged between the big toe and second toe as shown in the next photo. Item 2 is moleskin adhesive, placed over the potential bunion area as shown in the next photo.

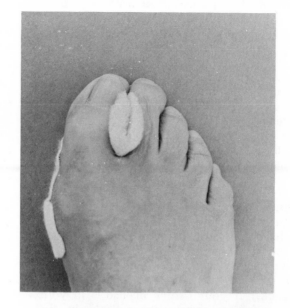

The polyurethane foam (after folding) is placed as shown. It is so light that you will soon forget it is there, yet it does the desired job of holding the big toe in a more normal position. The moleskin adhesive can be left in place for the entire trip. When you wash your feet just wash over it—no problem.

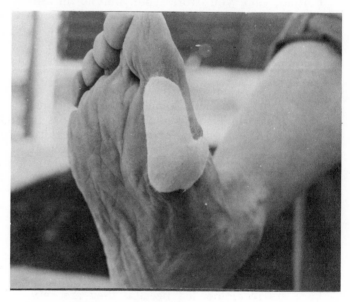

The moleskin adhesive in place. Use moleskin also on the top surface of certain toes, or any other places on the foot where you have experienced soreness or chafing on past hikes.

Such devices as this—a firm rubber form for accomplishing the job shown for the polyurethane foam—are not recommended. They are generally uncomfortable, and you will usually end up not using the device even though you have carried it with you.

hikers forget their packs.) In their anxiety to hit the trail, hikers sometimes leave canteens and other gear "safely" in the trunk of an automobile at the roadhead. To discover this after you are a few hours distant from the roadhead is very disconcerting, to say the least. Admittedly, it saves a certain amount of wear and tear on equipment to leave it at the car, but it is still not recommended.

There are a few items that should be left at the roadhead. For example, billfold, car keys, loose change, and similar items are normally of no use on the trail. If you should lose your car keys while on the trail, you have a problem over and above the nuisance of carrying them and keeping track of them while hiking. It is a good idea to have at least a spare ignition key hidden inside the car. One way of storing keys is to wrap them in foil and hide them under a rock near the car at the roadhead. (Don't forget which rock.) If your fishing license is in your billfold, and you store your billfold in the vehicle at the roadhead, remember to remove the license and take it with you.

PACKING

Don't wait until the day before the trip to pack your gear. With some minor exceptions, everything can be packed a week or more in advance. After you have reviewed your checklist a number of times and assured yourself that those items are what you need, you are ready to pack. Rather than having your pack a jumble of gear and having to turn it upside down to find some small item of equipment, most of your gear should be packed in heavy plastic bags, about 9 by 18 inches in size. Thus, except for large items, the contents of your pack should consist of a number of bags, which in turn contain the smaller items of equipment. Plastic bags are recommended because they are very light in weight and you can immediately see the contents without opening the bag. If it rains and some water gets into your packbag, they will help to keep your gear dry.

Only plastic bags that are new should be used. Do not see how much gear you can stuff into your packsack. As stated in Part 2, you should choose as large a packframe and packsack as possible, commensurate with your body build. This is not so that you can carry a heavy load, but rather because any normal load that is carried will be more comfortable using a large frame and large packsack. It will also be easier to pack your packsack and to find certain items later on when they are needed, if every "nook and cranny" of your packsack is not stuffed with gear.

In packing gear, the usual tendency is to put heavy items in the bottom of the pack. This is wrong. The heavy items should be as high in the pack (without making it top-heavy) and as close to the back as possible.

Do not tie canteens, cooking pans, and similar gear to the outside of your pack or packframe. Usually the only items that should be lashed to the packframe are the sleeping bag, tent (if you carry one), and sleeping pad. (In a large packbag there may be room inside the bag for the tent.) The sleeping pad roll is quite frequently carried under the large flap at the top of the packbag. The sleeping bag should always be carried in a high tear strength, waterproof stuff bag. Cooking pans, canteens, etc., if hung on the outside of the pack, will usually swing with each step you take and this is enough to drive most people crazy. If your gear is properly planned there should be room inside the pack for such equipment. Some fishermen will not have the special backpack fishing rods, with short sections of equal length, and this deserves special mention.

The individual sections of most fishing rods are too long to go inside the average packsack. Some backpackers carry their rod sections in an aluminum case and lash or tape the case on one side of their packframe. This case represents added weight and length, however, and is not usually necessary. Instead, it is recommended that you start by taping the rod sections together, simply lining up the sections in a parallel position, and then wrapping tape completely around the sections at several points. In addition, tie an 8- or 10-inch length of stout cord to one of the line guides of each section. Now lay the taped sections alongside one of the vertical outside frame members of your pack, so that the bottom of the rod sections is slightly higher than the bottom end of the packframe member. Then wind some more tape completely around the sections and the frame member, at several points, taping them fast. The short length of cord fastened to the line guide of each rod section is a safety cord and should be tied to the frame member also. Then if the tape should come loose, you will not lose the rod section. Some rod sections will protrude up to 6 inches or more above the topmost part of the pack frame, but if you are careful in passing under overhanging limbs this should not be a problem. Fishing reels and detachable handles go inside the pack.

First aid kits, pocketknife, eye glasses (if not worn), trail snacks, and other items that will probably be needed during the day, should go in the outside pockets of the packbag. Then they will be readily accessible. This includes your canteen or water bottle, and water purification tablets. The aluminum fuel bottle, containing fuel for the backpack stove, is also generally carried in an outside pocket. On many packbags one of the large outside pockets is just the right size for a typical quart fuel bottle. If your packbag has a separate lower compartment, with outside access, this is a good place to carry rain gear, tennis shoes for wading streams, and other large items that may be needed during the day. If your packbag does not have such a compartment then such items should be placed near the top of the load in the main compartment.

Take care in packing food bags that items that may tear or rub holes in the bags are kept away from them. Wrapping a towel or an item of clothing around the food bag will help to protect it. In packing a flashlight, reverse one of the batteries, so that the light does not accidentally come on while you are hiking. *Don't reverse both batteries* because some flashlights will still work with both batteries reversed.

Some items, like matches, soap, and so forth, are best packed by dividing the total supply into two or more parts and packing in separate packs. Keep one supply as a spare until the other is

An unbreakable plastic quart bottle makes a good water bottle and fits nicely in an outside pocket of many pack bags.

totally used up. Then if the one supply is misplaced or lost you will have the spare. This is another reason for taking a few minutes to police each campsite and lunch site before you leave it. A supply of matches or soap left at the last campsite isn't going to help when you are ten miles down the trail.

Avoid the use of brittle plastic boxes in packaging small items of equipment. With a little shopping you will find a good variety of unbreakable plastic and aluminum containers. I well remember a trip long ago where I carried a small, neat, brittle plastic box in my hip pocket. It contained fishing lures and supplies, including some small, very sharp treble hooks. The first inkling that all was not well, and that my hip pocket was a mess of broken plastic and balled-up lures, was a "pointed reminder" from some of those sharp treble hooks.

In a group that is using a backpack stove it is best for one person to carry the stove and fuel, and no food. In this way there can be no contamination of food on the trail from the fuel.

Specific items of common equipment should be assigned to the various members of a group on a *permanent* basis (for the trip). That is, they should be responsible for carrying those particular items for the entire trip and knowing at all times where the items are.

In packing camera film, place it in the packbag where it will be reasonably cool. On a hot day the heat from the sun may affect the exposure time of the film. Color characteristics may also be affected. Wrapping spare film in insulated paper bags and placing it near the center of the load in the main packbag compartment is a good precaution.

If you are coming out of a remote area the same way you go in, you may want to leave a cache of food along the way. A cache or two of food, set aside for the last few meals, will save you from carrying that food all the way in and most of the way out again. If you plan to do this, put the food for the cache in a separate bag (or bags) when you are doing your packing at home. A cache (temporary) can simply be a heavy plastic bag containing the food for a particular meal or two, hung from a tree limb 10 to 15 feet off the ground. Select a tree that will not be readily visible from the trail, and mark the trail at that spot so that you will not pass by it on the way out. Pick a small-diameter tree with no limbs close to the ground and a bear will not be so likely to climb it.

It is a good idea to keep some sketches and notes from trip to trip as to how you pack your gear. If you find that you changed certain items from one outside pocket to another, or changed the grouping or location of certain gear within the packbag, make a record of it. You can then pack more systematically to start with for your next trip.

PACK WEIGHT

In Part 10, "The Complete Pack Load," it was determined that the weight of the full pack for a week-long trip would be about 36 pounds. This was for a group of three persons. This weight can be reduced somewhat by eliminating all nonessentials. Also, the food load is reduced by about 1½ pounds per day, as the food is eaten.

In general a person of average physical strength and stamina can carry about 30 percent of his or her weight. This would mean about 48 pounds for a 160-pound man or 36 pounds for a 120-pound woman. Obviously persons in poor physical condition cannot carry this much. Neither does the rule apply to growing children. Also, there is a big difference in laboring up steep switchbacks with a 40-pound load and hiking over relatively easy terrain. Hiking in the cool of the morning will not sap your strength as will midday hiking in the heat of the sun. The length of hike each day and the frequency of layover days are also factors.

Another major factor in pack weight is the weather, or possible weather. If your backpacking is done in mild weather, you will not need the clothing and other protective gear that you do for backpacking in the rainy season, or when it is cold. It should also be emphasized that a good packframe and packbag, properly loaded, and good hiking boots, are major factors in determining the load that you can *comfortably* carry.

I know of persons of relatively small body build, who make their living as guides, who regularly pack 50-pound loads. For most persons, however, backpacking is a sport to which they turn in order to escape the routine of a sedentary job. Most of their backpack trips are from several days to a week in duration. They are not interested in setting endurance records and they couldn't care less how far they hike in a day as long as they are in scenic country and enjoying themselves.

Quite a few persons hike into a base camp and then make daily hikes from there. Others may change camps once or twice during a trip. It should be recognized that changing camps (setting up and taking down) in itself requires considerable energy and a backpack trip in which camp is changed daily can, for some, be a real "grind."

If you are backpacking with a formally organized group, it is quite possible that the group leader will specify a maximum weight for packs. He does this for a good reason. He knows the trail and the terrain which lies ahead, and he knows the size of pack that an average person in good health can carry over that trail, at a moderate pace, without undue fatigue. By all means observe the limits for pack weights, as well as any other rules, that are specified. If the leader says the maximum pack weight is 30 pounds, he doesn't want anyone showing up with a 35-pound pack. If in doubt, get clarification from the leader well in advance of the trip.

TAKE THE INITIATIVE

Well, that's about it. Three or more persons can go into a wilderness, or other remote area, each carrying a 30- to 40-pound pack, and live comfortably for a week, shut off from all outside communication. Backpacking is a sport with many challenges and many rewards. One of the challenges is to reduce the weight of the pack by a few ounces and still live comfortably and eat well. Each ounce becomes a little harder than the one before, but it's fun trying.

Like a lot of other endeavors, it is one thing to talk about backpacking and another thing to do it. It is recommended that your first few backpack trips be short ones, primarily for the purpose of checking out and getting acquainted with your gear and to test your own capabilities. As your technique improves, you can lengthen the trip and get further from the roadhead. A good winter project is to make complete plans and preparations for a spring or summer backpack trip, getting all packs and equipment checked over, taking preliminary hikes to check out your gear, and so forth.

If you like the out-of-doors, a well-planned backpack trip can be one of the outstanding experiences of a lifetime. So let's get going. We aren't getting any younger. The mountains were never more beautiful, and it would be a shame to let all of those trout die of old age. There are mountain summits to be climbed, intriguing canyons to be explored, winding trails to be pursued through pine forests, and meandering paths to be followed across mountain meadows and along rushing white water streams. As with any other sport, there will come a time in your life when you will be unable to participate because of physical limitations. Backpacking can provide some mighty fine memories for your old age. (It will also help to put off that old age.) *Take the initiative!* Use your ingenuity (and, hopefully, this book). Good luck. May the good Lord smile upon you, may you have many campfires ahead, and may you have a light pack and a light heart as you go tramping along the mountain trails. *Adios!*

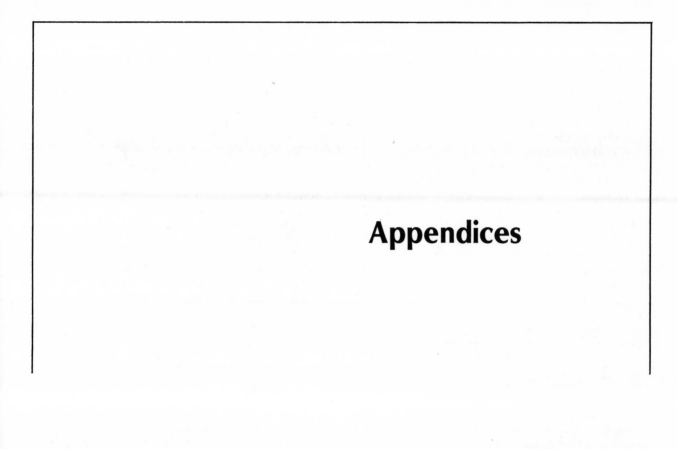

Appendices

APPENDIX A

SUPPLIERS SPECIALIZING IN BACKPACKING AND MOUNTAINEERING EQUIPMENT

Name	Address
Alp Sport	P.O. Box 1081, Boulder, Colo. 80302
Camp and Trail Outfitters	21 Park Place, New York, N. Y. 10007
Camp Trails	3920 West Clarendon Ave., Phoenix, Ariz. 85019
Cloud Cap Chalet	1127 S.W. Morrison St., Portland, Ore. 97205
Eastern Mountain Sports	1041 Commonwealth Ave., Boston, Mass. 02215
Highland Outfitters	3579 University Ave., Riverside, Calif. 92502
Holubar	Box 7, Boulder, Colo. 80301
Moor and Mountain	14 Main St., Concord, Mass. 01742
The North Face	308 Columbus Ave., San Francisco, Calif. 94133
Recreational Equipment Co.	1525 11th Ave., Seattle, Wash. 98122
Sierra Designs	4th and Addison St., Berkeley, Calif. 94710
The Ski Hut	1615 University Ave., Berkeley, Calif. 94703
The Smilie Company	575 Howard St., San Francisco, Calif. 94105
Sport Chalet	951 Foothill Blvd., LaCanada, Calif. 91011
Thomas Black and Sons	930 Ford St., Ogdensburg, N. Y. 13669
The Trading Post	86 Scollard St., Toronto 5, Ontario, Canada

SOURCES OF "DO-IT-YOURSELF" KITS FOR BACKPACKERS

Name	Address
Frostline Kits	P.O. Box 2190, Boulder, Colorado 80302
Carikit Outdoor Equipment	P.O. Box 1153, Boulder, Colorado 80302
Eastern Mountain Sports	1041 Commonwealth Ave., Boston, Massachusetts 02215

SOME SUPPLIERS OF GENERAL CAMPING EQUIPMENT
WHO CARRY SOME BACKPACKING EQUIPMENT

Name	Address
Eddie Bauer	P.O. Box 3700, Seattle, Washington 98124
L. L. Bean, Inc.	Freeport, Maine 04032
I. Goldberg	902 Chestnut Street, Philadelphia, Pennsylvania 19107
Herter's, Inc.	Waseca, Minnesota 56093
Morsan	# 810, Route 17, Paramus, New Jersey 07652

Note: Many of the large mail order firms, such as J.C. Penney, Sears Roebuck, and Montgomery Ward, also carry backpacking equipment in their catalogues and in some of their retail stores.

APPENDIX B

GENERAL SOURCES OF SPECIAL FOODS FOR BACKPACKING

Name	Address
Chuck Wagon Foods	176 Oak Street, Newton, Massachusetts 02164
Durkee Famous Foods	900 Union Commerce Building, Cleveland, Ohio 44101
Oregon Freeze Dry Foods	Albany, Oregon 97321
Perma-Pak	40 E. Robert Avenue, Salt Lake City, Utah 84115
Richmoor	P.O. Box 2728, Van Nuys, California 91404
Ad Seidel & Son, Inc.	2323 Pratt Boulevard, Elk Grove Village, Illinois 60007
Stow-A-Way Products Co.	103 Ripley Road, Cohasset, Massachusetts 02025
Trail Chef	1109 S. Wall Street, Los Angeles, California 90015
Wilson and Co., Inc.	Chicago, Illinois 60601

Note: Many of the suppliers of backpacking and mountaineering equipment listed in Appendix A, and many other firms which carry backpack equipment, stock dehydrated foods (including the brands of the companies listed above.)

APPENDIX C

ONE-MAN BACKPACK TENT

One primary reason for going backpacking is to be out-of-doors; that is, to live, cook, eat, and sleep in the open. We are really not getting maximum benefit from our backpacking experience if we coop ourselves up in a tent each night. Admittedly a conventional mountaineering tent is very desirable and even necessary for some backpack trips. However, in mild weather backpacking, at normal elevations, the tent described in the following paragraphs will serve very adequately.

Sleeping in the open, with nothing but the sky for a roof, is one of the great pleasures of backpacking. To lie in your sleeping bag and watch the starlit skies overhead before falling asleep is an exhilarating experience. Yet there are occasions when flies, mosquitoes, ants, and other "peskies" can definitely detract from the pleasure of such a night. There may also be times when you want to be away from camp for brief periods but would like to leave your bed and some items of clothing or gear on the ground without having them accessible to bugs, rodents, snakes, birds, etc.

The "tent" described here is lightweight and will provide protection from the nuisances mentioned above. Yet you will still retain that pleasurable feeling of sleeping in the open and won't feel "cooped up" when using this tent. It is made essentially of nylon mosquito netting, which is a rather strong but lightweight material. For rain protection you simply cover the nylon netting "tent" with a plastic fly sheet or a fly sheet made of waterproof coated nylon. (It has been pointed out that the best commercially made mountain tents are *not* waterproof. For absolute protection against rain a *separate fly-sheet* must be used.) It is not difficult to make a nylon netting tent. The sketch below

shows dimensions of the finished tent and paragraphs that follow describe the fabrication process.

MATERIALS

1. Nylon mosquito netting, about 5 square yards, is required for top and ends of tent. The netting is sold in varying widths, so note the width as listed in the catalogue and figure your requirements accordingly before ordering.

2. It is recommended that a waterproof floor of coated nylon be used. A "bathtub" construction is recommended, which will extend up the sides and ends of the tent from 4 to 6 inches. You can use a cheaper material and then treat it with a waterproofing compound but it will not be as satisfactory as coated nylon. As for the nylon netting, the nylon is sold in varying widths, so you will need to consider the width of the material in figuring your requirements. Recreational Equipment Co., The Ski Hut, and some of the other suppliers listed in Appendix A sell such materials by the yard.

3. The waterproof rain fly for the tent may be either polyethylene sheeting or coated nylon. Waterproof coated nylon is recommended as being more durable, lighter in weight, and easier to use. The fly should be about 10½ feet long, 6 feet 10 inches wide at the head end, and 4½ feet wide at the foot end.

CUTTING

Top. For the top you will need a piece of netting about 44 inches wide at one end, 64 inches wide at the other end, and 98 inches long.

Ends. Cut a triangular piece of netting which is 36 inches along the base (ground) edge and 34 inches along each of the other edges (about 29 inches high). Sew the two zippers onto this front end piece so that the open ends of the zippers meet about one inch down from the peak of the triangle. One zipper should be sewn to open from the outside, the other from the inside. The

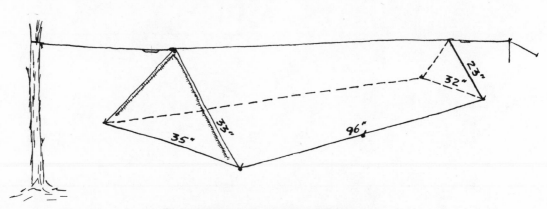

Sketch showing dimensions of finished tent

Backpack tent with plastic fly sheet for rain protection

Backpack tent with coated nylon cloth (waterproof) fly

Correct method of using shock cord in ridge line to provide "give"

foot end (before sewing) is a triangle 33 inches along the base and 24 inches along each of the other edges (about 17 inches high).

A small hole, about $1/8$-inch diameter, is needed at the peak of each end. The tent ridge line is installed inside the tent, passes through this small hole at each end, and is tied to cloth loops at the front and foot end of the tent.

Floor. The floor of the tent should be about 35 inches wide at the head end, 32 inches wide at the foot end, and 96 inches long. To each of these dimensions add 8 to 12 inches, to allow the "floor" to extend up the sides of the tent from 4 to 6 inches. Do not cut into the cloth at the corners of the tent where the floor extends up the sides. Simply *overlap* the cloth at these points and sew it in place. It will then be more waterproof than if you make a cut at the corners for a somewhat neater appearance.

Fly. In making the fly, sew the strips of cloth together so that the seams run *vertically* down from the peak, rather than horizontal to the ground. The fly will then shed water more readily. Provide cloth loops at the front peak and rear peak of the fly, for attaching a ridge line. Reinforce these points of attachment with 4-inch squares of cloth. Use similar squares of reinforcing cloth at the four corners of the fly and at two intermediate points along each ground edge, for attaching grommets.

SEWING. All of the sewing on this tent can be done on an ordinary household sewing machine. Sew a piece of cloth about 4 inches square to the netting at the top front of the tent and at the top foot end. Then sew small loops of cloth to these points for securing the ridge line. Sew three small loops for stakes, about 1 inch diameter, along each side of the floor (head end, foot end, and center). Before sewing the loops, sew on 4-inch squares of cloth at these points, for reinforcement. Next, using straight pins or a basting stitch, fasten the floor loosely to the top. When that is done it is suggested that you take the tent to a level spot in your yard, install it on a ridge line of proper slope, and stake out the ground edges. When you are satisfied that your pins or basting stitches are properly located, take the tent back to the sewing machine and sew the floor securely to the top.

Next sew the foot end to the tent, then the head end. If you want to be cautious, use the straight pin or basting stitch procedure, with another trial setup in the yard.

THE RIDGE LINE. It is recommended that you use parachute cord or an avalanche cord for a ridge line. Use a piece about 20 feet long and leave it permanently attached to the tent. It is secured by a knot to the cloth loops at the front top and foot end top of the tent. Erect the tent in the yard, and, with some trial and error, secure the ridge line so that when it is pulled taut the ridge of the tent material is smooth (free of wrinkles) but not stressed.

It is also recommended that you install about a 1-foot length of $1/8$-inch diameter shock cord in the ridge line, adjacent to the front and foot ends of the tent (outside). Install the shock cord by first tying one end of it securely at the desired point in the ridge line. Shock cord does not tie easily. Pull each part of the knot tight with pliers. Next, tie the other end of the shock cord into the ridge line at such distance from the first point that when the shock cord is stretched to the desired degree the ridge line will have a definite sag in it between these two points However, if the shock cord is stretched very much further, the ridge line becomes parallel to it and the ridge line takes the stress.

USE. Many tents require poles to be carried or two trees 10 to 15 feet apart, with a level area between. The latter are frequently difficult to find at the particular spot where you decide to camp. This tent only requires a tree or good-sized bush near the head end for fastening the ridge line. A short stick, near the foot end, will keep that end at the proper height. It is best to erect the rain fly on a separate ridge line about 1 foot higher than the tent ridge line. If you feel you may lack a tree or bush for tying the head end of the tent you can buy a single collapsible aluminum pole for this purpose. Both the ridge line near the front end of the tent and for the fly can be tied to this pole. Two additional lines tied at the top of the pole and angling to the ground will be required to hold the pole securely. The pole should be placed several feet out from the head end of the tent to allow room for entry.

APPENDIX D

ONE-WHEEL DUFFEL CARRIER

Some time ago I gave a talk and demonstration on backpacking to a Scoutmaster's round table group at Las Cruces, New Mexico. Afterward there was the usual question and answer session. One Scoutmaster raised the question, "How do I take a deserving and qualified Scout who happens to have such a small body build that he cannot possibly carry a pack of sufficient size to hold his gear on a full-scale backpack trip?" My answer was that I frankly did not know. However, for some time afterward I gave the matter some very serious thought. Why should such a Scout, or any other person for that matter, be denied the pleasure of a backwoods trip simply because his physical size and strength do not permit him to carry a large enough pack?

My first thought was that pack animals could be used. However, I have had considerable experience with pack animals, pack mules in particular, and I quickly realized that many persons would not have the knowledge and experience to successfully manage pack animals. I do not like to see mechanized equipment of any kind used on pack trips. However, after much deliberation and planning, I designed and built a one-wheel pack carrier or duffel carrier, which will be briefly described in the following paragraphs.

The chassis or main structure of this carrier consists of a two-by-four wood member mounted to a bicycle wheel. A new 16-inch bicycle wheel was purchased and a semipneumatic "flatproof" tire mounted to the rim. The tires are heated in hot water and forced onto the rim. There is no inner tube or valve stem. Strap iron members then were used to mount the two-by-four to the axle of the wheel. A "superstructure" was added to the two-by-four main member to provide a load-carrying surface 18 inches wide and 72 inches long. "Handles" were added front and aft.

I will readily admit that I have not used this one-wheel carrier for any full-scale backwoods trips. However it has been used for trail runs on nearby mountain trails. It will do the job of transporting gear over mountain trails, where a reasonably good trail is available. It will readily carry 125 to 150 pounds.

This duffel carrier can also be used by a backpacking family, where small children are involved who cannot carry packloads. I know of one such family that has built and used this carrier for backwoods trips. This particular family goes into an area where most of the trail in to their chosen site is good. They use the carrier to carry much of their gear for most of the distance through the woods. When they get to within about a mile of their destination the trail gets too rough for the carrier. (They operate from a fixed base during their stay.) They then stash the carrier in an out-of-the-way place and carry their gear from there. On the way out the carrier is retrieved and used for the trip back to the roadhead.

1

2

3

Stages of fabrication

1. Wheel assembled to chassis (two-by-four)
2. Top view, wheel and chassis
3. Finished carrier with load-carrying super-structure mounted on chassis.

Carrier in use

APPENDIX E

WILDERNESS AND PRIMITIVE AREAS IN THE NATIONAL FORESTS

State	National Forest	Headquarters	Total Acreage
ARIZONA			
Blue Range (also in New Mexico)	Apache	Springerville	180,139
Chiricahua	Coronado	Tucson	18,000
Galiuro	Coronado	Tucson	52,717
Mazatzal	Tonto	Phoenix	205,137
Mount Baldy	Apache	Springerville	7,106
Pine Mountain	Prescott	Prescott	16,399
	Tonto	Phoenix	
Sierra Ancha..................	Tonto	Phoenix	20,850
Superstition	Tonto	Phoenix	124,117
Sycamore Canyon	Coconino	Flagstaff	49,575
	Kaibab	Williams	
	Prescott	Prescott	
CALIFORNIA			
Agua Tibia	Cleveland	San Diego	25,995
Caribou	Lassen	Susanville	19,080
Cucamonga	San Bernardino	San Bernardino	9,022
Desolation	Eldorado	Placerville	41,343
Dome Land	Sequoia	Porterville	62,121
Emigrant	Stanislaus	Sonora	97,020
High Sierra	Sierra	Fresno	10,247
	Sequoia	Porterville	
Hoover	Toiyabe	Reno, Nev.	42,779
	Inyo	Bishop, Calif.	
John Muir....................	Sierra	Fresno	503,258
	Inyo	Bishop	
Marble Mountain	Klamath	Yreka	213,363
Minarets	Inyo	Bishop	109,484
	Sierra	Fresno	
Mokelumne...................	Eldorado	Placerville	50,400
	Stanislaus	Sonora	
Salmon Trinity Alps	Klamath	Yreka	223,340
	Shasta-Trinity	Redding	
San Gabriel	Angeles	Pasadena	36,137
San Gorgonio	San Bernardino	San Bernardino	34,644
San Jacinto	San Bernardino	San Bernardino	20,564
San Rafael	Los Padres	Santa Barbara	142,722
South Warner	Modoc	Alturas	68,507
Thousand Lakes	Lassen	Susanville	15,695
Ventana	Los Padres	Santa Barbara	52,769
Yolla Bolly-Middle Eel	Mendocino	Willows	108,451
	Shasta-Trinity	Redding	
COLORADO			
Flat Tops	White River	Glenwood Springs	102,124
Gore Range-Eagle Nest	Arapaho	Golden	61,101
	White River	Glenwood Springs	
La Garita	Gunnison	Gunnison	48,486
	Rio Grande	Monte Vista	
Maroon Bells-Snowmass	White River	Glenwood Springs	71,060
Mt. Zirkel...................	Routt	Steamboat Springs	72,472

State	National Forest	Headquarters	Total Acreage
Rawah	Roosevelt	Fort Collins	26,674
San Juan	San Juan	Durango	238,407
Uncompahgre	Uncompahgre	Delta	53,252
Upper Rio Grande	Rio Grande	Monte Vista	56,600
West Elk	Gunnison	Gunnison	61,412
Wilson Mountains	San Juan	Durango	27,347
	Uncompahgre	Delta	
IDAHO			
Idaho	Boise	Boise	1,224,733
	Challis	Challis	
	Salmon	Salmon	
	Payette	McCall	
Sawtooth	Boise	Boise	200,942
	Challis	Challis	
	Sawtooth	Twin Falls	
Salmon River Breaks	Nezperce	Grangeville	216,870
	Bitterroot	Hamilton, Mont.	
Selway-Bitterroot (see also Montana)	Clearwater	Orofino	988,655
	Nezperce	Grangeville	
	Bitterroot	Hamilton, Mont.	
MINNESOTA			
Boundary Waters Canoe Area	Superior	Duluth	747,128
MONTANA			
Absaroka	Gallatin	Bozeman	64,000
Anaconda-Pintlar	Beaverhead	Dillon	157,803
	Bitterroot	Hamilton	
	Deerlodge	Butte	
Beartooth	Gallatin	Bozeman	230,000
	Custer	Billings	
Bob Marshall	Flathead	Kalispell	950,000
	Lewis & Clark	Great Falls	
Cabinet Mountains	Kootenai	Libby	94,272
	Kaniksu	Sandpoint, Idaho	
Gates of the Mountains	Helena	Helena	28,562
Mission Mountains	Flathead	Kalispell	73,340
Selway-Bitterroot (see also Idaho)	Bitterroot	Hamilton	251,930
	Lolo	Missoula, Mont.	
Spanish Peaks	Gallatin	Bozeman	49,857
NEVADA			
Jarbidge	Humboldt	Elko	64,667
NEW HAMPSHIRE			
Great Gulf	White Mountain	Laconia	5,552
NEW MEXICO			
Black Range	Gila	Silver City	169,356
Blue Range (see also Arizona)	Apache	Springerville, Ariz.	36,598
Gila Wilderness	Gila	Silver City	433,690
Gila Primitive Area	Gila	Silver City	130,637
Pecos	Santa Fe	Santa Fe	167,416
	Carson	Taos	

State	National Forest	Headquarters	Total Acreage
San Pedro Parks	Santa Fe	Santa Fe	41,132
Wheeler Peak	Carson	Taos	6,027
White Mountain	Lincoln	Alamogordo	31,171
NORTH CAROLINA			
Linville Gorge	Pisgah	Asheville	7,575
Shining Rock	Pisgah	Asheville	13,350
OREGON			
Diamond Peak	Deschutes	Bend	35,440
	Willamette	Eugene	
Eagle Cap	Wallowa-Whitman	Baker	220,416
Gearhart Mountain	Fremont	Lakeview	18,709
Kalmiopsis	Siskiyou	Grants Pass	76,900
Mt. Hood	Mt. Hood	Portland	14,160
Mt. Jefferson	Deschutes	Bend	99,600
	Mt. Hood	Portland	
	Willamette	Eugene	
Mount Washington	Deschutes	Bend	46,655
	Willamette	Eugene	23,071
Mountain Lakes	Winema	Klamath Falls	33,003
Strawberry Mountain	Malheur	John Day	196,708
Three Sisters	Deschutes	Bend	
	Willamette	Eugene	
UTAH			
High Uintas	Ashley	Vernal	237,177
	Wasatch	Salt Lake City	
WASHINGTON			
Glacier Peak	Mt. Baker	Bellingham	464,219
	Wenatchee	Wenatchee	
Goat Rocks	Gifford Pinchot	Vancouver	82,680
	Snoqualmie	Seattle	
Mount Adams	Gifford Pinchot	Vancouver	42,411
Pasayten	Okanogan	Okanogan	518,000
	Mt. Baker	Bellingham	
WYOMING			
Bridger	Bridger	Kemmerer	383,300
Cloud Peak	Bighorn	Sheridan	137,000
Glacier	Shoshone	Cody	177,000
North Absaroka	Shoshone	Cody	351,104
Popo Agie	Shoshone	Cody	70,000
South Absaroka	Shoshone	Cody	483,130
Stratified	Shoshone	Cody	203,930
Teton	Teton	Jackson	563,500

APPENDIX F

SOURCES FOR MAPS, TRAIL INFOR-MATION, AND BACKPACKING INFORMA-TION

Adirondack Mountain Club
Gabriels, N. Y. 12939

Appalachian Mountain Club
5 Joy Street
Boston, Mass. 02108

The Appalachian Trail Conference
1718 N Street N.W.
Washington, D.C. 20036

Direccion de Geografia
y Meteorologia
Tacubaya, D.F., Mexico

Federation of Western Outdoor Clubs
201 S. Ashdale Street
West Covina, Calif. 94590

The Florida Trail Association
33 S.W. 18th Terrace
Miami, Fla. 33129

Greb Hiking Bureau
1 Adams Street
Kitchener, Ontario, Canada

Green Mountain Club
108 Merchants Row
Rutland, Vt. 05701

Mazamas
909 N.W. 19th Avenue
Portland, Ore. 97209

New York-New Jersey Trail Conference
G.P.O. Box 2250
New York, N. Y. 10001

The Sierra Club
1050 Mills Tower
San Francisco, Calif. 94104

U.S. Forest Service
Washington, D.C. 20240
(and Regional Forest Service Offices)

U.S. Geological Survey
1028 General Services, Administration Building
Washington, D.C. 20240

U.S. Geological Survey
Federal Center
Denver, Colo. 80204

Wilderness Society
729 15th Street N.W.
Washington, D.C. 20005

APPENDIX G

ORGANIZATIONS WHICH PROMOTE CONSERVATION OF NATURAL RESOURCES

The following is a partial list of some well-known organizations that are fighting the uphill battle of conservation, from one standpoint or another. You are urged to take an active interest in the programs of one or more of these organizations. If nothing more, you can at least become a dues-paying member. Don't delay! Write to them today!

American Forestry Association
919 17th Street N.W.
Washington, D.C. 20006

American Planning and Civic Association
901 Union Trust Building
Washington, D.C. 20005

Appalachian Trail Conference
1916 Sunderland Place
Washington, D.C. 20036

Defenders of Wildlife
731 Dupont Circle Building
Washington, D.C. 20036

General Federation of Women's Clubs
1734 N Street N.W.
Washington, D.C. 20036

The Izaak Walton League of America
1326 Waukegan Road
Glenview, Ill. 60025

National Association of Soil and Water
  Conservation Districts
1424 K Street N.W.
Washington, D.C. 20005

National Audubon Society
1130 Fifth Avenue
New York, N. Y. 10028

National Parks Association
1300 New Hampshire Avenue N.W.
Washington, D.C. 20036

National Parks and Conservation Association
1701 18th Street N.W.
Washington, D.C. 20009

National Wildlife Federation
1412 16th Street N.W.
Washington, D.C. 20036

The Nature Conservancy
1522 K Street, N.W.
Washington, D.C. 20005

The Sierra Club
1050 Mills Tower
San Francisco, Calif. 94104

The Wilderness Society
2144 P Street N.W.
Washington, D.C. 20037

Wildlife Management Institute
709 Wire Building
Washington, D.C. 20005

APPENDIX H

SURVIVAL

The aspect of survival usually implies that you have had an emergency of some sort in the woods or other remote area. Yet, when one starts thinking and talking about survival, the discussion almost invariably centers on precautions to take so that actual survival circumstances are not encountered. When we get right down to fundamentals, your knowledge and experience in backwoods travel (under various conditions) are the most important tools at your disposal for either preventing circumstances from developing into a situation that calls for survival techniques or for successfully getting out of an emergency situation if one does occur. A situation that might cause one individual or a group to go into semipanic might cause a more experienced individual or group only mild concern. Or, the latter might simply look upon the situation as an interesting challenge. So if you want to avoid a serious emergency in the woods, take every opportunity to add to your knowledge and experience. This especially concerns travel and living in foul weather, staying oriented at all times, knowing where the next water supply is, first aid, and preparedness for emergencies.

As your knowledge and experience grow, you will become more sure of yourself. This in turn will lead to a frame of mind and an attitude toward the backwoods that can save your life in an emergency. *Panic* has caused more persons to lose their lives under emergency situations than any other single factor. Many people who take to the woods are fine as long as the sun is shining and the birds are singing. But let a little foul weather move in or a slight emergency occur, and they start seeing hidden dangers behind every rock and tree. This is due to lack of knowledge and experience. There is nothing in the woods that can or will hurt you if you take reasonable precautions. You are in less danger there than in traveling around in a big city. That statement is made with full knowledge of a number of accidents that have involved campground bears, as well as certain other so-called "hazards" of the woods.

So take every opportunity to increase your knowledge and experience of the woods. If you are a beginner, when you go on a backpack trip try to go with persons who are knowledgeable. If this is not practical, go in an area which has well-marked and frequently used trails and don't get more than one or two days' travel away from the roadhead. Give some frequent thought to emergency situations that could occur, and

mentally plan, step by step, what you would do about them. Do this often enough that if the emergency does occur your reaction to the situation will be somewhat automatic, and it will not be such a shock to you.

Probably the most frequent mishap among backpackers that is likely to call for some survival techniques is to get lost. When you enter a remote area, you should not only have a good map but also a good mental picture of the area. Is the overall area bounded on one side by a road? How many hours' travel is it from the vicinity that you will be in? Perhaps there are one or more streams in the area. Do they eventually lead to a small town or other habitation? In what general direction do they lie with respect to your planned route and, again, how many hours' travel would be required to reach them? What are the most *prominent unmistakable landmarks* of the region? Are there occupied fire-spotting towers or survey stations in the area, and could you find your way to them if you had to?

A most important factor is *water.* If you were lost you might not be able to find your way to a spring or small lake, unless they were marked by very prominent landmarks. However, if you knew that a stream lay parallel to your general route of travel and about how many hours it would take to reach it, that could be extremely important information to your survival. You can live a long time without food, but your days are few if you don't have water.

Survival, under the conditions in which most backpackers would encounter the need for survival techniques, would probably be for a period of a few days or a week, at the most. Let's say that in a party of two or more backpackers one member gets sick or hurt. If the injured or sick person could not travel you would ordinarily make him as comfortable as possible and go for help. You would leave him in the care of a third member of the party, if there is a third member. There is nothing in the woods that will hurt him and, unless he is dying, he will be all right until you return with help. You would make certain that the injured person had ample water and, preferably, some food within reach.

You can backpack for years and never get lost. Most of our wilderness areas and National Forests have well-marked main trails. If you stay on or close to those main trails there is no reason to get lost. Backpackers being what they are, however, you will eventually want to push further into the backwoods, away from the main trails. (I admit to having been temporarily lost in the wilderness quite a few times.) When you leave the main, well-marked, frequently used trails, that is when you need to be alert to the possibility of getting lost and to be especially meticulous about keeping yourself oriented. Know where you are at all times with respect to major landmarks. As soon as you realize you are lost, try to backtrack if you can. That is, try to find your way back to a known trail, stream, or other landmark rather than to keep pushing ahead. Frequently a party will be "lost" with respect to where they are going but not in regard to where they are. That is, they have an objective in mind that lies somewhere ahead, but the trail has "vanished" and they don't know where to find it. Yet, if they face the truth in time, they will be able to find their way back to where they came from. The answer is — BACK-TRACK! Forget the objective for this particular trip. Wait until you can arrange for some assistance from someone who is familiar with the area.

Let's assume, however, that you are not only lost with respect to the way ahead, but you aren't too sure of the way back. When you know you are really lost, make a firm and immediate resolution that you are going to pay particular attention to your "frame of mind" or mental attitude until the ordeal is over. *Act slowly and very deliberately.* Don't move hastily or do anything else hastily. Haste often leads to panic under such circumstances. Remember that the human body has far more mental strength, as well as physical endurance, than most people have ever put to the test. The "old woodsman" books say to sit down on a log and smoke your pipe. If that's what it takes, do it. (Check your match supply first!)

One of the first things to consider when you realize you are lost is water. How much water do you have with you? How far must you go in a certain direction before you are fairly certain of coming to a water supply? Do you recall passing a stream, spring, or other water supply during the past few hours? If possible, head back for it now. When you have found a water supply, stay with it until you have developed a positive plan for getting out of your predicament. Your water supply is always a foremost consideration when backpacking. When you are lost, it should be constantly considered.

Do you have any kind of container, aside from perhaps a 1- or 2-quart canteen? If not, unless you are in an area where water is abundant, you had better plan to camp awhile near the water supply you have found. Set up your "headquarters" there. From that head-quarters you should carefully make short trips out in straight lines of travel in the most likely directions of picking up familiar landmarks. Mark your path out from your "headquarters" or

WATER CONTAINERS. The 1-gallon plastic jug and 2½-gallon plastic bag make good containers for an emergency water supply. They weigh (empty) 4 oz. and 8 oz. respectively.

base camp very carefully so that there will be no doubt about finding your way back again. Spend several days or more in making these reconnoiter trips if necessary. A little elevation can sometimes be a big help in orienting yourself. Try and find some higher ground from which you can scan the area you are in. If you find a tree in a favorable location that isn't too hard to climb, give that a try. In the meantime try to make some additional water containers. A sheet of plastic, a waterproof garment, or a ground cloth can be fashioned into a water pouch holding 1 to 3 gallons and carried on the end of a stick over your shoulder in "hobo" fashion. If you have a water supply and have fashioned a means of carrying more water, you now have the most important single item necessary to your survival.

Your knowledge and experience in backwoods travel are also very important, as stressed earlier. Hopefully you have substantial amounts of both; otherwise you should have stayed with the main, well-marked, frequently used trails. Other things to consider soon after you realize you are lost are protection from the elements and various ways of attracting attention, particularly from possible passing *aircraft*. There are very few areas in the United States these days that do not have an occasional passing aircraft. If you are in a National Forest or wilderness area, it is quite likely that there will be aircraft within view almost daily, primarily Forest Service patrol planes.

Now, how do you attract their attention? Hopefully, your normal backpack gear or your survival kit (which we will discuss later) contains a steel mirror. It is a very important item. A *mirror* is the most reliable means of attracting attention from passing aircraft. There are heavy glass mirrors, with sighting holes, made especially for signaling. However, with a little practice an ordinary steel mirror can be used and will be just as effective. (Do your practicing at home or on a routine hike, before the need for emergency use comes up.) The steel mirror will be lighter and will not be subject to breakage. The universal distress sign is *three of a kind:* a volley of three gunshots, three fires or three billows of smoke from one fire, three flashes of a mirror, etc. Lacking a mirror, you can use a knife blade or the shiny surface of a cooking utensil, metal container, etc. These are not nearly as dependable, however.

Another good attention getter, especially in a forest, is smoke. Forest Service planes make regular patrols for the purpose of spotting forest fires. Fire towers are scattered throughout many of our forests for the prime purpose of locating forest fires and fixing their position. If you can build a fire and make enough smoke for them to

see (it doesn't take much), you can be reasonably sure that the fire will be investigated. One problem, in the case of aircraft, is having the fire going and enough "greenery" available to make the necessary smoke at the particular moment that a plane comes into view. A solution to this is a smoke signal cartridge, of the type shown in Part 11 of this book. With such a cartridge you have instantaneous smoke in good quantity when you need it. Such a smoke cartridge (or several) is recommended as an item for the survival kit of every party that ventures into the remote sections of the forests or wilderness areas.

By this time you are probably wondering, "When do we eat?" For the most part, forget it. You can go a long time without eating. It is unlikely that the average survival situation which a backpacker would encounter would be of such duration that food would be a great problem. If you have some food with you it should be rationed from the beginning of your emergency. One substantial portion of food per day is better than three smaller portions or frequent "nibbling" under such conditions. Also, it is sometimes possible to eat off the land to some extent. Berries or nuts in season are obvious foods.

Hopefully, your normal gear or survival kit included fishing line and hooks. Catch yourself a fish if you can. In shallow streams fish or minnows can sometimes be driven into very shallow pockets and clubbed or beached. A log or stick entrance way or "funnel" to the shallow area will help keep them there. Minnows are eaten whole.

Deadfalls and snares for the trapping of animals are usually associated with survival periods of weeks in extremely remote areas

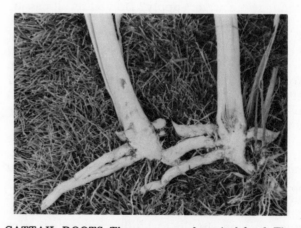

CATTAIL ROOTS. These are a good survival food. They occur over a large area of the country and cattail is easily recognized. The roots can be eaten raw or boiled (cooked).

and would not normally be applicable. However, if you should come across a porcupine take the time to "do him in" and take him along as a food supply. Also, snakes (including rattlesnakes) are a good source of food and can usually be easily killed if you see any. The best way to kill a rattlesnake is to use a stick 4 or 5 feet long and to strike the snake sharply just back of the head. It is very difficult to kill a rattlesnake by throwing stones at it. Also, don't follow a rattlesnake into dense cover. (You already have enough problems.) Frogs are a possibility, but don't eat toads. A rabbit will sometimes "freeze" in position hoping you don't see him, and you may be able to get one if you carry a stick or stone. Lastly, insects are an important source of food under such circumstances. Grubs (from rotted stumps or logs), grasshoppers, etc., are good food. Practically all flying insects are satisfactory food, and a small light or fire at night, in season, will attract large numbers. They can be eaten as is or roasted on a flat stone after the stone has been heated in a fire.

Let's say that after three or four days of living in your "headquarters" camp you have been unable to attract attention of aircraft, and you haven't been found by any surface-operating search parties. You have made regular reconnoitering trips out from your camp in straight line patterns like the spokes of a wheel. You have been unable to establish your position and pick up any firmly defined landmarks, although there are perhaps possibilities. You now have another decision to make. That is, whether to stay at your camp and make like Robinson Crusoe or to pack up all the water you can carry (along with a few other essentials) and strike out for "civilization."

Hopefully, in your "mind pattern" of the general area you will remember that there is a road paralleling the north-south border which should lie perhaps twenty miles due east. Or, it may be a railroad. Perhaps there is a logging area bordering the National Forest you are in that is operating, and you are reasonably certain you can find it. Or your best way out may be a stream in some other direction that you know will lead to habitation some thirty or forty miles distant. So you are ready to "pack up and head out." Avoid the choice of a destination that, if you *miss* it, will simply take you *deeper* into the woods. A long stretch of road, a river, or a railroad are good places to head for because your chances of missing them are not nearly so great as a pin-point objective such as a logging camp or small town. In packing up, forget the luxuries. Take all food, all the water you can carry (up to 3 or 4 gallons per person), your

survival kit, and necessary clothing. If the weather is hot, conserve your energy by traveling as soon as it is daylight and resting during the heat of the day. In hot weather it is just as important to keep your body cool as it is to ration your water. Avoid hurrying and any excessive exertion. Especially if your water is in short supply, take every precaution to avoid sweating (and loss of body water). Utilize shade when possible to save a few degrees in temperature (and water). Every time you come to a water supply fill up your water containers. Have your signaling mirror and smoke cartridges handy. If you are following a river you can of course dump most of your water supply while you are traveling with the stream. As soon as you leave the river, however, fill up all water containers.

Whether to follow mountain ridges or canyons in traveling is a question of terrain. Although there are exceptions, a lot of backpacking is done in fairly high country. To leave the country you will want to go down. If there is a canyon with a stream (or a trickle) of water at the bottom it will be very wise to stay with it, if it goes in the general direction you are heading. "Staying with it" does not necessarily mean walking in the bottom of the canyon. The canyon may be fairly wide at the bottom and provide relatively easy going, or it may be quite narrow, with possibly dangerous cliffs to be negotiated. In such cases it will be better to stay on higher ground, probably the first ridge on one or the other side of the canyon. Canyon bottoms may also have almost impenetrable thickets and undergrowth because the bottom gets more rain runoff. So, whether you travel the ridges or the canyon bottoms, or some of both, will depend upon the particular terrain. Again, if there is a trickle of water in that canyon bottom, keep it in sight as long as possible. You may also strike out through more "open" country. However, traveling through heavy timber without a trail to follow can be next to impossible. Downed timber and thickets will frequently be so dense as to simply rule this out. Also, attempting to travel in such a forest will probably get you "more lost" than you already are.

If you come to a trail and you are sure it is not a game trail, it will probably be best to follow it. That will depend on your knowledge of the area and where the trail may lead. Certainly if it is a well-used trail you would definitely follow it, rather than cross it and plunge into the woods again. The same applies to a road or a railroad, or a power line. You would follow it with the probability that it would lead to habitation. Which way to follow it

TRAIL MARKER. Lightweight cloth strips, made up at home and numbered with a felt tip pen, make excellent trail markers. They are tied to a tree limb or bush at conspicuous places along the trail, using a simple over-hand knot. A note on the back trail is made on a 3″ x 5″ card, or in a small notebook. The note is numbered to correspond with the number on the cloth strip marker.

would, again, depend upon your knowledge of the area. Normally, however, you would follow in the direction that takes you to predominantly a lower elevation. When you come to such a trail or road, it would be a good idea to impale a 3″ x 5″ note card (another item for the survival kit) or tie it on a branch with a string in plain view of persons who may travel the trail or road. The note card should give your name, address, phone number, and the fact that you are lost. Specify the date and the direction you are headed on the trail or road. Ask the reader to get in touch with certain family members or authorities, or both.

By following these procedures you may arrive back at civilization. It cannot be stressed too strongly that, before going into a remote area, some responsible person or persons should be notified in advance that you are going, the general area you will be in, and the date you will be back. They should also be told that if you are not back by that date you have met with an emergency and they are to notify authorities to start a search for you. This immediately makes it apparent that the most favored choice for survival is to set up camp very near the point you became lost and "make like Robinson Crusoe." Then the searchers will have perhaps a 10 or 20 square mile area to search for you instead of 100 or 200 square miles. You should

only try to travel out if, for some reason, the odds are all against your being found where you are. If you are embarrassed by being lost and that is about to cause you to strike out into unfamiliar country, forget it. That too could cost you your life. Statistics have proven time and time again that if you are thoroughly lost your best chance for survival is to "stay put." Find the best place for a "camp" in the area you are in, make yourself as comfortable as possible, and wait for rescue. Try to make camp in an area where there is open terrain nearby. In addition to a smoke signaling fire, stamp out a pattern in the snow (if there is snow), use fire ashes to make a pattern, stake out a bright colored tent or ground sheet, and use all other available means to aid aircraft in spotting your location.

And now some word about that survival kit. Some of the items mentioned are simply those that you would normally carry as part of your routine backpacking gear and they will be carried in a packsack pocket or wherever you normally carry them. However, a few items are "special," and it is recommended that you actually carry them in a small, separate kit, to be used only for survival purposes.

The following are items that are generally carried as a part of your normal backpacking gear. If not, they should be when you venture off the main trails of a Wilderness or Forest area:

1. Matches (several supplies stowed in different places in your pack(s) and more than normally carried).

2. Long-burning candles. Two or more candles that will burn six hours or longer. Save your match supply by lighting a candle and using it for starting a fire each time you need fire.

3. First aid kit (the more remote the area, the more complete it should be).

4. Extra water container(s). Several collapsible plastic, 1-gallon containers are good. During "normal" travel they will possibly be carried empty.

5. Heavy plastic or coated nylon (waterproof) tarp.

6. Cold weather clothing if there is a possibility of low temperatures.

7. Map. Also a good "homemade" sketch of the area that has been drawn with the aid of a person who is thoroughly familiar with the area. It should show all important trails, sources of water and recognizable landmarks that may not be included on a commercial map.

8. A good compass.

9. Canteen for each member of the party.

10. A good knife, and such items of cooking gear, equipment, and clothing as are normally

carried by an experienced backpacker.

11. Good flashlight(s) and extra bulb. At least one flashlight in party should be a "C" or "D" size. Extra batteries.

12. Mirror.

The following additional items should be carried and many of these might be contained in a special, specific "survival" container:

1. Three or more smoke cartridges for signaling (see Part 11 for photographs).

2. Some survival foods. Meatbars, jerky, pemmican, and nuts are good (concentrated and rich in protein and fat). Carry extra salt.

3. Note cards, 3" x 5" (fifteen or twenty cards). A wood pencil. Enough transparent, plastic map-covering material to cover ten or fifteen of the note cards and make them waterproof, after the note is written. Some stout cord for hanging note cards (with a written message) in a prominent place along your trail or at "camps" to aid a search party in finding you.

4. Trail markers. Strips of very lightweight cloth, with a number added.

5. About one square yard of nylon mosquito netting, preferably about 2 feet wide by 4 feet long to use for fashioning into a net to catch insects for food and for seining minnows or fish for food.

6. Some fish line, a few hooks, and some split shot (sinkers).

7. Some "picture frame" wire to possibly use for an animal snare.

8. Water purification tablets. (Iodine tablets are somewhat preferable to halazone.)

9. Whistle (shrill and loud, for signaling).

For a final bit of advice, don't let your pack get lost. (It has happened.) A hiker may throw off his pack and maybe walk to a certain vantage point for a better view, perhaps only a short distance away. He then returns for his pack and finds it isn't there. (It is still there but he didn't return to the exact spot where he left his pack.) Obviously this is a serious situation. Your pack is your "house" when you are in the woods, and keeping it with you may very well decide the difference between surviving and not surviving.

APPENDIX I

SUB-ZERO CAMPING

James (Gil) Phillips of Albuquerque, New Mexico, a good friend of the author, is one of the foremost experts in the United States on camping in sub-zero weather. When temperatures plunge to 30° or 40° below zero, Gil heads for Wolf Creek Pass in southern Colorado. For a number of years, Gil has taken groups of interested persons into that area in January to instruct them on camping out in sub-zero weather and thoroughly enjoying it. He has developed a complete line of clothing and cold weather gear for this type of camping, based on a unique approach to the problem of staying comfortable in cold weather, that many outdoorsmen are not familiar with. The purpose of the next few pages is not to make you an expert on cold weather camping but rather to briefly describe Gil's techniques and equipment, and perhaps spark your interest so that you will want to look into the subject further. Before describing the equipment in some detail, let's first briefly discuss some basic concepts that Gil has developed, largely through his own learning process of trial and error.

BASIC CONCEPTS

Fire. You do not need a fire or any source of artificial heat to keep warm at 40° below zero. As Gil says, suppose there was a blizzard or you could not find fire wood. You would be in real trouble if you had depended upon fire to keep you warm. The Eskimo never depends upon fire for warmth. Under certain conditions you may want a fire, but look upon it as a luxury, never as a necessity.

Food. You do not need hot food for such camping. You body derives no more energy from hot food than it does from cold food. That doesn't mean you can't have some hot meals, but, again, look upon hot food as a luxury, not a necessity.

Body Movements. The concept that you must work fast and move fast in such temperatures, in order to keep warm, is taboo. In such temperatures you move very slowly and deliberately. It takes five to seven times as long to perform simple camp jobs in such weather as it does in normal temperatures.

Sleep. Some outdoorsmen consider it a fact that if you go to sleep in sub-zero weather you may never wake up. Gil Phillips claims this is essentially impossible to do. He says if you get cold enough you will wake up—shivering—just as you do in normally cold temperatures.

Feet and Hands. The extremities of the body, the feet and hands, are usually the first to get cold. The head usually gets cold last. To prevent heat loss from the body you need to protect all areas from exposure. The saying "If your feet are cold, put your hat on" is not at all farfetched. Another point, if your hands, ears, or another part get frostbitten, you do not rub them with snow. You rub the affected part with your hands to restore circulation. Or, you place your feet (for example) against someone else's bare chest or stomach for warmth.

Plastic Foam and Plastic Sheeting. A basic part of Gil's approach to keeping warm in sub-zero temperatures involves the use of plastic foam (polyurethane foam) and plastic sheeting. The polyurethane foam is the basic thermal insulation and moisture remover. The plastic sheeting is the wind stop and vapor barrier at the bottom of the bed. He wraps a plastic sheet completely around his bed, as will be described later. He says if you should get low on air to breathe you will wake up—fighting. He claims that only babies who lack the strength to work their way free from such an enclosed plastic sheet are in danger of suffocation.

SLEEPING BAG. The sleeping bag which Gil uses for sub-zero camping, as for articles of clothing, is made of polyurethane foam. The right thickness for the sleeping bag is about 1 to 1½ inch. For some years Gil took Boy Scout troops on winter camping trips into the Pecos Wilderness of northern New Mexico. He taught the Scouts to make their own sleeping bags, as well as various articles of clothing, from polyurethane foam. Sleeping bags are always of mummy shape to conserve heat. The foam is glued together with automobile trim cement. A complete large-size sleeping bag weighs about 3½ pounds. In sub-zero temperatures you sleep with all clothes on and at 40° below zero such a sleeping bag will be comfortable. The manner in which this sleeping bag is made into a "bed" is quite unique and will be described in some detail.

A 12-foot-square plastic sheet, of about 4 mil thickness, is a basic part of the bed. A polyurethane pad (without cover), 24 by 72 by 1 inch thick, is also needed. Lastly, you need a piece of nylon cloth about the same size as the poly pad, or slightly larger. The polyurethane pad is not for the purpose of bone comfort but rather moisture comfort. It carries the ice-forming moisture away from the sleeping bag. The nylon cloth is placed beneath this pad and will be frozen stiff in the morning. It can be shaken out, hung in a breeze, and it will be dry—even in sub-zero temperatures.

The order of events in making up your bed for the night is as follows:

1. Lay the 12′ x 12′ plastic sheet down on the snow. The purpose of the plastic sheet is to

form a waterproof barrier between your bed (sleeping bag) and the snow. It is also part of your wind barrier.

2. Lay the piece of nylon cloth down along one side of the plastic sheet.

3. On top of the nylon cloth goes the 1-inch thick polyurethane pad. On top of this you place your sleeping bag.

4. You now fold the free side of your plastic sheet over the top of the sleeping bag and tuck it under that part of the same plastic sheet which is already beneath the sleeping bag.

5. Next, that part of the plastic ground sheet extending out from the foot end of the sleeping bag is tucked underneath. The sleeping bag is now completely enclosed in the plastic sheet, with the plastic sheet tucked under one side and the foot end of the overall bed. There is still a slip-through "tunnel" formed by the plastic sheet extending beyond the head end of the bed. You "maneuver" through this end and slide into the sleeping bag when you are ready to go to bed, tucking the plastic sheet back under the bed at the sides, where it probably came "untucked" while you were getting into bed. Your supply of breathing air for the night comes through the "tunnel" of plastic extending out from the head end of the bed.

6. When you get into one of these beds for the night, you really get "all the way" in. Head, face, mouth, and nose go inside the hood of the sleeping bag which is then drawn completely shut with the draw string, the string held by a simple knot or drawstring clamp. Air can pass freely through the foam as you breathe and there is no necessity of providing an opening at your face or nose.

Much of this procedure and technique seems contrary to the principles that many outdoorsmen, including myself, have long adhered to in using conventional sleeping bags of down, sleeping in small tents (if any shelter is used), fighting the problem of condensation, etc. A good goose down bag loses much of its insulating value when damp. The polyurethane sleeping bags apparently "eat up" the moisture. Gil Phillips explains the process like this:

"Moisture given off by your body during the night will pass into and through the polyurethane sleeping bag. The moisture from the sleeping bag then passes into the poly pad beneath the sleeping bag. The nylon cloth beneath the poly pad will soak up this moisture and may be frozen 'stiff' with frost in the morning. This is easily removed by 'beating' it out. It is dry 'water dust,' or sublimated evaporation. Also, the moisture that travels upward from your sleeping bag condenses on the inside surface of the cold plastic sheet. All of this moisture is 'dust' in the morning and is

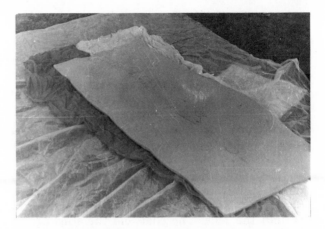

PREPARATION OF BED. A 12-foot by 12-foot plastic sheet is first laid on the ground (snow). A sheet of nylon cloth, slightly larger than the sleeping bag, goes next. A 1-inch-thick polyurethane pad goes on top of the nylon cloth. The sleeping bag is placed upon the foam pad. The free side of the plastic sheet is then folded over the top of the bed and tucked under at the side and foot end.

simply shaken from the plastic sheeting."

Booties. Your daytime footwear, the mukluks, are of course removed when you get into your sleeping bag. A foot "mitten" or "bootie" made of the polyurethane foam is worn at night to help keep the feet warm. Socks are not usually used, either for daytime use or at night.

CLOTHES. At temperatures below zero, 1-inch-thick polyurethane foam is a basic part of the clothing. It is worn as underclothing next to the skin. You can use very large, loose fitting mesh underwear to hold in place the panels of foam which are wrapped around the trunk of the body and around the thighs. The arms and legs are also wrapped in sheets of foam. Wool or synthetic (nylon) trousers and wool shirts are recommended rather than cotton. Again, they should be very large and loose fitting because of the bulkiness of the foam to be worn underneath. Now for a few remarks on outer clothing.

Waterproofing. For temperatures below freezing, clothing should not be waterproof. Our bodies require that moisture be emitted even at 50° below zero. If the clothing is waterproof this moisture is forced to stay in the clothing insulation. The moisture then reduces the effectiveness of the clothing in retaining body heat. You should use clothing that permits the continuous passage of moisture to the outside air as it is being formed. Poly foam has this characteristic, if it is not enclosed in a waterproof cover.

Coat. The coat should be large, loose fitting, and preferably long enough to reach well below the hips. Gil Phillips favors a quilted dacron type of coat with nylon outer cloth shell. A most important part of the coat is an attached hood. The hoods that you will normally find attached to such coats, if you find them at all, will be too light in weight (one layer of cloth) and too small. They must be large enough to accommodate a foam hat and possibly a face tunnel, which will be discussed in a moment. A suitable coat is so seldom found with a satisfactory hood that Gil finds it desirable to make his own hood and attach it to the coat after the coat is purchased. A quilted type of hood is best. A drawstring is very important, to fit the hood around the face. The coat and the arms of the coat must be large enough that you can pull both arms out of the coat sleeves and cross them over your chest.

Hat. The hat is made of 1-inch-thick polyurethane foam. It is to come well down on the forehead in front and to completely cover the back and sides of the neck.

Face Tunnel. The face tunnel might be considered part of the head gear. It is simply a piece of 1-inch-thick poly foam shaped into an essentially cylindrical form. Clothes hanger wire is used to give "shape" to the tunnel.

Mittens. Gloves are never used in sub-zero camping, always mittens. Your fingers need "companionship" to keep one another warm. The mittens are made of the 1-inch-thick poly foam, with generous gauntlets covering the cuffs of the coat. A very important part of the mittens is a substantial cord which goes around the neck and shoulders to connect with the mittens. Losing one or both mittens in sub-zero temperatures can be disastrous. You never lay your mittens in some "convenient spot" while working. They stay with you constantly. In doing various camp chores, eating, etc., you will slip your hands out of the mittens for a few minutes at a time, then back into the mittens when they start getting cold. They are like a portable pocket.

Mukluks. As in any other type of backpacking, your feet and the "shoes" that you put them in are of the utmost importance. In sub-zero hiking and camping, a new dimension is added (compared to normal backpacking)—the requirement to keep the feet warm. Thermal socks, leather boots, rubber boots, rubber boots with leather uppers, etc., are all left at home when camping in sub-zero temperatures. Gil Phillips has found that the only satisfactory footwear are mukluks. He makes his own mukluks from a pair of over-size galoshes, with attached canvas uppers reaching almost to the knees. The galoshes are lined with 1-inch-thick polyurethane foam. He does not use socks. He

takes a piece of 1-inch-thick polyurethane foam which is 29½ inches square and wraps each foot with this foam before inserting it in the mukluk. After a period of hiking the foam which is wrapped about the foot will tend to compress and wear in the area beneath the foot. Therefore, the foam is wrapped about the foot so that a different area falls beneath the sole of the foot each time the mukluks are put on.

MOISTURE CONTROL. Whether you are hiking, working in camp, or lying in your sleeping bag, you should take the necessary precautions to avoid perspiring. Whether you perspire will depend primarily on the weather temperature, amount of wind, and your level of exertion. If you find you are starting to perspire, slow down in your exertion, open up your clothing a bit, or remove some of your clothes (or do all of these). Remember to move very slowly and deliberately at sub-zero temperatures.

SHELTER. Gil never uses tents in his sub-zero camping. He frequently makes his bed right out in the open on the snow, using the procedure described above under "Sleeping Bag." When he does build a shelter it is most frequently a snow house. His course of instruction in sub-zero hiking and camping techniques always includes a considerable amount of time spent in building snow houses, which the students then live in. The snow houses are made with snow blocks, cut from the snow with an ordinary household saw. However, he does not consider a snow house or other such shelter to be really necessary, provided you are thoroughly trained and experienced in the other basic techniques. A snow cave can also be built and will provide a very adequate shelter. Gil sometimes builds igloos but he says that, in general, these take too much time. Incidentally, Gil is an electrical engineer and his work frequently takes him to the Aleutian Islands, off the coast of Alaska. A few years ago he took time off from his duties to instruct the Eskimos of the Barrow area on the building of igloos. (The use of igloos is primarily an art of the inhabitants of northeastern Canada, not Alaska.) He and his son then lived in the igloo for two weeks. He has on many occasions, after building an igloo or snow house, slept outside on the windswept snow, just to prove the adequacy of his clothing, sleeping bag, and technique.

TRAVEL. A conventional backpack is carried for winter camping, and Gil states that it need not weigh more than 30 to 35 pounds. All traveling is done on snowshoes. He particularly warns against use of skis unless you are very expert with them. There is too much danger of a

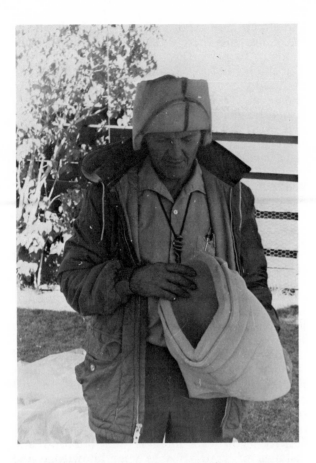

POLYURETHANE FOAM HAT AND FACE TUNNEL. Gil Phillips is shown here with a poly foam hat and face tunnel of the type he designed and has used for many years in his sub-zero backpacking and camping. Other articles of clothing, and sleeping bag, are made of the same polyurethane foam.

FACE TUNNEL. The face tunnel is used in this manner. The hood of the coat must be of generous size to accommodate the poly foam hat and face tunnel. The snow goggles, being worn here, are very important as a preventive measure against snow blindness. Note the heavy cord connecting the mittens. Loss of one or both mittens could be a disaster.

MUKLUK. The mukluk is the only satisfactory footwear for sub-zero temperatures and deep snow, according to Gil Phillips. This is the chosen footwear of the Eskimo.

twisted ankle or knee—or worse. About five miles per day is all that should normally be counted on in winter camping. The question of using a sled or toboggan for hauling gear is frequently brought up by his students. Gil does not recommend these except where it is known that the terrain will be open and level. Snow goggles are an important item of gear and are worn almost constantly when traveling and working about camp. Snow blindness can be very serious.

WATER SUPPLY. With snow covering the landscape one would think that water supply would be no problem. Yet there are difficulties in obtaining a water supply from snow, and Gil has a solution for this. In sub-zero temperatures all streams will probably be solidly frozen. Also, when the snow is several feet deep or more, the approach to a running stream, if it does exist, can be hazardous. You cannot "eat" enough snow to replace the water that your body uses every day. This amounts to a minimum of about 1½ quarts of water per day, and that is a lot of snow. To pass that much water through your mouth in the form of snow is essentially impossible. It will cause your lips to swell and crack, and you will have a terrible time. You could melt snow in a pan over a small stove used for backpacking, but Gil does not like to depend on fire or mechanical aids. His solution to the problem involves a large plastic bag with a wide-mouth opening. An ice bag with a large opening would be satisfactory. He stuffs this full of snow and puts it next to his body. The body heat causes the snow to melt as you hike along or work about camp. He stresses that it is important to put more snow into the bag before you pour out the water that is already in the bag. Carrying a bag of snow inside your shirt or close to your skin may not sound very comfortable, but Gil says that you soon get used to this.

FOOD. The choice of food is more important in winter wilderness travel than in the summer. When you cannot depend upon fire for cooking, your choice is narrowed considerably. The food chosen should be high in protein and fat. Sugar and starch base foods are poor sources of lasting body heat and energy. Gil considers unprocessed foods to be best. The food should be cut in bite size chunks before leaving home. It is terrible to be hungry and to try and bite or cut a piece of cheese at 20° below zero. (It makes excellent structural material at this temperature.) Cheese and dried fat beef are good foods. (Most commercial jerky is too lean for this usage.) Raisins, nuts, bacon, "Tang," dried milk, and shredded coconut are good. Fresh frozen fish and frozen beef can be eaten "as is" with some "practice." Soup and other common backpacking foods which require cooking should be considered "luxury" foods, rather than essential.

WHERE TO GO. A good place to go for your sub-zero backpacking and camping activity is to a ski area. In the dead of winter, in areas where sub-zero temperatures will be found, many roads will be hazardous or impassable. However, roads into ski areas will usually be kept open. After some persuasion, Gil frequently convinces a ski lift operator to haul him and his equipment to the top of a ski lift and he takes off from there. For those just starting to learn the sub-zero hiking and camping techniques it is a good idea to stay fairly close to "civilization," such as an operating ski resort. As with other backpacking activity, you can increase the duration and distance of your trips as your knowledge and experience grow.

That, very briefly, is a description of the unusual techniques, clothing, and accessories that Gil Phillips uses in his hobby of backpacking and camping in sub-zero temperatures. In closing, Gil asked that I stress the fact that, for the most part, he has simply adapted the principles that the Eskimos have used for many years, and to be sure and give the Eskimos their due credit. He is a most unusual and interesting person and you will be hearing more about him, I am sure. He is constantly experimenting, testing, and perfecting his gear and methods. If you would like to learn more about his techniques and equipment and have fun doing so, he will be glad to meet you at Wolf Creek Pass in southern Colorado—next January.

OTHER LITERATURE

Following is additional reading material dealing with some of the various aspects of backpacking with which you may want to become familiar.

1. *American Red Cross First Aid Textbook.* The American National Red Cross. 17th and D Streets, Washington, D.C. 20006.

2. *Appalachian Trailway News.* A magazine published three times yearly by the Appalachian Trail Conference, 1718 N Street N.W., Washington, D.C. 20036.

3. *Backpacker.* A magazine published four times yearly. Subscription address is 28 West 44th St., New York, N. Y. 10036.

4. *Basic Mountaineering.* San Diego Chapter of the Sierra Club, San Diego, Calif. 92112.

5. *Carters' Map and Compass Manual.* Published by Carters Manual Co., P.O. Box 186, Estacada, Ore. 97023.

6. Cunningham and Hansson, *Light Weight Camping Equipment and How to Make It.* (Available from any suppliers listed in Appendix A.)

7. Danielson, John A., *Winter Hiking and Camping.* The Adirondack Mountain Club, Glen Falls, N. Y. 12801.

8. Darvill, Fred T., Jr., M.D. *Mountaineering Medicine.* The Skagit Mountain Rescue Unit, Inc., P.O. Box 2, Mount Vernon, Wash. 98273.

9. *Fieldbook for Boys and Men.* Boy Scouts of America, New Brunswick, N. J. 08901.

10. *Going Light with Backpack or Burro.* The Sierra Club, 1050 Mills Tower, San Francisco, Calif. 94104.

11. Kjellstrom, Bjorn. *Be Expert With Map and Compass.* American Orienteering Service, LaPorte, Ind. 46350.

12. Lathrop, Theodore G., M.D., *Hypothermia: Killer of the Unprepared.* Booklet published by Mazamas, 909 N.W. 19th Avenue, Portland, Ore. 97209.

13. *Lightweight Equipment for Hiking, Camping, and Mountaineering.* The Potomac Appalachian Trail Club, 1718 N Street N.W., Washington, D.C. 20036.

14. Manning, Harvey, *Backpacking: One Step at a Time.* A particularly comprehensive discussion of backpacking equipment. Recreational Equipment, Inc., 1525 11th Ave., Seattle, Wash. 98122.

15. *1,000,000 Miles of Canoe and Hiking Routes.* Ohio Canoe Adventures, Inc., P.O. Box 2092, Sheffield Lake, Ohio 44054.

16. *Summit.* A mountaineering magazine published ten times yearly at Big Bear Lake, Calif. 92315.

17. *The Signpost.* A newsletter for backpackers and mountaineers, published at 16812 36th Avenue West, Lynwood, Wash. 98036.

18. *Trail Walker.* A newsletter published six times yearly by the New York-New Jersey Trail Conference, G.P.O. Box 2250, New York, N. Y. 10001.

19. *Wilderness Camping.* A magazine published six times yearly. Subscription address is P.O. Box 1186, Scotia, N. Y. 12302.

Index